Advancing the Regional Commons in the New East Asia

T0300529

Advancing the Regional Commons in the New East Asia highlights a number of interests which members of ASEAN and Plus Three countries collectively recognise. This set of common interests includes not only economic development but also social development. Written by nationals in their respective countries, the different chapters in this volume highlight the different foundations for such common interests and these reflect the different constructive ways in which ASEAN and Plus Three countries come to see a multi-strand cooperative partnership.

The task of advancing the regional commons will involve efforts to recognise and nurture ASEAN's and Plus Three's common interests in terms of broad social development, managing regional security issues, the development of a regional infrastructure, and ensuring collective progress for all member countries. ASEAN becomes a community in 2015 and the idea of embracing, protecting, sustaining and advancing the regional commons becomes a vital process. Concurrently, APT has also realised that its contribution to the achieving goal of community and promoting regional commons is absolutely critical for both ASEAN and the Plus Three countries.

Academics will find in this volume a clear analytical treatment of issues which regional groupings are currently facing and this can provide the basis for a comparative analysis. This volume will also be of interest to students and the general public looking for a systematic introduction to the successful implementation of cooperative ventures and also an assessment of the new collaborative energies which shape this dynamic region.

Siriporn Wajjwalku is Associate Professor of Political Science at Thammasat University, Thailand.

Kong Chong Ho is Associate Professor of Sociology at the National University of Singapore.

Osamu Yoshida is Professor of Political Science at Hiroshima University, Japan.

Politics in Asia

Advancing the Regional Commons in the New East Asia

Edited by
Siriporn Wajjwalku, Kong Chong Ho and
Osamu Yoshida

Routledge
Taylor & Francis Group

LONDON AND NEW YORK

First published 2016 by Routledge

2 Park Square, Milton Park, Abingdon, Oxfordshire OX14 4RN
711 Third Avenue, New York, NY10017

Routledge is an imprint of the Taylor & Francis Group, an informa business

First issued in paperback 2017

British Library Cataloguing in Publication Data
A catalogue record for this book is available from the British Library

Library of Congress Cataloging in Publication Data
Names: Siriporn Wajjwalku, editor. | Ho, Kong-Chong, 1955- editor. | Yoshida, Osamu, 1960- editor.
    Title: Advancing the regional commons in the new East Asia / edited by Siriporn Wajjawalku, Kong Chong Ho and Osamu Yoshida.
    Description: New York : Routledge, [2016] | Series: Politics in Asia | Includes bibliographical references and index.
    Identifiers: LCCN 2015030100| ISBN 9781138892507 (hardback) | ISBN 9781315709123 (e-book)
    Subjects: LCSH: Regionalism–East Asia. | Regionalism–Southeast Asia. | Institution building–East Asia. | Institution building–Southeast Asia. | East Asia–Politics and governmetn. | Southeast Asia–Politics and government. | ASEAN
    Classification: LCC JQ1499.A38 R43225 2016 | DDC 303.48/25–dc23
LC record available at http://lccn.loc.gov/2015030100

ISBN: 978-1-138-89250-7 (hbk)
ISBN: 978-0-8153-6875-5 (pbk)

Typeset in Galliard
by Taylor & Francis Books

Contents

List of figures

List of tables

Foreword

In Southeast Asia today, spaces of economic and political activity are seen to be the predominant and determinative sites of regional integration. Less heralded is the role of pedagogical materials, scholars and academic institutions in creating the knowledge and understanding required for effective and informed regionally oriented actors. Bringing together scholars from Brunei, Cambodia, China, Indonesia, Japan, Laos, the Philippines, Malaysia, Myanmar, Singapore, South Korea, Thailand and Vietnam (the "Association of South East Asian Nations Plus Three" or APT countries), the Community of East Asian Scholars project focuses on the potential of academic practice to promote an emergent and responsible regional consciousness.

Supported initially by Thammasat University in Bangkok and later by the first higher education grant awarded to an ASEAN-based project by the ASEAN Plus Three Fund, CEAS' aim was two-fold. The first goal was to commission papers by leading scholars from the ASEAN and APT community. They were asked to analyse, from their viewpoints of being in their respective countries and in the region, the key promises, issues and challenges faced by ASEAN and APT. The results of their work will appear in three edited volumes. This book, *Advancing the Regional Commons in the New East Asia*, will be joined soon by two forthcoming volumes, *Institutionalizing East Asia: Mapping and Reconfiguring Regional Cooperation* and *Regional Community Building in East Asia: Countries in Focus*. In providing rigorous and expert perspectives on the history, politics and institutional processes of Southeast and East Asia *by* Southeast and East Asian scholars, CEAS hopes to encourage mutual understanding among and of APT countries. As a teaching material and as a source of insight, this volume will equip younger generations in the region with an important lens on their own regional architecture.

The second aim of the project was to stimulate collaboration, as well as long-standing connections among scholars and academic institutions in APT countries. Indeed, one of the highlights of the project has been the process through which the three volumes were developed. In biannual workshops over the past three years, CEAS authors have shared, debated and modified chapter outlines and drafts. All three volumes reflect the collegial spirit of these workshops.

As our efforts become realised in print, CEAS would like to thank the ASEAN Plus Three Fund for its generous support. Special thanks also go to the Ministry of

Foreign Affairs of Thailand, particularly the ASEAN Department and the Permanent Nission of Thailand to ASEAN Secretariat, for its continuous efforts and coordination, without which the project would not have successfully achieved its goals. The editors recognize the invaluable assistance of Miyo Hanazawa and Malavika Reddy who kept the project on track with their efficient management of tasks and timely reminders. Finally, this volume, as well as the two forthcoming volumes, is the product of a long-term commitment by participant authors and editors for which CEAS would like to express its deep gratitude.

Community of East Asian Scholars
Thammasat University
Bangkok, Thailand

Preface

As I write the preface for the first ASEAN Plus Three funded book project, I cannot help but reflect on this volume's connection to ASEAN history. ASEAN began with five countries and expanded to include all ten countries of Southeast Asia, welcoming all and threatening none. Since our beginnings, we have managed our collective affairs well. We have grown our economies impressively. We have dealt with internal tensions. We have attracted sustained investment into our markets. Our regional community's advances are reflected in the interest that our East Asian, Pacific Rim and South Asian friends have demonstrated in partnering with us. Indeed, ASEAN is essential to the architecture of cooperation in the Asia-Pacific region.

The question now is how we propel ASEAN into the future. This is where the Community of East Asian Scholars (CEAS) and the present volume, *Advancing the Regional Commons in the New East Asia*, become especially significant. As *Advancing the Regional Commons in the New East Asia* discusses, common flows of goods, services and people, resources and challenges that transect national boundaries also bind together this region. Acknowledging these flows, resources and challenges as *shared* is required for continued regional engagement in the age of ASEAN and ASEAN Plus Three.

This vision of Asia that we have been building can only be fully realised if our younger generations – our children and our students – subscribe to and are motivated by this same vision. Because we are so diverse, from our varied linguistic, religious and cultural practices to our unique histories, norms and hopes, we have to educate our youth about the regional frameworks of which they are a part in order to sustain the sentiment of togetherness that has thus far characterised ASEAN. Towards these ends, collaborative research undertakings, like CEAS, will become increasingly influential catalysts of regional momentum, enhancing our own and our future generations' understandings of the uniqueness of this region.

Surin Pitsuwan
Former Secretary-General of ASEAN (2008–2012)

Contributors

Azmi Mat Akhir is currently a Senior Research Fellow and Deputy Executive Director (Academic) of the Asia-Europe Institute (AEI) of the University of Malaya in Kuala Lumpur. Prior to joining the AEI on 3 September 2007, he had had a long service with the ASEAN Secretariat in Jakarta since 1 January 1993, coordinating ASEAN regional economic and functional cooperation programmes and activities, including in higher education, which had made him very familiar with the ASEAN and ASEAN+3 processes.

Kong Chong Ho is Associate Professor of Sociology at the Faculty of Arts and Social Sciences, National University of Singapore. His research interests are in the political economy of cities, urban communities and higher education. He is an editorial board member of *Pacific Affairs* and the *International Journal of Comparative Sociology*. Kong Chong is co-author of *City-States in the Global Economy: Industrial Restructuring in Hong Kong and Singapore* (Westview, 1997); and co-editor of *Service Industries, Cities and Development Trajectories in the Asia-Pacific* (Routledge, 2005); *The City and Civil Society in Pacific Asian Cities* (Routledge, 2008), *New Economic Spaces in Asian Cities* (Routledge, 2012) and 'Globalising Higher Education and Cities in Asia and the Pacific' (*Asia Pacific Viewpoint*, 55(2), 2014).

Nor Azizan Idris (PhD, University of Wales, Aberystwyth) is Associate Professor in the International and Strategic Studies Programme and Head of Postgraduate Studies, School of History, Politics and Strategic Studies, Universiti Kebangsaan Malaysia UKM. His research interests are in the area of security and foreign policy studies, international organisation and the politics of development.

Harit Intakanok is a lecturer who has taught and researched in International Affairs, Political Economy, Global Economics and Geopolitics at International College, Khon Kaen University, Thailand. Educated in the UK from a very young age, Harit graduated from Durham University with a PhD in Geopolitics. His recent works cover energy security in ASEAN and ASEAN Plus Three and power dynamics in Southeast Asia.

Soparatana Jarusombat is Associate Professor in the Faculty of Political Science at Thammasat University, Bangkok. Having received a PhD in Urban Environmental Engineering and Management from the Asian Institute of Technology, her research interests are in sustainable natural resources management and urban environmental management. Soparatana is also Head of Public Administration at the Faculty of Political Science at Thammasat University. She can be contacted at s.jarusombat@gmail.com.

Heung Ju Kim is a professional researcher at the Institute for Poverty Alleviation and International Development (IPAID) at Yonsei University, Wonju Campus, South Korea. He can be reached at myutos78@hanmail.net.

Hyung Jun Kim is a socio-cultural anthropologist with a special focus on Indonesia. He is Professor in the Department of Cultural Anthropology, Kangwon National University, South Korea. He has published on the issues of Islam and socio-cultural changes in Indonesia, and is currently working at the Islamic organisation, Muhammadiyah.

Pan Suk Kim is Professor of Public Administration in the College of Government and Business at Yonsei University, Wonju Campus, South Korea. He is currently the president of the Asian Association for Public Administration (AAPA). He can be reached at pankim@gmail.com.

Anh Thu Nguyen received her PhD in Economics at the Yokohama National University, Japan, specialising in International Development. Currently, Nguyen Anh Thu is Associate Dean of and Lecturer in the Faculty of International Business and Economics, University of Economics and Business, Vietnam National University, Hanoi. Her key areas of research are international economic integration, particularly in ASEAN and Asia, international trade and green growth.

Hong Son Nguyen received his PhD in Political Economics at the National University of Moscow, Russia. As an expert on public policy and national development, he has presided over many research projects on the economic integration of Vietnam and Asia; the development of the service sector in Vietnam (education and training, science and technology, finance and banking services); and the international financial and monetary system. He has been the author of many books and papers published locally and internationally. Currently, he is Associate Professor and Rector of the University of Economics and Business, Vietnam National University, Hanoi.

Zarina Othman earned her PhD in International Studies from the University of Denver, Colorado in 2002. Associate Professor Othman is currently Head of the Program of Strategic Studies and International Relations, Universiti Kebangsaan Malaysia (UKM/National University of Malaysia), Bangi, Malaysia. She is a member of the Community of East Asian Scholars. Her research interests focus mainly on human security issues in Southeast Asia, non-traditional threats, East Asian community, regional security and human and drug trafficking. Her recent publications include: *Sity Daud, Zarina Othman and Rashila*

Raml, Human Security and Peace in Archipelagic Southeast Asia (Bangi: UKM Publishers, 2015).

Leng Leng Thang is a socio-cultural anthropologist with a special focus on Japan as well as other parts of Asia. She is Associate Professor and Head of the Department of Japanese Studies, National University of Singapore. Leng Leng has published on the issues of aging, gender, intergenerational relationships, family, gender and transnational migration, especially in Japan and Singapore.

Siriporn Wajjwalku is an Associate Professor in the Faculty of Political Science, Thammasat University, Bangkok, Thailand. She received a BA in Political Science from Thammasat University and an MA and PhD from Nagoya University, Japan. Her study focuses on Japan's foreign policy, international development and regional cooperation. The recent publications include "Japan: Politics and Political Institutions" (2014) and "Institutional Arrangement and Aid Effectiveness: Japan's Aid Provision to Mekong Countries" (2015). She was the former Dean of Faculty of Political Science, Thammasat University (February 2010 – January 2013). Currently, she is the President of the Japanese Studies Association of Thailand, as well as the acting Dean of the School of Social Innovation, Mae Fah Laung University, Chiang Rai, Thailand.

Osamu Yoshida is Professor in the Faculty of Law in the Graduate School of Social Sciences and the Graduate School for International Development and Cooperation at Hiroshima University, Japan. He is also Research Hub Leader of the university's Hiroshima Active Peacebuilding Research as well as Project Manager for the Hiroshima University Human Resource Development Project working with the Bangsamoro Government in the Philippines. He received his PhD from Jawaharlal Nehru University and an LLM from Nagoya University. He can be contacted at oyoshid@hiroshima-u.ac.jp.

Abbreviations

AADMER	ASEAN Agreement on Disaster Management and Emergency Response
ACCORD	ASEAN and China Cooperative Operations in Response to Dangerous Drugs
ACDM	ASEAN Committee on Disaster Management
ACE	ASEAN Centre for Energy
ACTS	ASEAN Credit Transfer System
AEC	ASEAN Economic Community
AEI-UM	Asia-Europe Institute, University of Malaya
AERR	ASEAN Emergency Rice Reserve
AFSIS	ASEAN Food Security Information System
AFSRB	ASEAN Food Security Reserve Board
AFSRS	ASEAN Food Security Reserve System
AHA Centre	ASEAN Coordinating Centre for Humanitarian Assistance
AIDS	Acquired Immunodeficiency Disease Syndrome
AIFS	ASEAN Integrated Food Security (framework)
AMAF	ASEAN Ministers of Agriculture and Forestry
APEC	Asia-Pacific Economic Cooperation
APG	ASEAN Power Grid
APSC	ASEAN Political-Security Community
APT	ASEAN Plus Three
APT-EMM	ASEAN Plus Three Education Ministers Meeting
APTERR	ASEAN Plus Three Emergency Rice Reserve
ASCC	ASEAN Socio-Cultural Community
ASCOE	ASEAN Sub-Committee on Education
ASEAN	Association of Southeast Asian Nations
ASEAN-PMC	ASEAN Post-Ministerial Conference
ASED	ASEAN Education Ministers Meeting
ASED+3	ASEAN Education Ministers Meeting Plus Three
ASEP	ASEAN Environmental Program
ASOD	ASEAN Senior Officials on Drug Matters
ASOEN	ASEAN Senior Officials on the Environment
ASP	ASEAN Studies Programme

ATIGA	ASEAN Trade in Goods Agreement
ATS	amphetamine-type stimulants
AUN	ASEAN University Network
BAGHUS	The Bangi Approach to Human Security
BOT	Board of Trustees
CEAS	Community of East Asian Scholars
CEPT	Common Effective Preferential Tariff Scheme
CMI	Chiang Mai Initiative
CSCAP	Council for Security Cooperation in the Asia-Pacific
EAERR	East Asia Emergency Rice Reserve
EAS	East Asia Summit
EAS–EMM	East Asia Summit Education Ministers Meeting
FDI	Foreign Direct Investment
FTA	Free Trade Agreement
HFA	Hyogo Framework of Action
HIV	Human Immunodeficiency Virus
NGO	Non-Governmental Organisation
RCA	Revealed Comparative Advantage
SOM-ED	Senior Officials Meeting on Education
TAGP	Trans-ASEAN Gas Pipeline
TC	Trade complementarity
UNDP	United Nations Development Programme
UNEP	United Nations Environment Program
UNODCCP	United Nations Office on Drugs Control and Crime Prevention
USD	United States Dollar

Introduction

Advancing the regional commons in the New East Asia

Siriporn Wajjwalku, Kong Chong Ho and Osamu Yoshida

East Asia is the region of great dynamism and regionalisation process is quite advanced. Apart from the Asia-Pacific Economic Cooperation (APEC), countries in East Asia have been involved in a number of regional cooperation schemes such as the Association of Southeast Asian Nations (ASEAN), ASEAN Plus Three (APT) and East Asian Summit (EAS).

A significant moment in regionalisation occurred during the economic crisis of 1997 that led to the creation of APT, together with a long-time attempt of exploring and experimenting a regional cooperation pattern, contributing to the evolvement of APT. With the limitations of ASEAN mechanism focusing on consensus and non-intervention, and the slow progress of APEC, APT became the answer for the regional architecture (Stubbs, 2002). Although the speed and scope of cooperation has not been fast and comprehensive, the ultimate goal of creating an East Asian Community is still far away and obstacles are waiting (Md Damiri, 2011), APT's past successful activities such as Chiang Mai Initiative, East Asia Emergence Rice Reserve, etc., prove that this arrangement can accomplish its mission and its future is still promising. In fact, it is witnessed that the longer APT cooperation continues, the broader and deeper the areas of cooperation become.[1]

Three important points can be made regarding the APT and ASEAN relationships. First, relationships within Plus Three elements of APT do not expand their areas of cooperation with each other so much as ASEAN elements do among member countries. Second, the competition among Plus Three countries for enhanced relationships with ASEAN has so far led to the increase in the field of integration such as ASEAN's free trade agreements with each of the Plus Three countries. And third, there is also an accompanying increase in cooperation between each of the ASEAN member countries and each of the APT countries. More interesting is the difference in each of the Plus Three's vantage points in engaging in cooperative ventures with ASEAN, such as Japan for a more sophisticated institutional and technological integration, China for a more flexible approach in trade and South Korea in between. Initiatives in particular fields made by one of the Plus Three tend to be caught up by the other two and, thus, the fields of cooperation and integration become broader. No less important are the opportunities provided by the APT framework for Plus Three countries to sit down together and discuss matters of mutual interest even when their bilateral relations are not very good.

While an East Asian Community as the ultimate goal of regional cooperation is still struggling to take shape and searching for an appropriate pattern and scheme of cooperation, ASEAN and APT have moved to create EAS as a parallel track and one step forward to achieving it. With the progress of economic cooperation, common interests and concerns, and shared perspectives, to some extent, can be made the "common thread" that twist the countries of the region together into an even thicker sense of a regional identity. As seen recently, APT is now moving forward to a new area of cooperation by emphasising cross-sector cooperation and cross-border issues which represent "commons" of the region.

Two qualities come together in the term "Commons": the property of "belonging equally to or shared equally by two or more"; and, the quality "of or relating to the community as a whole or public".[2] In East and Southeast Asia, the idea of regional commons is widely promoted, in particular for the use and management of natural resources. Ostrom (2008, 3) had defined the common-pool resources as "resources that are sufficiently large that it is difficult, but not impossible, to define who are the recognized users and to exclude others. Further, each person's use of such resources is subtractive of benefits that others might enjoy." Several cases of common-pool resources managed by communities within the country or cross-border between two countries or even by regional attempt can be seen in many parts of the region. The fisheries and coastal resources management in Cambodia, Thailand, Indonesia and the Philippines, and the Mekong River Commission are some examples that reflect several methods of governing the common in the region.[3] For APT in particular, it is interesting to note from an examination of declarations and agreements signed recently that collective management of regional commons such as food, energy, water and environment are priorities.[4]

In addition, this idea now has been expanded to include not only the nature and natural resources commons, but also economic commons, social and societal commons, cultural and knowledge commons, as well as digital commons. This illustrates that on one hand, there are some new norms and practices that countries in East and Southeast Asia, particularly ASEAN and APT members, would like to establish as "common values and practices" in the region such as liberalisation and common market, regional normative commons (diversity, human rights, human security) and community-based management. Such kinds of values and practices reflect the changing character of regional cooperation among ASEAN and APT.

It should also be observed that while national interests are still considered superior, new values and practices have become more accepted, which can be appreciated as advancing the regional commons. On the other hand, there are several issues which are regional challenges and need regional cooperation as a sustainable solution. Although this is not a new aspect of regional commons, ASEAN and APT members have better realised that without their collective action, the sustainable solution cannot be achieved. This leads to better and deeper cooperation among members, which also reflects advancing regional commons.

In titling this volume *Advancing the Regional Commons in the New East Asia*, our intention is to highlight a number of interests which members of ASEAN and APT collectively recognise. This set of common interests, as the chapters in this volume will elaborate, includes not only economic development but also social development. There are different foundations for such common interests and these reflect the different constructive ways in which ASEAN and APT countries come to see a multi-strand cooperative partnership. And the task of advancing the regional commons will involve efforts to recognise and nurture ASEAN's and APT's common interests in terms of broad social development, managing regional security issues, the development of a regional infrastructure and ensuring collective progress for all member countries. In 2015, ASEAN takes the first step to becoming a community and the idea of embracing, protecting, sustaining and advancing the regional commons becomes a vital process in strengthening this community. Concurrently, APT has also realised that its contribution to achieving the goal of community and promoting regional commons is absolutely critical for both ASEAN and the Plus Three countries. *Roadmap for an ASEAN Community 2009–2015*[5] by the ASEAN Secretariat highlights three community pillars: political security, socio-cultural and economic. The individual chapters in this volume highlight and analyse in greater detail the specific strategic and critical issues underlying these pillars in which ASEAN and APT countries have engaged and interacted.

The first set of chapters addresses the concept of human security[6] which is central to the political security pillar. If we adopt the United Nations Development Programme's broad definition that human security is freedom from fear and want,[7] then this is a common issue which needs to be addressed by the ASEAN community.

The mutual help that permeates through the ASEAN community is provided by the example of food security. ASEAN is comprised of a region which is susceptible to different types of natural disasters such as typhoons and flooding. Therefore, the idea of maintaining a regional stock of essential grains such as rice that can be deployed in the event of an emergency, when national stocks are under threat of being exhausted, is an important regional common. In Chapter 1, Siriporn Wajjwalku argues that food security is a critical path for regional integration. As food is a basic human need, food security represents a foundation and an enduring facet of inter-country mutual security arrangements.

The fear issue of human security is clearly addressed in Chapter 2 by Zarina Othman and Nor Azizan Idris on the problem of illicit drugs in ASEAN. Their analysis points to the multidimensional nature of the problem; how production of drugs is tied to weaker economies and enforcement problems, and how drug use is also tied to the spread of infectious diseases such as HIV. It is clear that the Southeast Asian drug industry is a regional problem which needs regional cooperation and the authors examine the various avenues where national enforcement agencies work with ASEAN and ASEAN Plus Three partners as well as international agencies such as Interpol to combat the drug problem.

Migration, both in the facilitation of the movement of people as well as in ensuring that visitors settle and integrate well in host countries, is an important mechanism for facilitating greater understanding and building solidarity at the grassroots level and in everyday life. In this regard, Hyung Jun Kim and Leng Leng Thang examine the movement of the young in education migration and the old in retirement migration in Chapter 3. Youths from Southeast Asia move to more developed education systems while elderly migrants tend to move in the opposite direction, from Northeast Asia (Japan and Korea) to warmer climates in Southeast Asia and where the cost of living is substantially lower. Thus, migration provides a common opportunity for ASEAN and Plus Three partners to mutually benefit from migration exchanges. Both streams create opportunity and risks in the host–guest relationship. Given that both groups are relatively long-term stayers, the opportunities to develop a deeper mutual understanding between hosts and guests certainly exists, but so too are the possibilities of misunderstandings and exploitation, especially when migrant groups reside in enclaves. Thus, while ASEAN and APT member countries develop inter-governmental institutional frameworks for mutual understanding and cooperation, the kinds of flows Kim and Thang document may well allow for a forging of solidarity and identity among the diverse groups and cultures of ASEAN and APT countries.

On the policy front of host governments, Chapter 4 by Pan Suk Kim and Heung Ju Kim stresses the importance of changing government policy from an assimilation model to a multicultural model which recognises the rights of migrants, where the migrant is treated with respect, and where the government is active in social integration. Domestic policies among member countries within a common region can reduce the costs and problems associated with movement, enabling a more supportive inter-state system to emerge which preserves the shared human capital of the region. The benefits of such human capital accrues to both sending and receiving countries, in the form of the fruits of labour, powering industry, sustaining innovations and allowing for elderly care as well as new family formation. In the process, a regional market that has already developed for migrants may be transformed to a regional community for people from a common region.

Economic development also involves sustained efforts to strengthen foundations. Many studies of the returns to education by economists have linked years of formal education to higher personal incomes. At the societal level, governments are often motivated to spend on education as human capital on the assumption that education is the key to developing a skilled labour force necessary to move the country forward economically, and that returns to such investments include societal benefits like a more tolerant and participative society. This latter point of tolerance and participation is at the root of the second ASEAN pillar which is socio-cultural development. It is concerned "with realising an ASEAN community that is people-centred and socially responsible with a view to achieving enduring solidarity and unity among the nations and peoples of ASEAN by forging a common identity and building a caring and sharing society".[8] Key to realising the social and cultural objectives of the ASEAN community is in the education of

ASEAN's youth. Chapter 5 by Azmi Mat Akhir examines efforts at regional cooperation in education within ASEAN, particularly for higher education, through quality assurance initiatives, credit transfers, collaborative research and the enhanced mobility of students and researchers between universities within the community. Akhir points out that such collaboration efforts are likely to lead to the strengthening of ASEAN as the mutual hosting of students in various universities is likely to lead to an enhanced understanding of both the host country as well as ASEAN as a whole.

ASEAN is comprised of countries which are at different levels and speed of development. An important objective is to create harmonious growth by ensuring that all countries and sub-regions partake in this process. This goal does not necessarily mean even growth. Some member countries will grow faster, and key cities will also grow faster as investments tend to be urban-centric. However, the goal of narrowing the development gap between countries and between cities and less-developed regions will mean that the benefits of economic development should be shared through a well-developed and integrated ASEAN education system accompanied by youth development and mobility schemes, as suggested by Akhir in Chapter 5. The future of ASEAN rests on the shoulders of its youth and therefore the development of ASEAN cannot afford to ignore the welfare of young people.

The focus of the third pillar is ensuring a strong ASEAN economic community by economic integration, making ASEAN more economically competitive, reducing the developmental divide and trade promotion.[9] These issues – economic integration, trade promotion, competitiveness and by inference reducing the developmental divide – are addressed by Nguyen Hong Son and Nguyen Anh Thu in Chapter 6. They show that while trade within ASEAN is increasing, the similarity in economic profiles (specifically import-export structure) of member countries means that ASEAN countries trade more significantly with the rest of the world than they do within ASEAN. Their analysis shows that the APT countries, particularly China and Japan, have growing trade with ASEAN, in part because of the ASEAN-Japan Comprehensive Partnership and ASEAN-China Free Trade Agreement. The statistics Son and Thu garner provide a fairly sanguine immediate economic future for ASEAN, particularly with further integration within ASEAN and between ASEAN and the Plus Three countries.

Several countries in ASEAN are oil producers. The issue raised by Harit Intakanok in Chapter 7 is how ASEAN members – oil as well as non-oil producers – can cooperate in ways such that the region can gain as a whole from such economic cooperative ventures. The energy security issue can be seen in terms of the joint development of an infrastructure for the mutual benefit of development partners. This orientation can be observed in plans involving the building of the ASEAN pipeline, representing an ambitious ASEAN infrastructure project which will enhance the delivery of oil. Ensuring an efficient energy delivery system can be seen as one example of regional economic cooperation. This example is seen to expand opportunities for all, enabling a momentum for growth to be sustained for member countries. On the other hand, harmonious growth requires efforts to narrow the economic gap between member countries by ensuring the low-income, less-developed member countries are helped in their development aspirations.

Common economic development issues do not just involve promotion but also regulation and prevention of what economists term negative externalities – problems which spill across the borders of member countries. Major sea lanes that connect Northeast Asia and South Asia, West Asia and Europe run through ASEAN. And as the ASEAN region develops economically, the density of marine traffic between major markets and key industrial production sites require ASEAN countries to use existing collaborative networks to develop a marine environment management system to effectively regulate a variety of issues that will ensure a good quality of life, preserving shared marine resources and preserving harmony within the ASEAN community. In Chapter 8, Soparatana Jarusombat shows how the ASEAN working group on Coastal and Marine Environment can move forward in addressing important environmental issues through raising awareness of issues which surface, better inter-agency cooperation, the assessment of environmental impacts and the adoption of measures that can be implemented.

It is clear from the individual chapters comprising this volume that within the ASEAN and APT, big strides have been made to identify commons shared by country members and make inroads in regional cooperative development. At the same time, the authors in these eight chapters have also highlighted the constraints as well as the slower progress of some of the projects. The collection not only highlights inter-state initiatives, but also focuses on the people-to-people relationships, both of which are crucial in the building of an ASEAN community as well as the ultimate goal of the East Asian Community. These moves create a multi-stranded approach which embraces the idea of a common fate, shared progress and collective development, stemming from the common stance of members sharing the commons. Academics will find in this volume clear analytical treatments of issues which confront regional groupings and this can provide the basis for a comparative analysis. This volume will also be of interest to students and the general public looking for a systematic introduction to the successful implementation of cooperative ventures and also an assessment of the new collaborative energies which shape this dynamic region.

Notes

1 See www.asean.org/asean/external-relations/asean-3.
2 See www.thefreedictionary.com.
3 "Communities and Forest Management in Southeast Asia", www.asiaforestnetwork.org; Torell and Salamanca 2002; Hirsch 2006.
4 See www.asean.org/asean/external-relations/asean-3.
5 Association of Southeast Asian Nations 2009.
6 Political security is an issue more comprehensively dealt with in the Institutions volume.
7 Gomez and Gasper 2012.
8 Association of Southeast Asian Nations 2009, 67.
9 Association of Southeast Asian Nations 2009, 21–2.

References

Association of Southeast Asian Nations. (2009) *Roadmap for an ASEAN Community 2009–2015*, ASEAN Secretariat. Available at: www.meti.go.jp/policy/trade_policy/east_asia/dl/ASEANblueprint.pdf.

Gomez, O. and D. Gasper. (2012) *Human Security: A Thematic Guidance Note for Regional and National Development Report Teams*, UNDP. Available at: http://hdr.undp.org/sites/default/files/human_security_guidance_note_r-nhdrs.pdf.

Hirsch, Philip. (2006) "Governing Water as a Common Good in the Mekong River Basin: Issues of Scale". *Transforming Cultures eJournal*, 1(2). Available at: http://epress.lib.uts.edu.au/journal/Tfc.

Md Damiri, Mohd Hajizzuddin. (2011) "Cooperation within the ASEAN Plus Three Context: Incidential or Coincidence?" Paper presented at the 4th International Conference on Southeast Asia, Kuala Lumpur.

Ostrom, Elinor. (2008) "Sustainable Development of Common-Pool Resources". Paper presented at the Workshop in Political Theory and Policy Analysis, Indiana University, Bloomington.

Stubbs, Richard. (2002) "ASEAN Plus Three: Emerging East Asian Regionalism?", *Asian Survey*, 42(3): 440–455.

Torell, Magnus and Albert M. Salamanca. (eds) (2002) *Institutional Issues and Perspectives in the Management of Fisheries and Coastal Resources in Southeast Asia*. Kuala Lumpur: ICLARM-World Fish Centre, Malaysia and Swedish International Development Cooperation Agency.

1 ASEAN and food security

A critical path for regional integration

Siriporn Wajjwalku

1 Introduction

In November 2013, typhoon Haiyan hit the Philippines causing huge damage, a large amount of displaced people and casualties. It was reported that more than 5,000 people died, more than 20,000 were injured, and almost 2,000 were missing. In addition, more than a million houses were damaged due to the heavy storm and floods, and the affected population was over 2 million. The area was under emergency for several weeks.

During the emergency, food, water, and other supplies were provided by several countries and international organisations. It was reported that six ASEAN member countries had supplied food, water, medicine and financial aid to the Philippines. These had been conducted bilaterally. Particularly relevant for the focus of this chapter, it was reported that the support from the Association of Southeast Asian Nations (ASEAN) came in the form of supplies delivered by two bodies of ASEAN, namely the ASEAN Plus Three Emergency Rice Reserve (APTERR) and the ASEAN Coordinating Centre for Humanitarian Assistance (AHA Centre).

APTERR is a regional cooperation scheme established in order to ensure food security in the region as well as to meet emergency requirements and achieve humanitarian purposes without distorting the normal international trade of rice. APTERR itself, with its earmarked reserve, does have a limited stockpile of food, and the government of the member country has to decide whether to release the supply through this scheme or not. In the case of typhoon Haiyan in the Philippines, the government of Japan, which is a member of APTERR, had decided to provide rice through the APTERR framework. Concurrently, the AHA Centre also works to provide humanitarian aid including food, water and other supplies. AHA fulfils these aims by coordination among ASEAN member states and with the United Nations and other international organisations for disaster management and emergency response. As mandated by the ASEAN Agreement on Disaster Management and Emergency Response, the AHA Centre is designed to be a regional hub for disaster risk monitoring and analysis, and a coordination engine to ensure ASEAN's fast and collective response to disaster within the region. With that mandate, AHA Centre has a stockpile which is ready to be delivered alongside efforts at a local procurement.

Although ASEAN had responded to the emergency in the Philippines, this operation exposed its limited and inefficient role. At the operational level, the mandate and function of APTERR and the AHA Centre brought out the question of duplication and a lack of coordination. At the policy level, the unclear policy and strategy on food security and disaster management regarding food aid created confusion. Specifically, there were two issues which inter-crossed and are operated by two different bodies, namely, food aid as humanitarian aid during emergency, and the longer-term goal of food security and poverty reduction.

In addition, food, especially rice, is a sensitive product due to different productivity and capacity, as well as the development stage of each ASEAN member country. One of the cornerstones of ASEAN is that it prioritises the national interests of its members and with this position comes the ASEAN norm of consensus and non-interference. The norm of consensus and especially non-interference makes it difficult for ASEAN to respond quickly during an emergency when a disaster strikes a member country as the usual protocols must be respected before aid is forthcoming. This problem makes emergency food aid as a cornerstone of food security a real issue for ASEAN.

In fact, food security is not the new issue among ASEAN member countries, but it has become more critical recently for several reasons. After the euphoria created by the Green Revolution, global warming and climate change and the increasing potential for crop damage and failure makes the question of food availability a critical issue again. Concurrently, the increasing frequency of disasters recently in the region also draws attention to food availability and accessibility for the affected countries. In addition, the food crisis in 2008 resulting from the high price of rice has heightened concerns on food accessibility for poorer countries, along with the related issues of poverty, inequality and injustice.

The core issue of food security is the method to secure and distribute food supply in times of emergency and normalcy. In general, as food is a basic need, it is the state's obligation to secure food, and therefore, food is also considered as national security because it relates to the country's survival. Basically, there are several ways for a state to secure food, such as self-sufficiency, by importing or food aid, and the delivery mechanism of each method varies according to the time and conditions of both provision and reception actors. In normal times, food can be secured by high domestic productivity or international trade and agricultural cooperation, while during an emergency, food can be secured by domestic reserve relief or international humanitarian aid. ASEAN members apply different policy and mechanisms in dealing with food security under different conditions.

Recently, the Plus Three countries have also paid attention to food security issues due to the increasing number of disasters in the region. Since the 2000s, the Plus Three, particularly Japan, has supported the food security policy and mechanism of ASEAN actively, in terms of budget, institutional arrangement and earmarked rice reserves. Several agreements were signed, a number of activities were conducted and the improvement of institutions and their functions have been seriously debated among ASEAN and the Plus Three members during the last decade. APTERR, which formally held the first meeting in March 2013, is the product of the cooperation among ASEAN and the Plus Three members. It is expected that this organisation will be a core body securing food supply both during emergency and normalcy.

However, due to the increasing amount and scale of disasters, ASEAN countries realise the necessity of having an agency which will take a direct responsibility on disaster management and humanitarian relief. In 2011, ASEAN members signed the Agreement on the Establishment of the ASEAN Coordinating Centre for Humanitarian Assistance on Disaster Management. Following this agreement, the AHA Centre was formally established with humanitarian relief (which includes food aid) as its main mission. Functioning as a coordinating centre and facilitation for joint emergency response, the AHA Centre will establish and maintain the regional standby arrangements for emergency response in which the food stockpile exists and data of earmarked assets and capacities available in the region for emergency response are accumulated. Ideally, it is expected that the AHA Centre will coordinate closely with APTERR on food aid delivery during the emergency. During normal times and for longer-term planning and activation, the AHA Centre will take a secondary role with APTERR taking the primary role to ensure food security in terms of poverty reduction through trade and agricultural coop-cration. As non-members of the AHA Centre, Plus Three countries will contribute to the AHA Centre on an individual country basis.

This chapter aims to explain the evolution and development of regional coop-eration on food security among ASEAN member states and the Plus Three coun-tries. It attempts to examine and understand the different perspectives between ASEAN and the Plus Three as well as their roles and contributions to policy direction, organisational structure and function, mechanism for coordination and outputs of the cooperation focusing on food security during emergency and nor-malcy. A critical set of organisations formed within ASEAN tasked with the objective of ensuring food security will be discussed (see Table 1.1). Indonesia and the Philippines are selected to be case studies of countries that have suffered from food insecurity due to natural disasters, while Thailand and Vietnam have been selected as case studies of countries that export food and have the capacity to donate food during emergency.

2 Self-sufficiency in food of ASEAN member countries

A key obligation for a country's government to its people is to ensure the food supply both during normalcy and emergency. Several factors contribute to food self-sufficiency of the country, including geographical location, climate, quantity and quality of existing natural resources for agricultural production, technological capacity and the economic development of the country. In the case of ASEAN, the situation of food security of ASEAN as a region and as individual country members is rather complicated due to geographical limitations, different levels and degrees of productivity, and economic disparity between members. This set of factors means that member countries face different types of food insecurity and in turn pursue different policies and plans to deal with the problems. Bello (2010)

Table 1.1 ASEAN's key organisations and functions regarding food security

Acronym	Full name	Year established	Key functions
AMAF	ASEAN Ministerial Meeting on Agriculture and Forestry	1979	A meeting of ASEAN Ministers of Agriculture to formulate policy regarding agricultural cooperation, including food security
AMAF+3	ASEAN Ministerial Meeting on Agriculture and Forestry and the Ministers of Agriculture of the People's Republic of China, Japan and the Republic of Korea	2001	A meeting of ASEAN Ministers of Agriculture and Ministers of Agriculture of the People's Republic of China, Japan and the Republic of Korea, to formulate policy regarding agricultural cooperation, including food security
SOM-AMAF	Senior Officials Meeting of ASEAN Ministerial Meeting on Agriculture and Forestry	1979	The main body under AMAF that oversees and facilitates the overall cooperation among members in food and agriculture, with the guidance of AMAF
AFSRB	ASEAN Food Security Reserve Board	1979	The body that formulates and provides policy direction for ASEAN members regarding food security
AERR	ASEAN Emergency Rice Reserve	1979	The scheme of rice reserve and release agreed by ASEAN members
EAERR	East Asia Emergency Rice Reserve	2003	The scheme of rice reserve and release agreed by ASEAN members and the Plus Three countries
APTERR	ASEAN Plus Three Emergency Rice Reserve	2011	The body under AMAF+3 that manages rice reserve and release during emergency
AFSIS	ASEAN Food Security Information System	2003	The project that provides and facilitates ASEAN members on agricultural information (collecting, interpreting and distributing)
AHA Centre	ASEAN Coordinating Center for Humanitarian Assistance	2011	The body that provides assistance to ASEAN members during emergency

Note: This table was created by the author with information from www.asean.org.

has divided the ASEAN members into three groups. The first group consists of the countries that are relatively more food secure. Singapore and Brunei are in this group with their small populations, high per-capita income and economic structures dominated by industry and trade. Due to their geographical limitations, in fact, these two countries are at food security risk, but owing to their economic capacity they can secure food supply by trade. The second group, except Vietnam and its socialist-orientated market economy, has adopted a market-oriented policy and industrialisation. Indonesia, Malaysia, the Philippines, Thailand and Vietnam are in this group. Thailand and Vietnam are food-exporting countries, while the rest are self-sufficient. However, due to the recent frequency of natural disasters, Indonesia and the Philippines now face the problem of food insecurity in terms of availability, accessibility and stability. The third group comprises the poorest countries of the region whose economies are in transition. Laos, Cambodia and Myanmar are in this group. While these countries attempt to restructure their economic systems, they are facing a number of difficulties. The food insecurity is also serious; therefore, they need a special policy to deal with the issue.

Table 1.2 shows the rice balance for the ten countries of ASEAN. The table shows that the largest rice exporters are Thailand and Vietnam, with Indonesia and Malaysia being the largest importers. In general, the poor countries (Cambodia, Laos and Myanmar), although self-sufficient in rice, are at risk of food insecurity due to poverty and a low level of development, and therefore will secure food supply through development mechanisms focusing on poverty reduction, while countries facing insufficiency during emergency due to disaster (Indonesia, the Philippines) will secure food supply by food aid as humanitarian relief. With

Table 1.2 Rice balance sheet of ASEAN countries, 2012 (milled rice) (unit: ton)

Countries	Supply		Demand	
	Production	Import	Domestic utilisation	Export
ASEAN	**125,531,202**	**3,660,663**	**113,060,181**	**18,544,295**
Brunei	1,463	31,988	34,662	–
Cambodia	5,617,794	–	3,302,496	1,948,412
Indonesia	39,925,652	1,620,000	41,216,303	1,000
Laos	2,131,200	15,383	2,105,304	20,883
Malaysia	1,774,011	1,143,292	2,552,445	–
Myanmar	18,103,183	–	19,532,052	789,000
Philippines	11,427,925	500,000	12,682,210	–
Singapore	–	350,000	270,000	85,000
Thailand	20,872,665	–	13,777,000	8,500,000
Vietnam	25,676,309	–	18,187,707	7,200,000

Source: From www.afsisnc.org/sites/default/files/publications/asean.pdf.

this realisation, ASEAN has developed a mechanism that is able to respond to the different demands of its members.

3 Regional cooperation on food security in ASEAN

3.1 ASEAN and ASEAN Plus Three cooperation on agriculture and food: policy evolution and development

Since its establishment, ASEAN has tried to promote regional cooperation on several issues, and food security is one of them. ASEAN has classified food security as a part of agricultural cooperation under the scope and framework of regional economic cooperation conducted by ASEAN ministers of agriculture and forestry. However, in 1968 when the agricultural cooperation was initiated, attention was focused on food production and food supply only. Later, in 1979, the scope was extended to cover cooperation on agriculture and forestry, and the Meeting of ASEAN Ministers on Agriculture and Forestry (AMAF) was set up as a mechanism to conduct the cooperation annually.

The year 1979 was considered as a turning point for agricultural cooperation and food security in ASEAN. At the first meeting, the Manila Consensus was delivered with the emphasis on regional cooperation on agriculture and food. Food security during emergency was raised as critical and, therefore, mechanism and structure to secure food supply during emergency was set up by the signing of the ASEAN Food Security Reserve Agreement in that year. Following the agreement, the ASEAN Food Security Reserve Board was appointed to implement the policy while the ASEAN Emergency Rice Reserve was set up by member countries to reserve rice within their countries as well. Concurrently, in order to promote food security in periods of non-emergency, AMAF also appointed the Committee on Food, Agriculture and Forestry, the Committee on Industry, Minerals and Energy, as well as setting the common policy direction on the ASEAN Quarantine Ring for Common Plant and Animal Protection. These activities aimed to support the agricultural production and increase productivity, which would indirectly contribute to food security through poverty reduction. The policies and activities reflected the different methods to secure food adopted by ASEAN members, namely food security during emergency was focused on a reserve and release system while food security for normalcy was achieved by increasing production and trade. In terms of the structure of cooperation, apart from AMAF, Senior Officials of Ministry of Agriculture and Forestry and several working groups were appointed to support AMAF as the operational units. An annual meeting was utilised as the main mechanism to operate the cooperation.

The significant developments of AMAF during the 1980s were the Protocol to Amend the Agreement on the ASEAN Food Security Reserve in 1982 adding a new paragraph in the annex to the agreement regarding ASEAN supply and demand for rice, the inclusion of Brunei in the ASEAN Food Security Reserve Agreement in 1985 and the increased amount of earmarked rice reserve from 50,000 metric tons to 53,000 metric tons in the same year. It is important to note that until 1994 there was no strategic plan and plan of action as guidelines for member countries to conduct their activities collectively. Member countries of AMAF generally were motivated to initiate and conduct activities by their own interests, either with or without regional planning.

The major breakthrough for the issue of food security came in 1994 with the Program of Action for ASEAN Cooperation in Food, Agriculture and Forestry 1995–1999, drafted and approved by AMAF. Owing to the creation of this strategic plan and plan of action on the agricultural cooperation, the role of AMAF and its direction became more clear, streamlined and institutionalised. As the first five-year plan, it focused on productivity in order to increase food supply and ensure food availability. Research, training and information sharing had also been promoted. As it was the first plan, there were limited initiatives and new mechanism invention. Instead, the existing mechanism was reviewed and improved, particularly the ASEAN Emergency Rice Reserve under the ASEAN Food Security Reserve Agreement.

In anticipation of the first plan coming to a close, ASEAN members agreed in 1997 to prepare the next plan. The Strategic Plan of Action on ASEAN Cooperation in Food, Agriculture and Forestry 1999–2004, or the Hanoi Plan of Action, was approved and enforced in 1999. This plan established new initiatives to promote food security and regional cooperation. Firstly, it was agreed to strengthen the regional database system to support ASEAN members for regional planning on production and trade. Secondly, the regional trade on food under AFTA would be reconsidered and analysed in order to increase trade on food both inter- and intra-ASEAN. Thirdly, the regional food market would be strengthened in order to increase regional food security. Fourthly, demand and supply of main food products, such as, rice, corn, beans and sugar, would be studied. Fifthly, it was agreed to establish the regional information system to support member countries to manage their food supply. And lastly, the realisation that the efficient management of food supply during emergency and for the self-insufficient countries was extremely significant, and the member countries agreed to reconsider the ASEAN Food Security Reserve Agreement in order to ensure the food supply worked, especially regarding rice.

Following this strategic plan, the ASEAN Food Security Information System was established in 2003 in order to collect data, analyse and disseminate to all members as a support mechanism for food security. It should be noted that the contribution of the Hanoi Plan was crucial in terms of the institutionalisation of AMAF and the regional cooperation on food and agriculture due to the trade openness and information sharing resulting from the plan implementation. In addition, as AFSIS was established with the support of the Plus Three countries, especially Japan, to be a facilitating agency for food security, it reflected the relations between ASEAN and the Plus Three countries as well as their different perspectives on cooperation in agriculture and food.

When the Strategic Plan of Action on ASEAN Cooperation in Food, Agriculture and Forestry 1999–2004 was approaching the final stage, the Strategic Plan of Action on ASEAN Cooperation in Food, Agriculture and Forestry 2005–2010, or Vientiane Action Program, had been drafted and approved in 2004, and was enforced in 2005. It was the third strategic action plan with the objective of promoting regional cooperation in order to achieve a regional community in 2015, particularly the ASEAN Economic Community. Under this plan, the AFSIS-2nd phase was continued, and the Early Warning Information Report, the Agricultural Commodity Outlook Report and the Annual Report were produced and disseminated. With the continuity of the Vientiane Plan with the expectation of information sharing regarding sensitive product, it was hoped that regional cooperation would become deeper and stronger.

Before the end of this plan, the ASEAN Integrated Food Security (AIFS) Framework and Strategic Plan of Action on ASEAN Food Security 2009–2013 had been set up. The AIFS had four main components: food security and emergency/shortage relief; sustainable food trade development; an integrated food security information system; and agricultural innovation. However, when the AIFS was carefully investigated, it was noted that although AIFS was designed to respond to both types of situations, namely the emergency or shortage of food and long-term food security, two thirds of the components reflected the priority of ensuring long-term food security by focusing on sustainable production and trade promotion.

The inclusion of the Plus Three countries in the existing regional cooperation framework in 2001 was another important development of regional cooperation on agriculture and food. After the economic crisis, the ASEAN Plus Three was created as a new mechanism to support ASEAN countries as well as to promote wider cooperation among countries of East and Southeast Asia. Through regular meetings, active engagement in various sectors and a leading role in several areas of cooperation, the ASEAN Plus Three became more institutionalised. Concurrently, with their active involvement in development and cooperation with ASEAN members, the Plus Three countries help to strengthen regional cooperation in several areas as well as contribute to the progress of regional integration.

The Plus Three countries also have been very active in agriculture and food cooperation. Similar to AMAF, the ASEAN Ministerial Meeting on Agriculture and Forestry and the ministers of agriculture of the People's Republic of China, Japan and the Republic of Korea, or AMAF+3, was created as the cooperation mechanism among ASEAN members and the Plus Three countries. Since the first meeting in 2001, the AMAF+3 meetings have been continued annually with new significant initiatives, such as the pilot project on East Asia Emergency Rice Reserve (EAERR), the ASEAN Plus Three Cooperation on Food Security and Bio-Energy Development, ASEAN Plus Three Bio-Mass Energy Forum and ASEAN Plus Three Roundtable on Food Security Cooperation Strategy. Sharing similar objectives to AMAF, AMAF+3 also aim to promote the regional cooperation in agriculture and food by emphasising food security and food reserve, as well as food information systems. However, compared with AMAF, AMAF+3 have given priority to food security during emergency by allocating huge effort and resources on the institutionalisation of the food reserve and release system.

While the emergency reserve is the priority, AMAF+3 do not neglect agricultural cooperation. With their advanced knowledge and technique, the Plus

Three countries contribute to the development of agricultural sectors of ASEAN countries through training and information sharing. These help ASEAN countries to increase their productivity and be able to secure food supply in long term. It is also noted that AMAF+3 pay more attention to sustainable agriculture, which is the core of food security in the long term. Therefore, environmentally friendly and climate change adaptation are promoted by AMAF+3 regarding agricultural development and cooperation. At the same time, with the realisation of crucial interrelations between food security and energy security, AMAF+3 have initiated and promoted bio-energy development. As biofuel has become a new source of energy, it could replace the food product due to a high demand of energy as well as the high income generated following that demand. This situation will weaken food security in the long term. Therefore, the Plus Three countries try to harmonise and promote both food security and energy security by several means, such as the ASEAN Plus Three Bio Mass Energy Forum, and the ASEAN Plus Three Comprehensive Strategy on Food Security and Bio-Energy Development 2011.

In 2007, the ASEAN Plus Three Cooperation Work Plan 2007–2017 was initiated and implemented as a guideline for enhancing and promoting cooperation among ASEAN and the Plus Three countries in a comprehensive and mutually beneficial manner. After five years of implementation, the ASEAN Plus Three Cooperation Work Plan 2007–2017 was reviewed at its mid-term in 2012, revised and adopted again in 2013. The ASEAN Plus Three Cooperation Work Plan 2013–2017 continued to focus on strengthening and deepening the cooperation among ASEAN members and the Plus Three countries by joint actions and measures through closer consultation and coordination among sectoral bodies of ASEAN and the Plus Three. The revised ASEAN Plus Three Cooperation Work Plan, as the master plan, covered five important issues including political and security cooperation, economic and financial cooperation, the environment, climate change and sustainable development cooperation, the socio-cultural and development cooperation and connectivity cooperation. Cooperation in food, agriculture, fisheries and forestry comes under economic and financial cooperation, with the main objective of forging and enhancing deeper and closer cooperation among members.

Food security during both normalcy and emergency is categorised as being under agricultural cooperation, which is in turn a part of economic cooperation. APTERR and AFSIS are referred to in this plan as the two main bodies functioning to facilitate and support regional food security, particularly during emergency while food aid is not mentioned as the emergency response categorised under disaster management and emergency response. It is surprising to note that although disaster management and emergency response is included in this plan, it does not mention and cover food aid as a part of food security during emergency. According to the plan, disaster management and emergency response has focused on early warning systems, information sharing and a public awareness campaign. In addition, it is also important to observe that this Plan is a master plan for ASEAN Plus Three countries, which provide guidelines to all issues regarding cooperation among the Plus Three countries and between the Plus Three and

ASEAN countries; it is not a specific plan for cooperation in food and agriculture only. Therefore, compared with AMAF, which has its own plan on cooperation in agriculture and food, AMAF+3 is not yet firmly institutionalised. Moreover, as the master plan, it was a product of ASEAN Plus Three Foreign Ministers' Meetings, in which the policy and direction was initiated and drafted by the ministries of foreign affairs, not by AMAF+3, while activities indicated in the Plan will be conducted by line ministries involved in those issues. This situation also signified the different degree and level of involvement of the Plus Three countries in regional agricultural cooperation. As AMAF+3 have given priority to emergency rice reserve which is different from AMAF, this reflects the different perspectives on food and national interests between the Plus Three and ASEAN countries.

Recently, another development of this issue can be seen in an arrangement of the ASEAN Rice Trade Forum. In 2011, AMAF endorsed a pilot project on the ASEAN Rice Trade Forum with the objective of being a platform for promoting a coherent and coordinated policy action on rice trade to advance the goal of food security in ASEAN. In concrete terms, the Forum will bring together representatives of ASEAN member countries and various stakeholders including agri-business groups, non-governmental organisations and international development agencies to collectively share and analyse rice market information, ensure better coordination of food policy and identify policy options to strengthen regional cooperation and supply chain investment for sustainable development of rice trade and food security. The forum was convened twice, in 2012 and 2013, on a pilot basis by AFSRB in coordination with the ASEAN Secretariat and Asian Development Bank. Although the output of the forum was not substantial due to its early stage, it should be noted that the emergence of the forum has confirmed the priority of AMAF regarding food security.

3.2 ASEAN and ASEAN Plus Three cooperation on the Emergency Rice Reserve: from AERR to APTERR

Although some ASEAN members are food producers and food exporters, it is very challenging for ASEAN to secure food supply of the region and of the individual member country during emergency. In principle, in order to secure food availability and accessibility during emergency, food reserve and especially the release system are crucial. Realising this, in 1979, ASEAN members agreed on the Agreement on the ASEAN Food Security Reserve under which the ASEAN Food Security Reserve System and the ASEAN Emergency Rice Reserve were established.

The AFSRS and AERR were operated by the ASEAN Food Security Reserve Board in which representatives from all member countries participated. The core idea of this agreement and the system was to support the member countries in case of emergency or food shortage caused by disasters through the agreed amount of rice reserve in each member country and agreed release mechanism of rice upon emergency requirement. The agreement was updated in 1982 and 1997 in order to reset the amount of rice reserve which was increased following the inclusion of new members of ASEAN.

Functioning as a board, the AFSRB provides policy direction for the AERR. The country representative participating in the board mainly are officials of governments' agencies related to agriculture or trade and commerce in their respective countries, and the Ministry of Commerce of Thailand serves as the AFSRB Secretariat. The board meeting is a main mechanism of AFSRB to run the body including initiating policy and calling for support or approval from member countries. The board meets only once a year but its focus is on trade policy rather than food security policy. Being government officials, the board's members have faced a number of limitations to pursue regional cooperation. Understandably, board members prioritise their own country's perspective and therefore it is difficult for the board's members who represent their countries to contribute to regional cooperation if that contribution goes against their national interests. In addition, as the main function of the board is to coordinate among members through the meeting, the board itself is weak and does not have authority over its members. As a result, with coordinating mechanism alone, it takes a long time for members to agree on any common policy or collective activity.

Apart from providing policy direction, the board is regularly updated by member countries as an early warning system. In general, the report covers national stockholding policy and programme, as well as other aspects of food supply and demand situations, particularly with rice, of the member countries. The information forms the basis for situation appraisal and outlook to be circulated to member countries, but otherwise is kept confidential.

The amount of rice reserved has been changed from time to time, particularly when ASEAN enlarged to include new members such as Brunei and the Indochinese states. Then, the amount of total earmarked reserve increased to 53,000 metric tons in 1985, again to 67,000 metric tons in 1997, and in 1999 to 87,000 metric tons (see Table 1.3). However, it should be noted that until 2003, the amount of rice reserve among ASEAN member countries did not change. This reflected the fact that the amount of rice reserve was agreed among members with the consultation in AFSRB with the willingness of member states; it was not the response to the predicted demand during emergency although each country committed to set the earmarked stocks for emergency reserve. The ASEAN country which suffers from food shortage must apply for a release by making a direct request to another ASEAN member country, while the AFSRB need only be notified of the request from the emergency reserve. By this system, therefore, the rice reserve which would be delivered to the affected countries upon request was not the humanitarian aid, but a purchased product with the bilateral agreed price. With this reserve and release system, it was noted that the AERR stocks were neither increased nor utilised until 2003.

Briones (2011) claimed that AERR was inefficient and unresponsive to emergency requirements due to several reasons. Firstly, the reserve was too small, equivalent to only 0.4 day consumption of ASEAN countries. Secondly, the bilateral negotiation process for rice release had duplicated the regular market or government-to-government transactions. And thirdly, the AFSRB was unable to operate AERR as a regional entity due to a lack of funding.

Table 1.3 Earmarked stock of ASEAN Emergency Rice Reserve

Countries	1979	1985	1997	1999
Indonesia	12,000	12,000	12,000	12,000
Malaysia	6,000	6,000	6,000	6,000
Philippines	12,000	12,000	12,000	12,000
Singapore	5,000	5,000	5,000	5,000
Thailand	15,000	15,000	15,000	15,000
Brunei	–	3,000	3,000	3,000
Vietnam	–	–	14,000	14,000
Myanmar	–	–	–	14,000
Laos	–	–	–	3,000
Cambodia	–	–	–	3,000
Total	**50,000**	**53,000**	**67,000**	**87,000**

Source: www.asean.org.

Considering the fact that none of the AERR stock was utilised, the plan to revive AERR came about and the idea to strengthen the implementation of the AERR scheme was crystallised in a special workshop on Food Security Cooperation and Rice Reserve Management System in East Asia in 2001 in Thailand. The recommendation from the workshop was to review the possibility of establishing a new rice reserve scheme in East Asia. The proposal was endorsed at the AMAF+3 meeting in Indonesia in 2001, and the Ministry of Agriculture and Cooperatives of Thailand was appointed to coordinate the feasibility study on food security and rice reserve system in East Asia with the support of Japan. The result of the study recommended that a pilot project of EAERR should be conducted. The establishment of this pilot project was approved in 2002 and reaffirmed in 2003; it then started to operate in 2004.

As a pilot project, EAERR was managed by a management team under the supervision of a project steering committee with financial support provided by Japan and in-kind support provided by Thailand, in cooperation with other ASEAN members and the Plus Three countries. The EAERR pilot project aimed to gain experience of the implementation and management of a rice reserve and release system during emergency in order to design and develop a permanent system in the future. Regarding the reserve mechanism, EAERR, similar to AERR, did not hold physical stock, but participating countries had earmarked rice stocks equal to the total amount of 787,000 metric tons from national reserves. However, with the assumption that this pilot project would try the new mechanism as a test for the future, EAERR had explored the possibility and planned to develop the physical stockpile in terms of rice as well as cash, which became an example for the APTERR reserve system later. Regarding the release process, when encountering a food shortage, a member country would report to the management team the extent of its rice shortage and the amount of rice it required. Then, the country purchased the rice from the reserve and paid transportation and operational costs.

If the member country required more than the earmarked quantity, it requested the management team to provide the additional amount from other countries' earmarked reserve stock.

In terms of structure and function, the difference between AERR and EAERR was that EAERR had the project steering committee and management team to facilitate the process of rice release during emergency while AERR did not. With these two committees, it was expected that efficiency and effectiveness would be increased. Another difference between AERR and EAERR was the amount of total earmarked reserve. With the huge amount of earmarked reserve from the Plus Three countries, the total amount of earmarked reserve increased sharply to 787,000 metric tons, as shown in Table 1.4. This change reflected the relations between ASEAN and the Plus Three countries.

Although AERR and EAERR had shared the common practices of reserve and release mechanism, in comparison, EAERR had accomplished several missions during 2004–10. Details in Table 1.5 illustrate this situation. As can be seen from Table 1.5, the focus of the missions were on emergency food aid to mainly smaller towns and rural provinces affected by natural disasters such as typhoons and flooding. There was only one instance of a longer-term programme of poverty alleviation, and this was in Laos in 2004–5 involving a small group of urban poor households in Vientiane.

In addition to EAERR, AMAF+3 also established the ASEAN Food Security Information System (AFSIS), a supporting body to EAERR and food security policy. The main objective of the project was to strengthen regional food security through the systematic collection, analysis and dissemination of food

Table 1.4 Earmarked stock of East Asia Emergency Rice Reserve 2003

Countries	EAERR earmarked stock (tons) 2003
Indonesia	12,000
Malaysia	6,000
Philippines	12,000
Singapore	5,000
Thailand	15,000
Brunei	3,000
Vietnam	14,000
Myanmar	14,000
Laos	3,000
Cambodia	3,000
PRC	300,000
Japan	250,000
Rep. Korea	150,000
Total	**787,000**

Source: www.asean.org.

Table 1.5 EAERR accomplishment 2004–10

Duration	Programme	Country	Total quantity of rice (metric tons)	Beneficiaries
December 2004–June 2005	Poverty-alleviation programme	Laos	13.37	87 households and students in Vientiane province
November 2005–November 2006	Relief programme to help people affected by flood and rehabilitation programme	Indonesia	100	9,992 people in Sampang district and 22,825 people in Jember district
July 2006–December 2006	Relief programme to help people affected by volcanic eruption and typhoons	Philippines	930.24	154,500 households in Leyte, Cebu, Davao and Manila City
July 2007–January 2008	Relief programme to help people affected by flood and poverty-alleviation programme	Cambodia	379.76	11,798 households in Kampong Thom, Ratanakiri, Kandal, Kompong Chhnang and Takeo provinces
March 2008–May 2009	Relief programme to help people affected by flood	Indonesia	186.5	18,182 households in Central Java and East Java
November 2008–January 2009	Rehabilitation programme to help people affected by cyclone Nargis	Myanmar	164	13,120 people in Laputta and Bogalay townships
November 2009–February 2010	Rehabilitation programme to help people affected by typhoon Ketsana and flash floods	Philippines	520	7,137 households in Metro Manila and Ifugao provinces
July 2010–October 2010	Rehabilitation programme to help people affected by typhoon Ketsana	Laos	347	9,207 villages in Saravan and Attapeu provinces

Source: www.apterr.org/about-us/how-we-work/apterr-accomplishment.

security-related information. While Thailand hosts the office of AFSIS, Japan has provided financial support for the project. During the second phase (2008–12), the project's objective was extended to enhance the regional food security information system and increase capacities of member countries in providing the required information. In addition, three new elements were included in the project, namely, the Early Warning Information Report, Agricultural Commodity

Outlook and Mutual Technical Cooperation. The activities of AFSIS contained two main components: human resource development and information network development, and during the second phase the enrichment of the database and data analysis were emphasised.

Briones (2011) pointed out that the EAERR marked a significant improvement of AERR in terms of the amount of rice reserve and release, and a solution for the administrative bottleneck of financial as well as managerial support. With the positive result of the EAERR experiment, ASEAN and the Plus Three countries agreed to establish the permanent scheme of emergency rice reserve following the EAERR model. Therefore, after several meetings and discussions, the ASEAN Plus Three Emergency Rice Reserve (APTERR) was formally established in 2011.

APTERR is a regional cooperation scheme with the aim of strengthening food security and reducing poverty within the ASEAN members and Plus Three countries. The main objective of APTERR is to meet emergency requirements and achieve humanitarian purposes without distorting the normal international trade of rice. To enable APTERR to function, financial and other resources, including stockpiled or earmarked rice as well as management support, are sources from cash and in-kind assistance provided by member countries. Other countries and donor organisations may provide donations for the stockpiled emergency rice reserves.

The APTERR reserve and release mechanism is made in case of emergency through three APTERR programmes by using APTERR stocks. There are two types of rice reserve provided under APTERR. First, the earmarked emergency rice reserve is a specific quantity of milled rice which remains owned and/or controlled by the government of the earmarking country for the purpose of meeting emergency requirements of one or more APTERR member countries. The amount of this earmarked reserve has been continued as with those of EAERR (see Table 1.6). Second, the stockpiled emergency rice reserve is rice voluntarily donated to APTERR in the form of cash (termed stockpiled cash) and/or physical rice stocks (termed stockpiled rice) which are owned collectively by the APTERR member countries and managed by the APTERR Secretariat under the supervision of the APTERR council. With the establishment of stockpiled reserve, there is no necessity for APT members to increase or change the amount of earmarked reserve.

Regarding the release mechanism, following the case of EAERR, there are three programmes for the release of APTERR stocks. Tier 1 involves the release of earmarked stocks under a pre-arrangement to address problems of food availability; it is designed for anticipated emergency. The pre-arranged release of rice reserve is formalised as a forward contract, indicating the specific quantity and grade of rice, pricing method, terms of payment and delivery, and other requirements between the supplying and affected countries. Tier 2 involves the release of earmarked stocks for emergency not addressed by Tier 1; it is designed for unanticipated emergencies. Delivery follows an on-the-spot arrangement between the supplying and affected countries. Payment can be made in cash or through long-term loans or grants based on a mutual agreement between the countries involved. Tier 3 involves the release of stockpiled emergency rice reserve to address problems of food accessibility; it is designed for acute emergency and other humanitarian responses to food insecurity. This release is the donation of rice as humanitarian assistance to affected countries upon their requests. In special cases, rice distribution can be fast-tracked under an automatic trigger. In addition, the release of rice may also be possible for poverty alleviation and malnourishment eradication programmes to address other humanitarian purposes.

During the two years of its existence, APTERR conducted several activities. It was noted that the rice released from APTERR was utilised for both purposes of emergency response and poverty reduction. Table 1.7 is a summary of APTERR's accomplishments, noting that the annual interventions are similar to its

Table 1.6 Earmarked stock of ASEAN Plus Three Emergency Rice Reserve 2011

Countries	APTERR earmarked stock (tons) 2011
Indonesia	12,000
Malaysia	6,000
Philippines	12,000
Singapore	5,000
Thailand	15,000
Brunei	3,000
Vietnam	14,000
Myanmar	14,000
Laos	3,000
Cambodia	3,000
PRC	300,000
Japan	250,000
Rep. Korea	150,000
Total	**787,000**

Source: www.asean.org and www.apterr.org.

Table 1.7 APTERR accomplishment 2011–12

Duration	Programme	Country	Total quantity of rice (metric tons)	Beneficiaries
November 2011– December 2011	Emergency relief programme to help people affected by flood	Thailand	50 MT of milled rice and 31,000 cans of cooked rice	8,100 households in Central region
October 2012– December 2012	Food assistance for poverty alleviation and malnutrition-eradication programme	Indonesia	200	20,000 households in Yogyakarta, Central Java, Banten and East Java provinces

Source: www.apterr.org/about-us/how-we-work/apterr-accomplishment.

predecessor EAERR (see Table 1.5). The scale of aid, in terms of volume of rice and number of household beneficiaries, also looks promising.

Aside from these accomplishments, APTERR continues to face challenges. Briones (2011) has mentioned three crucial issues which may prevent APTERR from following its mandate: the reserve and release system, financial and administrative support, and lastly, the harmonisation of rules and regulations among member countries. These issues are difficult to solve. Regarding the reserve system, although the current reserve is huge, it is an earmarked and not a stockpiled reserve. The actual reserve which is stockpiled reserve is very small, and this affects the timeliness of the delivery process which is critical during emergency. It should be noted that stockpiled reserve is a standby arrangement which member countries, particularly exporting countries, have a low motivation to invest in. Crucially, the rice to be released as humanitarian aid during emergency is small and not sufficient because it will come from stockpiled reserve. In cases where a larger amount of rice is needed, the release must come from the earmarked reserve, and releasing this is time consuming. In order to improve the efficiency and effectiveness of APTERR during emergency, a larger stockpiled reserve for release under emergency humanitarian aid must be promoted. However, this seems unlikely to happen as long as the exporting countries are not motivated. In addition, as APTERR was established as a permanent scheme with the administrative structure to take responsibility of operation during both day-to-day and emergency situations, financial support for the overhead cost becomes critical. Although member countries agreed to provide support according to their ability, in reality it seems very difficult to collect the budget sufficient to cover the cost. For exporting countries, this will be an additional burden on top of rice reserve, while, for disaster-prone countries, as the efficiency and effectiveness of APTERR is not promising, supporting the overhead cost becomes an additional burden on top of their suffering. The affected countries prefer either to receive humanitarian aid as a grant or to improve their self-sufficiency in order to secure food availability or to respond to emergency. Lastly, although APTERR provides rice for emergency response, it is different from food aid categorised as a part of humanitarian aid. As the number of disasters has been increasing and humanitarian assistance has become more important, APTERR is unable to fulfil the demand properly. It is noted that although APTERR has reflected an attempt of regional cooperation among ASEAN and the Plus Three countries, it is only an incomplete job.

3.3 ASEAN regional disaster management framework and AHA Centre

After the Tsunami in 2004, ASEAN agreed with the Declaration on Action to Strengthen Emergency Relief, Rehabilitation, Reconstruction and Prevention on the Aftermath of Earthquake and Tsunami Disaster 2004. And in 2005, ASEAN concluded the ASEAN Agreement on Disaster Management and Emergency Response (AADMER).

AADMER fortified the regional policy backbone on disaster management by giving priority to disaster risk reduction. AADMER is a proactive regional framework for cooperation, coordination, technical assistance and resource mobilisation in all aspects of disaster management. It also affirmed ASEAN commitment to the Hyogo Framework of Action (HFA) and is the first legally binding HFA-related instrument in the world. Being comprehensive, the AADMER Work Programme 2010–2015 covered all aspects of disaster management and thus outlined a detailed roadmap for four strategic components, namely regional warning and monitoring, prevention and mitigation, preparedness and response, and recovery. However, surprisingly, regarding earmarked assets for the ASEAN Standby Arrangement, there is no specification of food reserve as a part of earmarked assets under this work programme.

In order to implement and monitor the AADMER work programme, several ASEAN bodies have been involved. The ASEAN Committee on Disaster Management (ACDM) has provided policy oversight and supervision in the implementation process. In particular, ACDM provides leadership and guidance towards fulfilling the goals and objectives of AADMER in the persuasion of the vision of disaster-resilient nations and safer communities within ASEAN by 2015. Under ACDM, subsidiary thematic working groups have been organised to lead the implementation of the AADMER work programme activities. In view of this, the working groups will initiate setting indicators for the monitoring and evaluation of the progress of the implementation process, make recommendations on specific technical areas of the AADMER work programme based on monitoring and evaluation reports, periodically report to the ACDM and provide technical guidance to the AHA Centre.

The AHA Centre has been identified as the main operational engine in executing the activities in the AADMER work programme. It is an intergovernmental organisation which aims to facilitate cooperation and coordination among ASEAN member countries and with other international organisations for disaster management and emergency response in the ASEAN region. The Centre was established in 2011 by the signing of the Agreement on the Establishment of the ASEAN Coordinating Centre for Humanitarian Assistance on Disaster Management.

At the operational level, the critical problem facing the AHA Centre recently is the coordination between APTERR and the AHA Centre during emergency. As mentioned earlier, while APTERR has operated the rice reserve and release system, the AHA Centre also is expected to conduct a similar activity during emergency. While APTERR has both earmarked and stockpiled rice reserves, the AHA Centre also has a mandate to provide food aid as humanitarian assistance. Therefore, the mobilisation of food is also done by the AHA Centre during emergency. However, with this duplicated function of two bodies, data from interviews suggested that in reality, affected countries received humanitarian assistance neither from APTERR nor the AHA Centre, but from international organisations and donor countries based on a bilateral basis. Comments from the affected countries on the regional cooperation scheme included the time-consuming procedure of bilateral negotiation and the mobilisation of food, as well as the limitations regarding manpower, and national rules and regulations related to the entry of supplies. Certainly, this reflects the weakness of the regional cooperation scheme of ASEAN.

4 ASEAN and food security during normalcy: the future path

While ASEAN cooperation in food security during emergency has been struggling for better efficiency and effectiveness, cooperation in food security during normal times also needs to be reconsidered. Kuntjoro and Jamil (2008) point out that there is not a *one-fits-all policy* to the issue of food security, meaning that each country generally designs its national policy and plan responding to its food security issue according to its own conditions and capabilities. Regional cooperation will be one measure among others which the country may select as its method to secure food availability and accessibility.

For food-exporting countries, securing food by trade openness and promotion is preferable due to the expected economic benefits because, for them, food, particularly rice, is not only staple food but also a high-value commodity which is an essential source of national income. Therefore, regional cooperation in agriculture and food focusing on increasing productivity, common policy on food price and technological innovation and transfer is highly supported by member countries. However, for rice-importing countries, relying on food trade only will be very risky due to the unexpected situations preventing trade flow, which include both political and economic conditions. Therefore, realising that food security is national security, increasing self-sufficiency in food becomes a priority policy for many importing countries, rather than trade promotion. From this perspective, regional cooperation will not be selected as a tool to promote food security for these countries.

For ASEAN member countries, although regional cooperation in agriculture and food has been promoted and institutionalised for a long time, witnessed by AMAF and several strategic and action plans, due to the diversity and disparity among them, each country has applied different methods to secure food. Food self-sufficiency policy, particularly on rice, is still highly promoted in some countries, such as Indonesia and the Philippines. While regional cooperation has been developed, which signifies that food can be secured by intra-food trade, it is very important for ASEAN members to balance a food self-sufficiency policy and the promotion of intra-food trade. Bello (2010, 105) has suggested that ASEAN member countries need to reach a common understanding on basic issues before progress can be made:

> If regional integration and cooperation means moving towards a common goal using a common strategy, then it is essential that the ASEAN member countries agree on what food security collectively means to them, and what food items are important to each of them and the region in general, so that regional integration and cooperation under the auspices of ASEAN can be better promoted.

In addition, it is also significant for ASEAN members to realise that food insecurity is a regional problem that can be best tackled by a regional approach. Although a self-sufficiency policy has been promoted, not all countries can secure their food availability by themselves due to geographical location, climate and natural resources. In this case, while their national policy and plan on food security may not be sufficient and efficient enough to tackle the problem, ASEAN members may find that a regional mechanism is vital and helpful in ensuring food security, as suggested by Kuntjoro and Jamil (2008).

While the balanced policy between trade openness and self-sufficiency among ASEAN member countries is critical, the balance between national and regional interests among them must also be reconsidered. It is important to note that the experience during the food crisis of 2007–8 among ASEAN member countries reflected the existing discrepancy between ASEAN's objective as a regional organisation and its member countries' national economic interests. Consequently, this led to uncertainty and disappointment among ASEAN members towards regional cooperation, as Chandra and Lontoh (2010, 3) explained:

> What was clear during the global food crisis, however, was that there was little in way of solidarity to ensure food security in the region, despite ASEAN's intention to establish an ASEAN Economic Community in 2015. For example, in search for greater economic gain from inflated global food prices, rice producing nations in the region, such as Cambodia, Thailand, and Vietnam, opted to supply global food demand at the expense of ensuring the food supplies of other ASEAN rice importing countries.

This regional response was a surprise to many people within and outside the region. It should be noted that without the common understanding on regional interests, it seems very difficult to convince member countries to promote and strengthen regional cooperation even at the expense of suffering some loss in export earnings. For a strong regional action to occur, all members must put the regional norm of ensuring food security first, even if this means some setbacks for short-term national economic interests.

The last issue related to food security in ASEAN is with the small-scale farmers and their livelihoods. Food is not only a product or commodity, but it is a way of life. Concurrently food security also links closely with poverty and rural development. To secure food as a long-term policy, poverty reduction through maintaining the rural livelihood of small farmers is key. In 2011, at the 44th ASEAN Ministerial Meeting, ASEAN member countries raised this issue and shared the view that cooperation in the agricultural sector must also touch upon the livelihood of small farmers to help those farmers to secure food means to eradicate poverty. Within this context, it is hoped that the regional cooperation of ASEAN will benefit the rural poor through the development of small and medium enterprises, access to financial resources, the market and new technology. These concerns push ASEAN member countries to start looking at food security from a new perspective.

References

Bello, Amelia L.. (2010) "Ensuring Food Security: A Case for ASEAN Integration". *Asian Journal for Agriculture and Development*, 2(1–2).

Briones, Roehlano M. (2011) "Regional Cooperation for Food Security: The Case of Emergency Rice Reserves in the ASEAN Plus Three". ADB Sustainable Development Working Paper Series, Asian Development Bank.

Chandra, Alexander C. and Lucky A. Lontoh. (2010) *Regional Food Security and Trade Policy in Southeast Asia: The Role of ASEAN*. Winnipeg: International Institute for Sustainable Development.

Kuntjoro, Irene A. and Sofiah Jamil. (2008) "Food Security: Another Case for Human Security in ASEAN". Paper presented at NTS-Asia 2nd Annual Convention, Beijing, November.

Documents

AADMER Work Program, Phase 1, 2.

Agreement on the ASEAN Food Security Reserve, October 1979.

ASEAN Agreement on Disaster Management and Emergency Response, 2005.

ASEAN Agreement on the Establishment of the ASEAN Coordinating Centre for Humanitarian Assistance on Disaster Management, 2011.

ASEAN Declaration on Enhancing Cooperation in Disaster Management, 2013.

ASEAN Declaration on Mutual Assistance on Natural Disaster, 1976.

The ASEAN Integrated Food Security (AIFS) Framework 2009 and Strategic Plan of Action on Food Security in the ASEAN Region (SPA-FS) 2009–2013.

ASEAN Plus Three Emergency Rice Reserve Agreement, 2011.

ASEAN Standby Arrangement for Disaster Relief and Emergency Response.

Joint Communique of the 44th ASEAN Foreign Ministers Meeting, 19 July 2011.

The Program of Action for ASEAN Cooperation in Food, Agriculture, and Forestry 1995–1999.

Protocol to Amend the Agreement on the ASEAN Food Security Reserve, October 1982.

The Second Protocol to Amend the Agreement on the ASEAN Food Security Reserve, July 1997.

List of interviewees

Officials of Agriculture, Industries, and Natural Resources Division, Finance, Industry and Infrastructure Directorate, ASEAN Economic Community, ASEAN Secretariat .

Officials of AHA Center.

Officials of the Office of Agricultural Economics, Ministry of Agriculture and Cooperatives, Thailand.

Officials of Perum BULOG, Indonesia.

Officials of Philippines Statistics Authority, Bureau of Agricultural Statistics, Philippines.

ACO Committee members of Indonesia and Vietnam.

2 Illicit drugs as a human security threat in East Asia

Zarina Othman and Nor Azizan Idris

1 Introduction

The Cold War ended abruptly in 1989 followed by the disintegration of the Soviet Union in 1991. Instead of focusing on weapons of mass destruction, the world now gave deeper and broader attention to the survival and well-being of individual human beings. Threats to the people have attracted greater attention among scholars, especially after the concept of "human security" was introduced in a United Nations Development Programme (UNDP) publication in 1994. Since then, the UNDP has continued to refine the concept, and in its *Human Development 1997* report, it called attention to human development as part of human security, and spoke of this as a "people-centred approach" to security (UNDP 1997).

The UNDP defines human security as, "First, safety from such chronic threats as hunger, disease and repression. Second, as protection from sudden and hurtful disruption in the pattern of daily life – whether in homes, in jobs or communities" (UNDP 1997). It divides overall security into seven categories: economic, food, health, environmental, personal, community and political. Further, the UNDP lists numerous factors that can become a threat to human security – famine, ethnic conflict, terrorism, pollution and illicit drug trafficking, to name just a few. Based on this definition, human security suggests a concern with quality of life, including economic growth and access to resources, rather than a concern with weapons and defence against outside forces. In short, human security does indeed mean putting the people first (Daud et al. 2015).

Food, jobs and income insecurity, human rights violations, ethnic and religious "cleansing", inequality and ratio of military spending are among those factors proposed as useful indicators for early warning of threats to human security. It describes a condition of existence in which basic material needs are met and in which human dignity, including meaningful participation in the life and governance of the community, can be realised. One definition refers to human security as "freedom from fear and freedom from want" (UNDP 1997, 16–17).

In Northeast Asia, Japan's initiatives helped to launch the United Nations Trust Fund for Human Security in 1999. The funding goes to components of human development such as education, health and small-scale infrastructure development

(United Nations Trust Fund for Human Security 2006). In 2003, the Commission of Human Security submitted its report, "Human Security Now", which emphasised "protecting people from critical and pervasive threats and situations, building on their strengths and aspirations. It also means creating systems that give people the building blocks of survival, dignity and livelihood."

Meanwhile in Southeast Asia, the human security discourse at first appeared as part of a critique of comprehensive security (Caballero-Anthony 2002). Closer assessment revealed that while many non-traditional issues were being newly considered as threats, there still appeared to be no common understanding of what human security is all about. Thailand remains the only East Asian member of the Human Security Network, an informal group of countries that encourages the resolution of international issues that present immediate threat to human beings. Following the Asian Economic Crisis in the late 1990s, Thailand established what is known as its Ministry of Social Development and Human Security, which is in charge of the country's social and economic affairs, including such goals as eradicating poverty (Daud and Othman 2005, 193).

At the regional level, at the ASEAN Post-Ministerial Conference (PMC) in Manila, ASEAN created an ASEAN-PMC Caucus on Human Security in 1998. Later, another ASEAN-PMC Caucus was established on Social Safety Nets (Capie and Evans 2002, 44), and ASEAN further took a proactive approach when it announced its ASEAN Vision 2020, focusing on human security within a context of societal security. ASEAN continued to assimilate the human security approach when it included it in its Asia-Pacific Economic Cooperation meeting in Bangkok in 2003 (Othman 2009a). These East Asian efforts all suggest that the acknowledgement and concern with threats to human life has become more important among policy makers.

The purpose of this chapter is to better understand one specific transnational threat to human security: illicit drug trafficking. Focusing on the selected cases of several East Asian countries – Malaysia, Myanmar, Thailand and China – this chapter is an attempt to understand why East Asia is increasingly vulnerable to illicit drug trafficking, and what has been done. Although the root causes of the problem may originate in one country, the impact of illicit drug trafficking is transnational in nature. In this chapter, we contend that illicit drug trafficking threatens human security – the health, freedom and overall well-being – even the very survival – of the individual citizens of a state. With insights derived from studying this threat, it is hoped that new strategies can be designed to address this and other threats to human security that should be seen as a common problem not only to all peoples within the states involved, but also a threat to the entity of the state itself, in the traditional sense.

2 Methodology

The primary data gathered for this study were collected from interviews with informants selected for their experience and expertise concerning illicit drug trafficking and human security. The interviews were conducted between 2012 and

2013 in Malaysia. The informants include 1) experts, mainly scholars in related fields, such as international relations scholars; 2) drug addicts and prisoners; 3) persons representing governmental authorities, including the police; and 4) non-governmental organisations (NGOs). Meanwhile the secondary data in this study is derived from published research and reports from the United Nations, the Malaysian, Thai and Chinese governments, books, theses and dissertations, monographs, published articles and research. Multiple sources of evidence were consulted to ensure the validity of the data gathered.

3 Background

Drug abuse is a global phenomenon, affecting almost every country, but its extent and characteristics differ somewhat from one region to another. Illicit drug use not only affects the health and lives of individuals, but also undermines the political, social and cultural foundation of all countries. Problems with drug dependence are extremely costly to all societies in terms of lost productivity, transmission of infectious diseases, family and social disorder, crime and increased healthcare costs (Othman and Druis 2014). Such threats that transcend national borders are not new, even though some scholars refer to them as "new security issues" because they crossed borders and involved non-state actors. However, the changing international scene has created conditions that give this type of threat a new importance and attention on the world stage. For example, criminal organisations involved in illegal transnational trafficking of various kinds (arms, goods and human beings, as well as drugs) have benefited from increased global interdependence and new technologies. The expansion of trade, tourism, means of transportation and communication and various kinds of networks have all made it possible for drug-trafficking organisations to distribute illicit drugs more widely, easily and profitably. In addition, a growing integration of global financial systems has provided more opportunities to "launder" drug money (converting illegally gained money to make it appear legitimate, by moving it into ordinary legal businesses such as hotels and real estate) (Schaeffer 1997; Othman et al. 2013).

All this is the background for the increase of drug abuse around the world and the problems that multiply because of it. One major problem is the role drug abuse plays in the world's epidemic of acquired immunodeficiency disease syndrome (AIDS), which is caused by the human immunodeficiency virus (HIV), and has become one of the threats to human security. It is estimated that more than 70 million people (90 per cent of the population in the developing world) have been infected with HIV. In 2012, the AIDS epidemic claimed more than 3 million lives, including 610,000 children, and an estimated 5 million persons had newly acquired HIV, bringing to 42 million the number of people globally living with the virus, with some unknown number already having the full-blown disease of AIDS (Kulsudjarit 2004, 455–6). The rapid rise in the disease was due in part to the number of new drug abusers among young people, who may become addicted quickly and often do not realise the dangers involved, particularly if they share contaminated needles and other equipment in injecting certain drugs.

In many parts of the world, especially in urban areas, a shift toward the use of drugs that are injected (such as heroin) has been the major mode of HIV transmission. Research has shown the injection of drugs (contaminated needle sharing, etc.) to be the main source of infection with HIV in Malaysia, China, Vietnam and Northeast India, and a major cause in Thailand and Myanmar. In 2002 about 57 per cent of all intravenous drug users tested in Myanmar showed positive for the HIV/AIDS virus. In Cambodia an additional cause has been documented: unsafe sexual practices while under the influence of drugs that impair judgement (Kulsudjarit 2004).

Also, a massive rise in the use of amphetamine-type stimulants (ATS) in Southeast Asia has led to an alarming increase in HIV/AIDS. While the development of some synthetic drugs (such as methadone, a synthetic opioid) has somewhat reduced the demand for illicit opiate drugs, opium is still needed for medicinal purposes, which allows some countries to continue to justify growing it on a large scale. Like the plant-based opiate drugs, synthetic drugs are also abused, as stated in the *World Drug Report 1997* (UNODCCP 1997, 39). This trend toward preference for synthetic drugs can be seen in Southeast Asia, where methamphetamines have been reported as the most abused of the synthetic drugs (UNODCCP 2000, 54). Within the group of ATS drugs, amphetamine and methamphetamine are the most widely abused, followed by the drug ecstasy (UNIDCP 2000, 56). There has been a massive rise in ATS and the combination of methamphetamine and sex has led to an alarming increase in HIV/AIDS in Southeast Asia overall. A shift to intravenous heroin injection has resulted in a spiralling HIV infection rate. In 2002 about 57 per cent of all intravenous drug users in Myanmar tested positive for the HIV/AIDS virus (Kulsudjarit 2004, 455–6). In Cambodia, there is a rise in HIV/AIDS through intravenous drug use and, to a much larger degree, unsafe sexual practices while under the influence of drugs. In Indonesia, more than 80 per cent of drug users are using the injecting method, with the majority also sharing contaminated injecting equipment, and about 43,000 drug addicts were reported to have HIV, particularly in urban areas where injecting drugs is a growing phenomenon. For instance, in Thailand, more than 50 per cent of injecting drug addicts were reported to be infected with HIV (Kulsudjarit 2004).

The seriousness of the illicit drug-trafficking problems in Southeast Asia caused ASEAN to officially acknowledge in 1998 that the problems were threatening the region's security, stability and resilience. Since at least 1972 there have been several "cooperative" efforts to tackle the illicit drug-trafficking problem in Southeast Asia. In 1984, the ASEAN Senior Officials on Drug Matters (ASOD) was formed, with the primary mission of coordinating anti-drug activities in the region. ASEAN also signed the Joint Declaration for a Drug-Free ASEAN, which committed them to eradicate the problem of illicit drug trafficking – including drug production, processing and abuse – by the year 2020. Later, in an international congress held in Bangkok in October 2000, the target date for a drug-free ASEAN was shifted to the year 2015. That declaration shows that the region is committed to combating the illicit drug problem, but it also shows they had no

Table 2.1 Drug-related arrests in East Asia, 2006–10

Country/Year	2006	2007	2008	2009	2010
Brunei Darussalam	475	772	591	556	565
Cambodia	608	263	294	615	648
China	56,217	68,109	73,360	91,859	101,748
Hong Kong	4,980	6,971	8,089	7,009	5,432
Indonesia	25,012	38,235	40,569	26,721	23,401
Japan	14,440	14,790	14,288	14,947	14,536
Laos	479	182	418	718	1,007
Malaysia	22,811	14,489	12,352	15,736	23,642
Myanmar	3,865	3,074	3,368	4,743	3,465
Philippines	11,535	10,710	10,530	9,052	8,259
Rep. Korea	7,709	10,649	9,898	11,875	9,732
Singapore	1,218	2,211	2,537	2,616	2,887
Thailand	86,197	104,347	149,915	135,976	174,725
Vietnam	16,686	14,800	24,739	21,086	23,497

Source: Drug Abuse Information Network for Asia and the Pacific (DAINAP, 2010).

idea how difficult it would be. Table 2.1 shows the drug-related arrests in East Asian countries from 2006 to 2010. It demonstrates that all countries are vulnerable to illicit drug use and trafficking in one way or another, and that the problems have only grown larger with time.

4 Illicit drugs as a common regional human issue

Although East Asian countries in general have adopted a comprehensive security approach, focusing on both military and non-military threats, the way they tackle human security issues such as illicit drug trafficking varies greatly from one country to another, partly because the region does not face a common immediate threat to its collective security. Nevertheless, the nature of illegal drug use and trafficking has made it an important human security issue (interview: Guenter Brauch, 7 December 2012). Cases from selected East Asian countries are discussed here.

4.1 Malaysia

The use of illicit drugs (known as *dadah*) in Malaysia dates back to the 19th century, when large amounts of opium were brought in by immigrant labourers from China. For a long time thereafter, British rulers ignored the growing problem. Opium had been used previously by a small group of people, mostly as pain relief by the elderly. However, in the early 1970s there were indications that the numbers of drug abusers had increased to include the misuse of cannabis, morphine and heroin (*International Narcotics Control Board* 1976, 15). In 1983, the Malaysian government declared that the problem had become increasingly serious and transferred the responsibility from the Ministry of Social Welfare Services to the Ministry of Home Affairs. The illicit drug problem since then has been officially identified as one of the threats to Malaysian national security (Othman and Druis 2014).

Nevertheless, after more than three decades the threat continues, although Malaysia is not a drug-producing country. Yet, data suggest that the number of drug addicts in Malaysia is among the highest in Asia despite Malaysia's mandatory death penalty for drug traffickers. Malaysia's geographic location is near the Golden Triangle, Southeast Asia's main illicit drug-producing area, which has meant that drugs are easily smuggled into Malaysian ports through sea routes, especially to Penang Island (located at the northeast of the Malaysian peninsular), as well as through the entire undeveloped jungle border areas between south Thailand and the northern area of the Malaysian peninsular (interview: Jamaludin Kudin, 8 November 2012). Recidivism among rehabilitated drug addicts remains high, even though Malaysian efforts to combat illicit drug trafficking have been considered as being somewhat successful and the rate of drug abuse has been declining (Scorzelli 1992, 171). In short, it is less effective (interview: Helmi, 4 November 2012; Yunus Pathi, 10 May 2013).

Malaysia continues to be a transit country for drugs en route to international destinations. However, drugs like heroin, opium, syabu, amphetamines and ketamine seized by both the Royal Malaysian Police and the Royal Malaysian Customs are evidence of the demand for these drugs within Malaysia. As of 2010, 792 Malaysians were still being detained in other countries for various drug offenses, while 976 foreigners had been arrested in Malaysia for the same (Othman and Druis 2014). There were also increasing rates of drug-related violence and crime – including burglary, pick-pocketing and purse snatching, car thefts, extortion, mugging and assaults on women and school children in order to steal their money and valuables (Othman and Druis 2014). This demonstrates a threat to personal and community security, important sectors of human security as a whole (interview: Adeeba Kamarulzaman, 10 March 2013). The Malaysian government allocates millions of dollars to finance rehabilitation centres and to combat drug trafficking. Considering that Malaysia is a small and still-developing country, this is a great

Table 2.2 Comparison of abusers detected in 2010 and 2009

Status of case	Jan–Dec 2010	Percentage	Jan–Dec 2009	Difference 2010/2009
New abusers (detected for the first time)	17,238	72.9%	7,123	142.00%
Repeat abusers	6,404	27.1%	8,613	−25.65%
Total number of addicts	23,642	100.0%	15,736	50.24%

Source: Malaysia's Country Report, 2010, 9, www.aipasecretariat.org.

burden, because it uses resources that would otherwise be available for development. Consequently, drug testing has become mandatory for all professionals, who can be fired from their jobs if suspected of drug abuse.

The number of drug abusers arrested by Southeast Royal Malaysian Police also increased from 49,762 in 2009 to 63,466 in 2010 (*Malaysia's Country Report,* 2010; see also Table 2.2). As an effort to ensure human security survival, Malaysia has established what is known as "1 Malaysia Cure and Care Clinics". Their aim is to "reduce harm" through various kinds of interventions to help drug users and their families and employers. They can walk in any time to get treatment and rehabilitation from medical specialists, social workers and counsellors without having to go through the legal system. Malaysia's Ministry of Health supports the system of clinics, which also offers methadone maintenance therapy to prevent relapse of drug users who are trying to get free of their addictions (interview: Harris Wong, 4 December 2012). The clinics also provide clean needles and equipment for those who inject their drugs, which saves both lives and money by reducing the rate of HIV, hepatitis and other infections.

It was reported in 2010 that the opiate-based drug heroin was abused by 27.4 per cent of all drug users, and morphine, which was used by about 21.9 per cent of the total, remained the main type of drug used. Ganja/cannabis was used by 12.7 per cent of drug users and 36.1 per cent used ATS (Othman and Druis 2014). According to the 2010 report, approximately 97.5 per cent of illicit drug users in Malaysia were male, and only 2.5 per cent were female. People between 19 and 39 years old were the largest age group of drug users, representing 72.4 per cent of the total. Adults 40 and older accounted for 18.3 per cent and 9.3 per cent were teenagers between 13 and 18 years old (Othman and Druis 2014).

In Malaysia it is the Narcotics Crime and Investigations Department of the Royal Malaysia Police that acts as the main agency for the enforcement of drug laws. The National Anti-Drugs Agency, under the Ministry of Home Affairs, is the lead agency responsible for the formulation of policies relating to drugs. In addition, the Cabinet Committee on the Eradication of Drugs is chaired by the Deputy Prime Minister, and reports directly to the Prime Minister. The fact that there is a mandatory death penalty signals that protecting human security is an important objective in Malaysia (interview: Zainal Abidn, 4 November 2012).

4.2 Myanmar

In Myanmar, early reference to opium dates from 1519 CE. But opium is believed to have reached the area in 1366, when the law code of Siam (Thailand) banned opium use in the kingdom east of the Irrawaddy River (Renard 1996, 14). Myanmar is today one of the countries that form the infamous Golden Triangle. In addition, tribal groups migrating from the mountainous provinces of southwestern China also brought the knowledge and practice of opium cultivation into the jungle plateaus and valleys of the Shan state, in the northeastern part of Myanmar. Monsoon rains make the area relatively inaccessible for several months each year, which makes it difficult to enforce narcotics laws. The hill tribes are poor; and for most, opium cultivation partly provides their income (Othman 2009b).

However, an increase in opium production was marked under the British, who conquered Burma after three bloody Anglo-Burmese wars (1824–6; 1852; 1886), which resulted with Burma becoming a territory completely ruled by the British as part of the British–India colony. When the British ruled, they first started to have opium farming taxed in Tenasserim, in the southern part of Burma; and by 1886, opium farms had become institutionalised all across Burma. It is thought that opium consumption in British Burma might have been higher than it ever was in British-India proper (cited in Renard 1996, 313). If true, that would signify that Burma's opium was an important commodity for the British Empire, and it also demonstrated that Burma's geography was most suitable for opium growing. In 1878, the British imposed the Opium Act, which banned the social use of opium except to "registered users". To the British, those registered users were ones who had no hope of recovering from their opium-smoking habit.

The opium trade grew more rapidly in Burma following British efforts to sell opium in China. Although Buddhists were against opium consumption, the British promoted its use anyway. At the same time, the British allowed opium cultivation in the Shan and Kachin states, both located in the northeast part of the country. The Shan chiefdoms, or *saopha* (also *sawba* or "hereditary rulers") had been encouraged by the British in 1886 to introduce the opium poppy into their territories, and retail shops had been licensed to sell opium to certain addicts. Although there were some efforts to replace opium with other crops – e.g. peanuts, tea, coffee – and to promote livestock development, none were successful (Renard 1996, 52).

Many Southeast Asian countries, including Burma, were for a brief period of time occupied by the Japanese Army. During the two years of their occupation over Burma, the Japanese were seriously opposed to the use of opium and established a plan to abolish it (Renard 1996, 41). But Japanese rule did not last long enough to carry out their plan. The British returned to Burma after World War II had ended and the British post-war opium policy remained the same as it had been earlier. Opium remained legal in the Kokang and the Wa Hills areas of the northeast part of the country. Meanwhile, the Shan state became a battleground (Lintner 1991). Shan's economy had already been devastated – having first been victimised by the events of World War II and later from the Chinese *Kuomintang* (KMT) invasion.

Meanwhile, mainland China became a communist state in 1949. The remnants of the KMT settled in Taiwan. Others fled to nearby areas, including the Shan state in northeast Burma. There, the KMT turned to opium trafficking for business revenue since it was the only means for the guerrillas to achieve their goal. The KMT began creating close connections with the Chinese networks that distributed opium and heroin beyond the region (Othman 2009b). Burma tried hard to abandon its opium field, but conflict in the border area made it difficult to achieve their target. In 1953, Burma established an "Opium Enquiry Committee" to reduce opium cultivation but met with little success. In 1961, Burma signed the Single Convention on Narcotics Drugs with the United Nations, which restricted drug use in Burma to medical purposes only. However, the opium trade continued (Renard 1996, 41). In 1962, Burma demanded that the UN approve regions in the Trans-Salween states as sites for legal poppy cultivation, citing the need for farmers to have this as a legitimate source of income. But Burma's appeal was denied, and cultivation continued illegally.

At the regional level, in 1991, the Burmese government adopted the Instrument of Accession to the United Nations Convention against Illicit Trafficking in Narcotics, Drugs and Psychotropic Substances. Thus, the UN was free to promote a regional programme to cooperate in dealing with narcotics issues in the country (Renard 1996, 326). The UN has played a major role in helping the country to reduce or eradicate the illegal opium and to develop other means of economic sustenance in the rural areas (Renard 1996, 86). Crop substitution was introduced by the United Nations Fund for Drug Abuse Control in the mid-1970s but failed. Similarly, the UNDP has funded several alternative development projects, substituting other crops in the drug-producing areas, such as in the Wa area.

In Myanmar, opiates are the most common illicit drug, with heroin being the most prevalent. According to a UNODCCP report, in 2010 there were 66,000 heroin users and about 67,000 opium users. In 2009 alone, Myanmar produced 330 tons of opiates while methamphetamine seizures increased from 1 million in 2008 to 23 million in 2009 (Table 2.3). Most had been illegally produced in the northeastern part of the country, in the remote Shan and border areas of the state, where there is limited government control. It was reported also to be easy to find cheap illegal drugs. In the border areas of the Shan and Kachin states, about 1.5 per cent of the adult population was reported to be addicted to drugs (UNODCCP 2009).

In general, Myanmar's opium trafficking and use appears to have been declining as of 2004, while the use of heroin, which had declined between 1998 and 2001 (see Figure 2.1), has been steadily rising again since then. According to a report by the government of Myanmar (2012), an estimated 75,000 people in the country were using drugs by injection (UNODCCP 2005). In relation to drugs, it is important to note that in the early 1990s, Myanmar's HIV infections were at their peak, with over 70 per cent of drug users infected, but the number has decreased since then. Eventually illicit drugs and HIV/Aids became a threat to health security in Myanmar. Myanmar's government recognised the role of injecting drug use in the spread of HIV, and Myanmar was among the first countries in East Asia to initiate a programme providing clean needles and syringes. In 2008, there were about 36 needle and syringe programmes located throughout the country (UNODCCP 2009).

4.3 Thailand

In the three Golden Triangle states, northern Thailand produces the smallest amount of illicit opium. Thailand has been one of the countries that has successfully substituted alternative crops on the opium poppy plantations – growing fruits

Table 2.3 Seizures of selected illicit drugs in Myanmar, 2007–11

Drug type	Measurement	2007	2008	2009	2010	2011
Methamphetamine pills	Pills	1,666,141	1,102,199	23,899,156	2,192,263	5,894,188
Crystalline methamphetamine	Kg	3.4	15.9	124.3	226.1	33.4
Methamphetamine powder*	Kg	470.8	3.9	339.0	0	20.2
Ecstasy	Pills	2,690	108	5	0	0
Heroin	Kg	68.4	88.2	1,076.1	88.5	42.4
Morphine	Kg	1,121.0	205.1	325.7	98.2	36.9
Opium, high grade	Kg	1,173.8	1,463.4	752	922	828.3
Opium, low grade	Kg	10,972	2,453	465	148	281.6
Opium oil	Kg	56.3	80.1	27.5	35.5	60.0
Cannabis**	Kg	104.3	170.2	284.6	205.6	196.4
Kratom	Kg	407.0	308.5	597.5***	375	969.5
Ketamine	Kg	n.a	n.a	14.9	n.a	1.4

Source: DAINAP 2010, CCDAC 2012a.

Notes: n.a = not available; * intermediary form in processing into methamphetamine pills; ** combined herb and resin; *** plus two litres of liquid speciose.

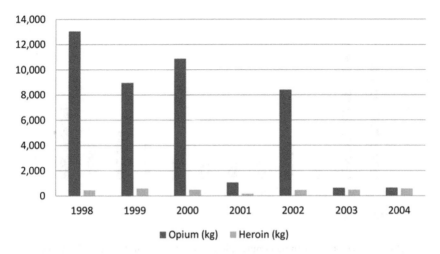

Figure 2.1 Myanmar opium and heroin seizures, 1998–2004
Source: World *Drug Report* 2005.

and vegetables, including cabbage, tomatoes, potatoes and apricots. They also
grow commercial flowers (UNODCCP 2000, 149). Although Thailand's opium
poppy production problem has been greatly reduced, Thailand ranks among the
highest in Southeast Asia in the number of drug addicts. When opium was no
longer so available, a new trend began in amphetamine addiction.

In Thailand, the most commonly abused drug in 2002 was methamphetamine.
Methamphetamine (*yaba* and *ice*) abuse is epidemic, fuelled by ample supply of
the low-cost drug, with prices running around Baht 100 or USD 2.50 per tablet.
Addiction was widespread, across all socio-economic levels and all age groups. An
estimated 5 per cent of Thailand's 62 million people are addicted to it and in 2002
an estimated 800 million tablets a year were being smuggled in to the country and
sold (see Figure 2.2). Of particular concern were school-aged children who were
getting the drug and becoming addicted. However, there appeared to be a
decrease in methamphetamine abuse in 2002 compared with the previous year,
particularly among recreational users. Although the abuse of ecstasy appears to
have increased in use among teenagers and entertainment workers, as well as
among commercial sex workers, the number of users was probably somewhat
limited due to its expensive price (Baht 500–800 or USD 12–19 a tablet). Rapid
expansion in the availability and use of both cocaine and ketamine was also noted.
Cocaine abuse in Thailand is still limited to adults and youth from wealthy families. A gram of cocaine costs Baht 3,000–3,500 or USD 72–83 compared with
Baht 100 or USD 2.50 for 50mg of ketamine. The low price of ketamine made it
widely used by many groups, but it was most popular among those who used
ecstasy; however, the abuse of volatile substances, popular among street children,
was stable in 2002.

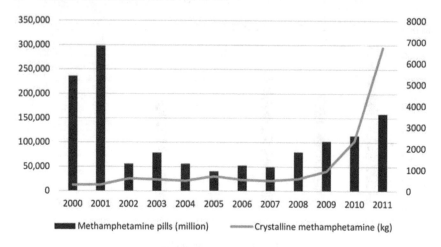

Figure 2.2 Seizures of methamphetamine (pill and crystalline) in Thailand, 2000–11
Source: DAINAP 2010; ONCB 2012.

According to the Thanyarak Institute for Drug Abuse in Bangkok, about 72 per cent of patients were methamphetamine addicts, 30 per cent of whom were between the ages of 15 and 19. Peer pressure appeared to be the primary reason for methamphetamine addiction among youth in Thailand and inhaling its fumes was the preferred method of methamphetamine use because it delivers the substance directly to the brain. It was thought that use of this kind of drug spread so quickly among Thai youth because it was cheap and readily available for those who saw it as a way to fit socially (Kulsudjarit 2004, 454). It shows how people are vulnerable to illicit drug trafficking.

Beyrer's (2008, 246–7) work shows the close connection between heroin use and HIV in Thailand:

> The HIV epidemic was first detected among injecting drug users (IDUs) in Bangkok in 1988 (Weniger et al. 1991). It was an explosive outbreak with clear links to incarcerated IDUs and spread initially among low-income, urban [homosexual] male residents who were ethnic Thais. However, HIV rapidly spread among Thai IDUs nationwide and within a year HIV rates of 20–40 percent were the norm. The IDU-related HIV epidemic was followed by a heterosexual outbreak of HIV that involved many more people. However, while the rate of infection of heterosexuals and other groups at risk declined after the period 1995–1996, that of IDUs overall did not decline (Thailand, Ministry of Health, 2001).

There have been several reports of pilot projects and successful programmes in Asia, including reports from India, Nepal, Thailand and Vietnam. Much of that work has focused on harm reduction and needle and syringe exchange programmes, the basic aims of most reported interventions. And this strategy is likely to produce positive results. As cited by Beyrer (2008, 253), the Thai working group predicted that "a decline in needle-sharing from 20 to 10 percent among Thai IDUs would avert 21,774 new cases of HIV/AIDs infections by 2006, and 81,761 infections by 2020. That would constitute the single largest number of infections averted for any one intervention strategy. By 2006, roughly 3,800 of the expected 22,000 infections nationwide would be averted by the intervention alone." The Office of Narcotics Control of Thailand is the agency responsible for fighting drug traffickers. Under Thailand's Narcotics Act, appointed officials have the right to search the premises and detain a person suspected of involvement with illicit drugs and they can seize any drugs or any property used in that involvement. Like Malaysia, Thailand has passed laws mandating the death penalty for drug traffickers. This is testimony to the seriousness of these countries' governments in their wanting to make Southeast Asia drug free by 2015.

4.4 People's Republic of China

Dupont (1999, 445–6) describes the illicit drug situation in China (see also Figure 2.3 and Table 2.4) in the following paragraph:

China is emblematic of this emerging East Asian drug security problem. In 1949, there were estimated to be 20 million drug addicts in China. The opium trade was ruthlessly stamped out by the communists to such an extent that in the mid-1960s China proudly claimed itself to be a country without narcotics. However, drug trafficking and opium addiction has re-emerged as a serious issue since the watershed 1979 modernization campaign began to transform the political and social climate in China. Initially, the drug problem was confined to the provinces adjacent to the Golden Triangle and China's Xinjiang Province in the far west of the country. The latter is the natural point of entry for Central Asian drugs. As China's modernization gathered steam, high-grade heroin began to make its appearance throughout the country especially in the larger cities like Beijing and Shanghai as well as Fujian Province. By the mid-1990s, the drug problem had become serious enough to attract the attention of senior Party officials in Beijing. A nationwide, anti-drug campaign was launched in April 1997, and in May of that year, Ruan Zhengyi, the deputy director of China's Public Security Bureau, acknowledged that the "the problem of drugs has returned to China with a vengeance".

Dupont (1999, 452) goes on to add that:

in the first quarter of 1998, 1.5 tons of heroin were seized by law enforcement agencies in China, a 58.6% increase over the same period in 1997. The National Narcotics Control Commission (NNCC) reported that there were 540,000 registered addicts in China at the end of 1997, 65% of them under 25. These figures are extremely conservative and almost certainly understate the real level of dependency.

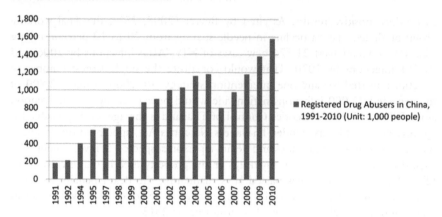

Figure 2.3 Registered drug abusers in China, 1991–2010 (unit: 1,000 people)
Source: National Narcotics Control Commission Annual Report on Drug Control in China, 2000–2011, from the Brookings Institution.

Table 2.4 Types of drugs seized in selected East Asian countries, 2011

Types of drugs	Malaysia	Thailand	Myanmar	China
Methamphetamine pills (mill.)	364,909	49,365,700	5,894,188	61,942,559
Crystalline methamphetamine (kg)	1,235.6	1,232	33.4	4,458
Methamphetamine powder (kg)	N/A	N/A	20.2	N/A
Ecstasy (pills)	98,751	21,115	0	317,886
Cannabis herb (kg)	1,054	14,302	Herbs and resin = 196.4	2,600
Cannabis resin (kg)	N/A	72.5	N/A	980
Cocaine (kg)	3.5	31.8	N/A	48
Codeine (kg)	1,573.8	4.1	N/A	N/A
Heroin (kg)	755.5	547.5	42.4	7,080
Inhalants (kg)	N/A	100.2	N/A	N/A
Ketamine (kg)	202.5	32,913	1.4	5,380
Opium (raw and prepared)	0.9	42.7	High: 828.3 Low: 281.6 Oil: 60	823
Morphine (kg)	N/A	N/A	36.9	N/A
Kratom (kg)	1,440.4	N/A	969.5	N/A
Benzodiazepines (pills)	1,773,875	N/A	N/A	N/A

Source: Adapted from CCDAC 2012a; National Anti-Drugs Agency 2010, 2011; Royal Malaysian Police 2010, 2011; UNODCCP 2013; ONCB 2012.

In 2000, an international research team published the findings of its investigations of the causes of HIV infections along the four heroin-trafficking routes leading from Laos and Myanmar to China, India, Thailand and Vietnam (Beyrer, 2008, 245).

Beyrer (2008, 245, 247, 249) provides the following account of the drug problem in China's border regions:

> The fearful symmetry of heroin trafficking and the spread of HIV can perhaps best be illustrated by the HIV epidemic in Yunnan Province of China, which is east of Myanmar and the first destination of overland exports of heroin from Myanmar to the rest of China. The farthest province from China's booming coastal cities, Yunnan has the highest HIV infection rate in China (Shao et al. 1998) ... As heroin spread among the young people of Yunnan and a rapid transition to injecting took place, there was a predictable rise in HIV infection. Equally predictable was the subsequent spread of infection to the non-IDU sexual partners, wives and children of the largely young adult male IDU population. Yunnan had the largest HIV epidemic in China ... China's emerging epidemic remains overwhelmingly due to needle sharing among IDU and the three most HIV-affected provinces of China (in order of prevalence, Yunnan, Xinjiang, and Guangxi) have all experienced IDU-related outbreaks along the major heroin routes ... Another heroin-related epidemic is currently being experienced by China. The Xinjiang Uighur Autonomous Region is the only Muslim majority region of China. Xinjiang shares borders with Afghanistan, Kazakhstan, and Siberia (part of the Russian Federation). The region is linked to the rest of China by the Silk Road (Joint United Nations Programme on HIV/AIDS, 2000). It has China's second highest rate of HIV infection by province, after Yunnan in the far south. More than 78 percent of the HIV infections in Xinjiang are owing to injection drug use involving heroin. Tragically, more than 90 percent of IDUs in the two largest cities in Xianjiang are ethnic Uighur, which means that the HIV infections in this large province are largely among young Muslims (Shao et al., 1998).

China, together with Japan and South Korea, are cooperating with ASEAN to make the region drug free by the year 2015. The China National Narcotics Control Commission has been actively engaged with their Southeast Asian counterparts in the field of intelligence exchange and joint law related to drug trafficking (Anti-Drug Law of People's Republic of China).

5 Human security framework

The human security model that we are recommending in this chapter is known as "The Bangi Approach to Human Security", known as BAGHUS for short. As argued by Ramli et al. (2012, 577), although the concept put forth by the UN is useful and comprehensive, in practice the implementation of the human security framework needs to be modified when applied to specific regions or countries, by taking into account the specifics of the region. While the UNDP suggested seven categories of security under their framework, and UNESCO later added "cultural security" as an eighth, BAGHUS presents nine security dimensions (Table 2.5).

Within these three frameworks, the definition for each category is discussed as follows:

- Environmental security is defined as the conditions in which social systems interact with ecological systems in sustainable ways, so that all individuals have fair and reasonable access to environmental goods, and mechanisms exist to address environmental crises and conflicts. Environmental scarcity (or "insecurity"), in interaction with other political, economic and social factors can generate conflict and instability.
- Economic security is defined as having a source of income you can count on, that is enough to cover food, clean water, adequate clothing and shelter (housing and utilities), plus necessary transportation, healthcare and education costs, with enough left over to save as a cushion in case of an emergency, and to pay for insurance, repairs, fees for necessary licenses and services, and other miscellaneous expenses necessary for life and well-being.
- Food security is defined as a state in which all people at all times have access to safe and nutritious food sufficient to maintain a healthy and active life for all ages. Food security also means that the food supply is maintained and monitored for both quality and quantity so that people do not have to fear dangerous changes (e.g., shortages, contamination or famine) will take place in the future.
- Health security can be understood as the action needed to reduce the vulnerability of all people to events and conditions that threaten their overall health and well-being. It means that medical care and treatment are available and accessible to all who become ill, diseased or disabled; that both the beginning and ending of life is attended with healthcare that is in the best interests of both the individual and of society, including the healthy mental

Table 2.5 A comparison of human security frameworks

Elements of human security	UNDP	UNESCO	BAGHUS
Environmental security	X	X	X
Economic security	X	X	X
Food security	X	X	X
Health security	X	X	X
Political security	X	X	X
Personal security	X	X	X
Community security	X	X	X
Cultural security		X	X
Social security			X

Source: Daud et al. 2015.

and physical development of mothers and their children; that systems to maintain sanitation and safety, along with other disease-prevention measures, are routinely maintained in all communities; and that an ongoing effort is made to educate the public, as well as public health and safety personnel, about how to maintain a safe and healthy community. It is noted that a lack of health security has an impact on other components of human security, including economic security and food security.

- Political security has been interpreted as the protection against threats imposed by the state on the people in general, and the protection of basic human rights for all. It illustrates the relationship between the state (government) on the one hand, as coordinator of the state's activities, and citizens on the other, as the stakeholders who must bear the consequences of the state's actions. Thus, political security is concerned with such state actions as the prosecution or persecution of an individual or a group of people for political reasons, or by restricting or preventing their ability to take part in the political life of society. Political security also provides ways for all groups to share power in the governance of a country, without discrimination based on religion, ethnicity, race, gender or socio-economic status.

- Personal security and community security are often seen as inseparable; therefore, taken together they are defined as the protection of one individual or group from physical violence, crime, manipulation, torture or domestic abuse, from state and non-state actors. In particular, personal and community security includes the protection of women and children, as well as men, from the negative impacts of modernisation and globalisation, such as child labour.

- Cultural security, in agreement with UNESCO, is defined as the general need to respect life, equality between women and men and the celebration of diversity in belief systems, language, lifestyle, traditions, value systems and religion. Cultural security is not only about protecting certain ethnic groups or minorities, but it is also about protecting gender equality and equity, which are central to sustainable development of a civil society in which each member respects others and has the opportunity to both fulfil their own potential (in the development of individual gifts/talents/abilities), while also contributing to their community/society in positive ways.

- Social security refers to public programmes designed to provide a "safety net" of income and services to individuals and families in times of extreme need. These can include help in the event of natural or man-made disasters (e.g., fire, earthquakes, hurricanes/typhoons, tsunamis, tornadoes, floods, epidemics, famine, war, etc.); and also in other times of hardship caused by sickness or disease, temporary or permanent injury and/or disability; a death in the family, especially of a breadwinner and/or parent; pregnancy, childbirth and its aftermath; a need for urgent and expensive medical care; unemployment, or underemployment (a job that is less than the person's qualifications would merit, or that pays less than is needed to support a family); any situation calling for subsidies to maintain the health of children and elderly members, including childcare and elder care when needed to allow qualified family members to earn income; loss of a home, or the inability to afford utilities or transportation necessary for health and well-being and holding a job. Social security also should include the establishment and maintenance of public parks and recreation facilities, as well as educational facilities (schools, institutes, museums, etc.) available to all (Daud et al. 2015).

To sum up, threats to human security can be understood as in Figure 2.4.

Security threats from sources external to a country's boundaries of course continue to be a concern, even as more attention is given to domestic matters of human security. However, because threats to people in an increasing interdependent world are increasing due to many changes that are taking place in today's international politics, the very survival of many states may depend on the quality of life of their people. After all, if we acknowledge that the people are the heart and soul of a nation, and that their work and patriotic spirit is necessary for a nation to prosper, then surely the well-being of those people – and the nurturing of their minds as well as their bodies – must be highly respected and protected.

6 ASEAN and East Asian regional cooperation in combating narcotics problems

The problem of transnational crime in East Asia is severe and this includes the narcotics trade. Acknowledging the seriousness of the issue, ASEAN works together with the International Police, the Colombo Plan and the UNDP in its effort to combat the drug problem in the region. Within larger East Asia, an important

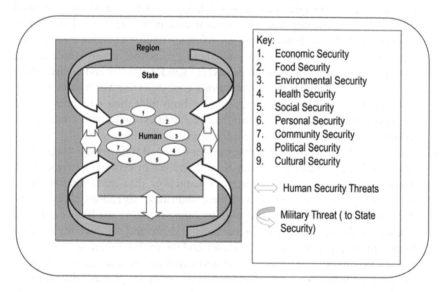

Figure 2.4 Common threats to human security
Source: Ramli et al. 2012.

effort was the drafting of the "Memorandum of Understanding" regarding cooperation and collaboration in drug control, which was signed in 1993 by Myanmar,
China, Laos, Thailand, Cambodia and Vietnam (UNIDCP 1998).

The 2012 Annual Report of the International Narcotics Control Board provided
the following summary for the East Asia region (2012, 77):

> In 2011, East and Southeast Asia continued to be the region with the second
> largest total area under illicit opium poppy cultivation, accounting for over 20
> per cent of illicit opium poppy cultivation worldwide. Increased illicit opium
> poppy cultivation was reported by the Lao People's Democratic Republic and
> Myanmar for six consecutive years, beginning in 2007. From 2011 to 2012,
> the total estimated area under cultivation in the two countries increased by
> approximately 66 per cent and 17 per cent, respectively, indicating potential
> growth in opium production ... East and Southeast Asia has continued to be a
> manufacturing hub and a growing illicit market for amphetamine-type stimu-
> lants, in particular methamphetamine. Seizures of methamphetamine in East
> Asia accounted for almost half of the global total in 2010. In 2011, most
> countries of the region continued to report increased seizures of metham-
> phetamine. Furthermore, evidence has shown that the illicit manufacture of
> amphetamine-type stimulants has expanded from traditional manufacturing
> countries such as China and Myanmar to other countries, including Cambodia,
> Indonesia, Malaysia, the Philippines and Thailand.

The illicit trafficking of drugs not only constitutes threats to state security by under-
mining national authorities and the rule of law; more importantly, they also threaten
the security and well-being of individuals and societies. Addressing these complex
problems therefore requires a transnational response. Yet regional cooperation in
this area is often complicated by sensitive issues that impinge on domestic jurisdictions, such as the need to share information, extradition laws and problems of
corruption. Nevertheless, regional efforts in fighting transnational crime can already
be seen on several fronts (Caballero-Anthony 2007, 6; Parameswaran 1998).

ASEAN has, since the 1970s, been the primary regional vehicle to respond
institutionally to the problem of drug trafficking. Emmers (2007, 512, 513)
assesses its development:

> Drug trafficking was discussed at the first ASEAN Summit of Heads of State
> and Government held in Bali in February 1976 and mentioned in the ASEAN
> Concord. Following the prioritization of the issue at the highest diplomatic
> level, the ASEAN Declaration of Principles to Combat the Abuse of Narcotic
> Drugs was adopted in Manila on 26 June 1976. Nevertheless, ASEAN's
> initiatives in these early years did not reach the primary producers in Southeast
> Asia;[1] ASEAN's drug control efforts were further eventually institutionalized
> in the 1990s to include all ten Southeast Asian countries. The adoption of the
> ASEAN Plan of Action on Drug Abuse Control in October 1994 led to new
> efforts to tackle the narcotics problem (ASEAN 1994). The Plan of Action ...

introduced ten specific projects on drug control to reduce narcotics demand and supply. Four training centres were also established to complement ASOD's[2] efforts to carry out the work programme. The foreign ministers issued a Joint Declaration for a Drug-Free ASEAN during their 1998 ASEAN Ministerial Meeting (AMM) stipulating the members' commitment to eliminate illicit drugs by 2020 (ASEAN 1997). Fourteen measures were recommended. The Joint Declaration did not, however, address problems of funding, monitoring and implementation as well as failed to establish a compliance mechanism. Despite these shortcomings, the schedule for creating a drug-free region was later brought forward to 2015 during the AMM in Bangkok (ASEAN 2000).

In addition to that, the ASEAN Ministerial Meeting on Transnational Crime, ASEAN Chiefs of National Police and ASOD focus on the exchange of information, enhancing legal and law enforcement cooperation, training, institution building and collaboration with extramural actors (Caballero-Anthony 2007, 6).

Myanmar and Thailand have also entered into an agreement calling for the exchange of information on heroin-production areas in Myanmar, and to undertake development efforts in several rural areas, making the people there aware of HIV infection dangers from injecting drugs as a human security issue. In addition, an NGO, the Council for Security Cooperation in the Asia-Pacific (CSCAP), which was established in 1993, also gives priority to security issues in the region, including arms trafficking, illegal immigrants, terrorism, transnational crimes and illicit drug production and trafficking (including amphetamines). CSCAP activities include workshops that address various transnational threats, including illicit drug trafficking, in the region (Ball 2000).

Besides these ongoing intra-ASEAN initiatives, ASEAN has also worked with its regional partners to enhance international cooperation in combating the narcotics problem. The most ambitious regional attempt at tackling the problem of narcotics has brought together the ten Southeast Asian countries and China. In October 2000, ASEAN, in association with the United Nations Office for Drug Control and Crime Prevention (UNODCCP), organised in Bangkok the International Congress in Pursuit of a Drug-Free ASEAN 2015. This resulted in the formulation of the Bangkok Political Declaration in Pursuit of a Drug-Free ASEAN 2015 and to the adoption of a plan of action, the ASEAN and China Cooperative Operations in Response to Dangerous Drugs (ACCORD). The latter was meant to eradicate, or at least seriously reduce, the production, trafficking and consumption of narcotics in Southeast Asia by 2015 (Emmers 2009, 52).

According to Caballero-Anthony (2006, 6):

The ACCORD outlines work plans toward a drug-free region and identifies priority projects and other cooperative measures including the sharing of information and best practices (mutual learning). Communication networks have also been set up among specialized agencies to facilitate better regional coordination in combating the drug problem. In short, beyond the exhortatory injunctions about transnational crime, the ACCORD tries to complement domestic efforts against the illicit trafficking and abuse of drugs by establishing an institutional framework for cooperation.

At its second meeting held in Beijing in 2005, ACCORD built on this initiative and constructed a Plan of Action 2005–2010 seeking to address the problem of illicit narcotics in four theatres: civic awareness, demand reduction, law enforcement and alternative development. If properly implemented, the plan could be an important step in establishing an anti-drugs cooperative process (Emmers 2009, 53). While ACCORD is only a declaration of intent, it addresses two key issues absent from the previous ASEAN initiatives. First, it regionalises cooperation against narcotics beyond Southeast Asia by including China. It therefore recognises that the regional production, trafficking and consumption of narcotics should be viewed as a wider East Asian problem rather than simply a Southeast Asian one. An effective response is said therefore to require broader regional cooperative structures. The primacy and leadership role of China here should be noted. Second, ACCORD seeks to confront the issue of oversight by establishing a monitoring mechanism and introducing target dates. The Plan of Action is also supported by UNODCCP and other UN agencies, as well as by individual countries in terms of funding, technical cooperation, joint programmes and other issues (Emmers 2009, 53).

Miao et al. (2005, 4, 20) has highlighted the positive cooperation between China and ASEAN on managing the drug problem. For example, China, Laos, Myanmar and Thailand worked together in combating illicit drug traffickers in 2003. Their efforts included exchanging information and identifying drug areas, in addition to intelligence exchange especially in the Mekong area. This cooperation between them is important to tackle this transnational issue.

In terms of continuing efforts to combat the drug situation, the 2012 Annual Report of the International Narcotics Control Board reported the following significant efforts (2012, 78):

> The Fifth ASEAN Plus Three Ministerial Meeting on Transnational Crime, for ASEAN members plus China, Japan and the Republic of Korea, was convened in Bali Indonesia, in October 2011. Delegates at the meeting reaffirmed the commitment of their countries to consolidating cooperation between ASEAN member States and China, Japan and the Republic of Korea in combating transnational crime. In addition, a plan of action to implement the memorandum of understanding between ASEAN and China on cooperation on non-traditional security issues, including the issue of drug trafficking, was adopted to further enhance cooperation between two parties in the areas of information exchange, personnel training, law enforcement, and research and analysis ... At the twentieth ASEAN Summit held in Phnom Penh in April 2012, Heads of State and Government of ASEAN member states adopted a declaration in which they affirmed the goal of a drug-free ASEAN Community by 2015 and decided that relevant ministers should accelerate the implementation of the ASEAN Work Plan on Combating Illicit Drug Production, Trafficking and Use (2009–2015). The leaders also decided that

annual reports on the progress of the implementation in the area of drug control should be submitted to ASEAN. Furthermore, they stressed the importance of sharing information and best practices of law enforcement and the necessity of enhancing cooperation with ASEAN external partners.

The 34th ASOD, which Myanmar hosted for the second time, opened in Yangon on 24 September 2013. The four-day meeting was attended by officials from the ASEAN Secretariat, ASEAN member countries, representatives from ASEAN dialogue partners – China, Japan, South Korea and India and those from the Drug Enforcement Administration of the United States, Australian Federal Police and UNODCCP. To eliminate opium production in Myanmar, three alternative development programmes are being implemented in collaboration with Thailand, China and UNODCCP. The programmes are aimed at reducing poverty and improving social welfare, health and the education status of local people and opium farmers (*Insight Southeast Asia* 2013).

7 Conclusion

Today, illicit drug production, trafficking and use are some of many human security issues. For many years, the problem of illicit drugs has been tackled from the perspective of traditional security. It is not surprising that East Asia, especially Southeast Asian countries, have imposed the toughest drug laws on earth, with a mandatory death sentence for anyone caught dealing drugs. Although illicit drugs may originate in one country, the problems they create impact the overall security of the people in the region. However, with increasing economic integration, the problem has increased and worsened. Based on the discussion presented, it is therefore more appropriate to shift the approach from national security to human security in dealing with the issue of illicit drugs, especially when it involves the most vulnerable groups, including tribal people, women, children and the poor.

In practical terms, although stricter border controls are needed, along with stiff penalties for those who are caught trafficking or colluding with traffickers, regional cooperation, information sharing, as well as collaboration with NGOs and private sectors are recommended. Not only people but also the state becomes the victim of the syndicates who gain control of whole communities and businesses, and profit by manipulating sophisticated modern network systems. It is recommended that students in social science disciplines, such as political science, international relations, sociology, economics, economic and social development and public policy and administration, among others, do in-depth research in order to reveal and report the ongoing impact of these issues on people. In the long term it will create more awareness, a more civil society and perhaps eventually a region that is at least relatively drug free.

Notes

1 Especially Myanmar and, to a lesser extent, Laos.
2 ASEAN Senior Officials on Drug Matters, formed in 1984.

References

Ball, Desmond. 2000. The Council for Security Cooperation in the Asia Pacific: Its Record and Its Prospects. Canberra: Strategic and Defence Studies Centre.

Beyrer, Chris. 2008. "Human Immunodeficiency Virus (HIV) Infection Rates and Heroin Trafficking: Fearful Symmetries", in Y. F Thomes et al. (eds), *Geography and Drug Addiction*. New York: Springer.

Caballero-Anthony, M. 2002. "Human Security in the Asia-Pacific: Current Trends and Prospects", in D. Dickens (ed.), *The Human Face of Security: Asia-Pacific Perspectives*. Canberra: Strategic and Defence Studies Centre.

Caballero-Anthony, M. 2007. "Nontraditional Security and Multilateralism in Asia: Reshaping the Contours of Regional Security Architecture?" Policy Brief. Stanley Foundation, June.

Capie, David and Paul Evans. 2002. *The Asia-Pacific Security Lexicon*. Singapore: ISEAS.

DAINAP. 2010. "Drug Information Network for Asia and the Pacific". Available at: www. apaic.org/dainap.

Daud, Sity and Zarina Othman. (eds) 2005. *Politik dan Keselamtan*. Bangi: UKM Publishers.

Daud, Sity, Zarina Othman and Rashila Ramli. 2015. *Peace and Human Security in Archipelagic Southeast Asia*. Bangi: UKM Publishers.

Dupont, Alan. 1999. "Transnational Crime, Drugs, and Security in East Asia". *Asian Survey*, XXXIX(3 May/June).

Emmers, Ralf. 2009. "Functional Cooperation against Human and Drug Trafficking in East Asia", in See Seng Tan (ed.), *Collaboration under Anarchy: Functional Regionalism and the Security of East Asia*. Singapore: S. Rajaratnam School of International Studies.

Government of Myanmar. 2012. "Central Committee for Drug Abuse Control". Available at: www.modins.net/myanmarinfo/ministry/home.

Human Security Network. Available at: actionguide.info/m/inits/26/.

Insight Southeast Asia. 2013. 2(5). Available at: www.idsa/in/isa.html.

International Narcotics Control Board. 1976. Available at: www.incb.org.

International Narcotics Control Board. 2012. Available at: www.incb.org.

International Narcotics Control Board. 2013 *Report of the International Narcotics Control Board 2012*. New York: United Nations.

Kulsudjarit, Kongpetch. 2004. "Drug Problem in Southeast Asia and Southwest Asia". *New York Academy of Sciences*, 1025: 446–457.

Lintner, Bertil. 1991. *Cross Border Drug Trade in the Golden Triangle*. Durham: University of Durham.

Miao, He, Melissa Curley and Nicholas Thomas. 2005. *Drug Control Cooperation between China and ASEAN: Past, Present, and Future*. Honk Kong: University of Hong Kong, Centre of Asian Studies.

National Anti-Drugs Agency. 2010. *Network for Alcohol and Drug Agency*. Available at: www.healthinfornet.ecu.edu.au/.

National Anti-Drugs Agency. 2011. *Network for Alcohol and Drug Agency*. Available at: www.healthinfornet.ecu.edu.au/.

National Narcotics Control Commission Annual Report on Drug Control in China. 2000–2011. Available at: www.brookings.edu/reserach/opinions.

ONCB. 2012. *Office of the Narcotics Control Board*. Available at: www.oncb.go.th/docum ent/act.

Othman, Zarina. 2009a. "Human Security Concepts, Debates and Approaches in Southeast Asia", in G. Brauch, U. O. Spring, J. Grin, C. Mesjaz, P. K. Mbote, N. C. Behera,

B. Chourou and H. Krummenacher (eds), *Facing Global Environmental Change: Environmental, Human, Energy, Food, Health and Water Security Concepts* (vol. 4). Berlin: AFES-Springer Press, 1037–1048.

Othman, Zarina. 2009b. "Burma (Myanmar): Born to Be a Narco State?" *Asian Profile*, 37(1): 67–88.

Othman, Zarina and Mohamad Daud Druis. 2014. "Illicit Drug Syndication: Threat towards Juveniles in Malaysia". *Journal of Social and Development Sciences*, 5(4): 284–291.

Othman, Zarina, Nur Ruhana Nasuha Adullah Jian and Abdul Halim Mahamud. 2013. "Non Traditional Security Issues and the Stability of Southeast Asia". *Jurnal Kajian Wilayah*, 4(2): 150–164.

Parameswaran, Pratap. 1998. *ASEAN Solidarity on the Prevention of Drug and Substance Abuse*. Jakarta: ASEAN Secretariat.

Ramli, Rashila, Zarina Othman, Nor Azizan Idris and Sity Daud. 2012. "Towards a Modified Approach of Human Security in Southeast Asia: A Perspective from Bangi". *Pertanika Journal of Social Sciences and Humanities*, 20(3): 577–588.

Renard, Ronald. 1996. *The Burmese Connection: Illegal Drugs and the Making of the Golden Triangle*. Boulder, CO: Lynn Rienner Publishers.

Royal Malaysian Police. 2010, 2011. Availabe at: www.rmp.gov.my.

Schaeffer, Robert K. 1997. *Understanding Globalisation: The Social Consequences of Political, Economic and Environmental Change*. Lanham, MD and New York: Rowman and Littlefield.

Scorzelli, James F. 1992. "Has Malaysia's Antidrug Efforts Been Effective?" *Journal of Substance Abuse Treat*, 9(2): 171–176.

UNDP. 1997. *Human Development Report*. New York: Oxford University Press.

UNIDCP. 1998. *United Nations International Drug Control Programme*. New York: University Press.

UNIDCP. 2000. *United Nations International Drug Control Programme*. New York: University Press.

United Nations Trust Fund for Human Security. 2006. Available at: www.unfoundation.org.

UNODCCP. 1997. *World Drug Report 1997*. New York: Oxford University Press.

UNODCCP. 2000. *World Drug Report 2000*. New York: Oxford University Press.

UNODCCP. 2005. *World Drug Report 2005*. New York: Oxford University Press.

UNODCCP. 2009. *United Nations Office on Drugs and Crime*. Available at: www.unodc.org/.

UNODCCP. 2013. *World Drug Report 2013*. New York: Oxford University Press.

Interviews

Abdul Sani, 14 November 2012 (not real name), drug trafficker/prisoner.

Adeeba Kamarulzaman, 10 March 2013, medical doctor, University Malaya.

Guenter Brauch, 7 December 2012, Professor of Human Security, Free University of Berlin.

Halim Wong Abdullah, 4 December 2012, Royal Malaysian police officer.

Jamaludin Kudip, 8 November 2012, Royal Malaysian police officer.

Yunus Pathi, 10 May 2013, President, PENGASIH (NGO rehabilitation centre).

Zainal Abidin, 4 November 2012, Royal Malaysian Customs.

3 Regional mobility from East Asia to Southeast Asia

The case of education and retirement migration

Hyung Jun Kim and Leng Leng Thang

1 Introduction

Intra-Asia movements are predicted to increase in significance (Hugo 1996). In terms of the flows between East Asia (China, South Korea and Japan) and Southeast Asia, one dominant flow is obviously the out-migration of labour for higher income and better life for their families left behind. They constitute predominantly the non-skilled labourers from Southeast Asia to East Asia, especially to Japan and South Korea (Douglass 2006). In recent decades, where more varied flows have been observed, besides the movement of the unskilled working population, there are also increasing flows of skilled and semi-skilled forms of migration, such as the presence of Indonesian caregivers in Japan (Ogawa 2010) and elite professionals from Southeast Asia working in East Asian cities (Yeoh and Willis 2005). Douglass, in examining transnational flows in Pacific Asia from the framework of global householding, notes that besides migrating for jobs including domestic workers and caregivers for elders and children, there are also increasing trans-border mobility for the purpose of marriage, where "these days, the so-called 'mail order brides' from Asia are more likely to go to Taiwan, Singapore, Korea and Japan than to the West (2006, 428)". In addition, he also identifies movements for education among children and their mothers, and retirement especially by older people from high-income East Asian countries to Southeast Asia.

This chapter particularly focuses on the phenomenon of such education and retirement flows from East Asia to Southeast Asia.[1] Douglass (2006) has alerted us to the recent attempts of Korean and Japanese governments to increase the number of foreign students studying in the respective countries motivated by low fertility rates, which have led to a fall in tertiary student enrolment in Korean and Japanese universities. While the launching of new university programmes such as four-year degrees conducted in the English language in these countries offered new options to students from Southeast Asia who have conventionally looked favourably to higher education in America, Australia and the United Kingdom, in this chapter we would like to examine educational migration in the reverse direction of East Asia to Southeast Asia, a phenomenon that has become increasingly visible in the recent decade, especially among middle-class families in South Korea and China. Similarly, the reverse retirement flow is discussed as another recent phenomenon triggered by increasing longevity in East Asia.

We contend that these less-discussed forms of migratory flows add new dimensions to human security issues in East Asia. Compared to conventional labour migration, the economic position of transnational retirees and students is more secure in that they usually bring their economic resources from home. Their cultural and social positions, however, are less stable. They are usually in their teens or in their late fifties and above, and it is important to understand how these groups adapt to a foreign environment. In cultural terms, for example, retirees are less equipped with linguistic capacity to acquire basic communicative skills to mix with a new community in their host country. In social terms, teenagers are severed from the most important relationship needed for their transition from adolescence to adulthood – the family. As belonging to age groups for which familiarity may matter more than "challenge", retirees and teenagers may be exposed to different forms of security problems which conventional transmigrants have not experienced intensively. At the same time, the length and type of their stay in local communities make them different from shorter-term visitors like tourists, and the potential for positive local-host interactions are significant. Hence, they bring new understanding to the role of migration in ASEAN community building.

It should be noted that although the discussion of such flows is limited to the direction of East Asia to Southeast Asia here, it is necessary to recognise that these are by no means a unidirectional flow. Within the region of Southeast Asia and East Asia, too, the velocity and intensity of migratory movements exist in different forms, including a blurring of what defines migration with the daily crossing of borders for work in the borderland regions. Education and retirement migration prevails within these regions, with Koreans and Chinese constituting the biggest student population in Japan, Malaysians and Indonesians as common sights among school children in Singapore, students from Indo-Chinese countries studying in Thailand and Singaporeans retiring in Malaysia.

Following Douglass (2006, 2012), we consider the concept of global householding useful in providing a framework to understand such newer forms of transnational flows. By focusing on the trans-border features that are increasingly common in "householding" – a term which is used to underscore the "way in which creating and sustaining a household is a continuous process of social reproduction that covers all life-cycle stages and extends beyond the family" (Douglass 2006, 421), the concept addresses the shortcoming in international migration studies which tends to overlook the family in its analysis of individual migrants. While students and seniors may appear as quite unrelated individuals in migration, our discussion will show that despite migrating to fulfil different objectives and hence resulting in different implications for the families, the movement of one may sometimes trigger mobility in another, resulting in the orchestrated movement of grandparents and grandchildren transnationally.

Douglass summarises the typical elements of householding in household life cycles into the following order of marriage/patterning, bearing, raising and educating children (and adults), the daily maintenance of the households, labour division and income pooling through livelihood activities and the caring of elders and other non-working members in the household (Douglass 2006, 423). By focusing on the young and the old in the process of global householding, we further hope to offer new insights on how they may implicate one another, although remaining largely as independent flows to the host countries. Furthermore, besides impacting on the migrants and their families, the interactions with local society led by such flows affect the nature of local society and residents as they experience globalisation on their doorstep. Thus, the onset of educational and retirement migration may shed new light on the impact of transnational mobility on local, national and regional community, and at the same time, on human security issues in East Asia.

In this chapter, we begin first with the discussion of education migration, focusing mostly on Korean students as a case of movement from East Asia to Southeast Asia, and including also a brief discussion of Chinese students and their mothers to Singapore relating to the phenomenon of the "study mother". Following this, retirement migration will be explored with the cases of Japanese and Korean retirees moving to Southeast Asia. In the final section, we discuss such transnational movements in the light of human security issues and the role of ASEAN and the East Asian economy before our concluding remarks.

2 Education migration: the flow of East Asian children and mothers to Southeast Asia

Since the 1990s, with economic growth, fewer numbers of children per household and an expanded income among middle-class families in urban East Asia, education of children has become a significant "project" for these families, deemed as an important pathway for the accumulation of cultural and social capital that will improve a family's well-being and upward social mobility (Huang and Yeoh 2005, 2011; Waters 2005; Lee and Koo 2006). It is common for "studying overseas" to mean studying in the United States, the United Kingdom, Canada, Australia or New Zealand for Asian students, and usually referring to those moving for secondary and tertiary education. Since the late 1990s, there has been increasing visibility of the presence of younger East Asian children, often with a parent (usually mothers), migrating to Southeast Asian cities to pursue an education.

The desire to improve English proficiency is the main reason triggering the movement of East Asian children overseas. While Western countries remain the preferred choice, Southeast Asian cities are increasingly considered a desirable second-choice destination because of the lower cost of living and educational expenses, the availability of suitable schools (e.g. international schools with teachers from Western countries) and incentives from host countries (such as a more relaxed visa policy) aimed at attracting foreign students. Malaysia and Singapore, for example, are two Southeast Asian countries which have emerged strongly in the global education market (Cheng et al. 2013). Among the students from East Asia, besides Chinese students who inevitably constitute a large number overseas due to the sheer size of the Chinese population, Koreans have also gained prominence recently as significant numbers have chosen to study in various Southeast Asian countries. This section largely focuses on the phenomenon of the temporary migration of Koreans for education to Southeast Asia but also includes Chinese students in the discussion of Singapore, highlighting the phenomenon of "study mothers" among the Chinese in Singapore.[2]

2.1 Korean students in Southeast Asia

Studying abroad has been a dream of many Korean students. This attitude seemed to originate from the late 19th century with the impact of Western science and technology. After the colonisation of Korea, Japan became the favourite destination, and after independence and the Korean War, the US came to the fore. Before the 1990s when the fruits of rapid economic development were not yet felt by ordinary Koreans, studying abroad was confined to a small number of students, especially those at the graduate level. In the 1990s, the demand for overseas education increased dramatically and students venturing overseas became much younger. At the end of the 1990s, Korean primary and secondary students studying abroad increased remarkably, and since the 2000s, overseas study for this age group has been no longer extraordinary.

The popularity and rapid expansion of studying abroad are closely related to the English language, which is not just a foreign language but a symbol of personal excellence and competence (Moon 2009). This significance of English suggests that the favourite destination for Korean students is English-speaking countries. The US has been the top favourite for decades, followed by Canada, the UK, Australia and New Zealand. Since the late 1990s, there have emerged new destinations, which, following Kachru (1985), can be classified as the "outer circle" of English, namely the former colonies of the English-speaking West. The Philippines, with its geographical proximity, became a popular place for learning English and Malaysia and India were also designated as suitable places.

In the Philippines, the influx of Korean students since 2000 is regarded as the second wave in Korean migration to the Philippines after the first wave of Korean businesses made inroads into the Philippines economy (Miralao 2007). Besides entering tertiary education, where Koreans constitute the highest proportion of foreign students in the Philippines' colleges and universities, there is also a sizable number of Korean children (including their mothers) in various educational arrangements, such as short-term English language schools, local schools and international schools. For example, in Cebu, a popular tourist destination for Koreans, Koreans dominate the foreign student population, making up 88 per cent of the 5,065 special study permit holders, outnumbering the second largest group, the Japanese, by almost 20 times (Palaubsanon 2010). Besides the Philippines and other former English-speaking colonies, Korean students are also present in international schools and English language schools in the major cities in Thailand, including international schools in Chiangmai city in northern Thailand.

The major reasons pointed out as advantages of studying English in Southeast Asia are the low costs of education and living. An advertisement of a consulting firm explains the advantages of learning English in the Philippines as follows:[3]

> The reason why studying in the Philippines is popular is that ... you can attend more classes with relatively cheap price. You can also concentrate on your study, not bothered by such everyday chores as cooking and laundry ... Differing from other [English-speaking] countries, classes in the Philippines are conducted mainly with the method of 1:1. If you wish to take such classes in other countries, you would have to pay an enormous amount of money.

Low costs of education and living are also stated as major advantages of study in Malaysia (Cheng et al. 2013). A close examination of advertisements on study in Malaysia, however, can help us to find a slightly different perspective and, for this, three quotes are presented:[4]

> Malaysia is a multi-ethnic country, which provides a social atmosphere in which people of every ethnic background can live without discrimination ... This environment makes it possible to learn both English and Chinese and to contact with people of diverse backgrounds and cultures.
> Many Korean firms operate in Malaysia and many more are planning to come to Malaysia ... Malaysia is the industrial and economic hub of Southeast Asia. Studying there, you can harmonize your vision with our national goal to advance into Southeast Asia.
> The national religion of Malaysia is Islam ... Islam demands moderation and self-control, which are the reasons why decadent entertainment industry has not developed ... This safe educational environment is one of the reasons why Malaysia is chosen as a destination for studying abroad at the primary and secondary level.

The advantages of studying in Malaysia include elements which are related distinctively to Malaysia. Meeting people of diverse backgrounds and obtaining better qualifications to work in Southeast Asia are viewed to be merits Malaysia can provide. In this framework, Malaysia is perceived not just as a place which satisfies the educational needs of Koreans who cannot afford to study in the US. Instead, it is considered as having its own excellences which the traditional favourite destinations cannot provide. These explanations indicate an emergence of a new perspective to evaluating study in Malaysia in particular, and study in Southeast Asia in general.[5]

2.2 Korean primary and secondary students in the Philippines

In analysing the development of Korean primary and secondary students' temporary migration to Southeast Asia, we examine the trends among Korean students studying abroad between 2003 and 2010. As shown in Figure 3.1, in 2010

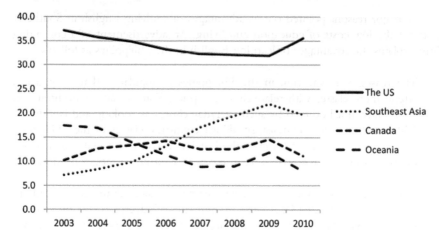

Figure 3.1 Primary and secondary Korean students studying abroad (unit: %)
Source: Korean Ministry of Education, Science and Technology (a).

their most favourite place for study is the US. Somewhat surprisingly, Southeast Asia is ranked as second with 19.7 per cent of the total.

The data show that Southeast Asia has established itself as an important destination in the market of studying abroad. Its ranking has risen from fourth position in 2003, to third in 2005, and then to second in 2006. Since 2006, the gap between Southeast Asia and the US has narrowed, while that between Southeast Asia and Canada and Oceania widened. Given that the parents, usually the mother, would accompany their children to the destination, the total number of Korean temporary migrants to Southeast Asia for educational purposes surely exceeds that of the number of Korean primary and secondary students to the region.

2.3 Korean students in tertiary education in the Philippines

The situation differs with the case of students studying abroad in tertiary education. The portion of Southeast Asia represented by the Philippines is far lower than that of the US. In 2010, the percentage of students to the Philippines is 9.9 per cent of the total (Figure 3.2). Moreover, as the majority of Korean students are enrolled in private non-formal institutions, their stay in the country is far shorter than primary- and secondary-school students. In 2011, for example, of approximately 30,000 Korean college students in the Philippines, only 2,653 are enrolled in universities.

Although the number of students enrolled in universities in the Philippines is relatively small, their absolute number is quite substantive. Only the US, Japan, China, Germany, Australia, New Zealand and the UK hosted more Korean students than the Philippines. Moreover, over the last decade, the number of students in the Philippines shows a rapid increase, from 300 in 2000 to 2,653 in 2010. These facts indicate that quantitative expansion in human flows can lead to

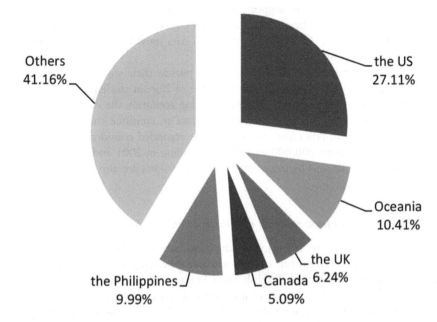

Figure 3.2 Korean tertiary-level students abroad in 2010 (formal and informal institutions)
Source: Korean Ministry of Education, Science and Technology (b).

qualitative change. As more Koreans have the chance to visit and stay in the Philippines, more decide to continue their tertiary education there.

2.4 Korean students in Malaysia and other Southeast Asian countries

The cases of primary and secondary Korean students in Malaysia suggest that non-educational flows can lead to the acceleration of educational flows. Talking about their reasons for choosing Malaysia, students and their parents mention such factors as having relatives in Malaysia, the recommendation of people in Malaysia and their previous experience of visiting Malaysia as tourists. There are also cases showing a dimension of global householding when retirement migration and education migration interacted to motivate each other's move, as in the case of Hong's informants (2009, 248):

> E who is to retire soon decides to send his children to Malaysia where he is going to seek for a new job or business opportunity, and F who is to retire in two to three years is planning to open a business in Malaysia by the time their children will finish secondary school and enter university there.

The cases of Korean students in Malaysia reveal that activities in conventional fields such as business and tourism may accelerate Koreans' flow into the region as students. This possibility is supported by a gradual increase in the number of Koreans enrolled in Southeast Asian universities which do not employ English as their medium of study. In Table 3.1, the 2010 data show the number of students studying in Southeast Asia.

A substantial number of Korean students pursue their studies in Indonesia, Thailand and Vietnam. Although the presence of Korean students in the region cannot be comparable to that in English-speaking countries, the data indicate that more Koreans consider Southeast Asia as a place to continue their study at the tertiary level. Korean flows into the region have expanded considerably during the last two decades, from 200,000 in 1991 to a million in 2001 and to 3 million in 2010 (Korean Tourism Organization); educational flows are also likely to expand in the near future.

2.5 Korean and Chinese students and their mothers in Singapore

Singapore, a relatively well-developed education hub in Southeast Asia, is another popular destination for Korean families who regard Singapore as ideal for its educational system offering both English and Chinese language learning. Korean students are among the top sources of international students in Singapore, alongside China, India, Indonesia, Malaysia and Vietnam. Koreans' interest in Singapore education began in 2003 with active marketing by the Singapore Tourism Board[6] of its education in Seoul. In 2005, there were 1,500 Korean students in Singapore government schools ranging from primary to higher secondary schools; by 2008 the number had jumped to 5,000 (Lee 2008).

Compared with education migration among tertiary students who are usually independent, mothers tend to accompany their children, especially when their children are of primary-school age. In Singapore, as in other parts of Southeast Asia, Korean mothers are typically middle-class family housewives where they lead

Table 3.1 Korean students enrolled in Southeast Asian tertiary institutions (2010)

	Undergraduate	*Graduate*	*Total*
Brunei	0	0	0
Cambodia	56	0	56
Indonesia	135	7	142
Laos	6	1	7
Malaysia	218	22	240
Myanmar	24	0	24
Philippines	2,653	0	2,653
Singapore	64	13	77
Thailand	358	45	403
Vietnam	206	20	226

Source: Korean Ministry of Education, Science and Technology (b).

an active life in their hobbies, learn English or are committed to church activities while living in Singapore (Lee 2008). Korean fathers, on the other hand, are much like the "astronaut" Hong Kong fathers who have relocated their wives and children in Western countries but still work in Hong Kong and reunite with the family through periodic visits (Lam 1994), shuttling regularly between Korea and Singapore.

Among the transnational education migrants in Singapore, the mothers of children from China, popularly referred to as "study mothers",[7] are a group that have received much attention – usually negative – in the Singapore media. Compared with the Korean housewife mothers who are less visible in public spaces, Chinese study mothers have gained much visibility as most seek employment to sustain their stay in Singapore. While there has not been any official release on the exact numbers of Chinese study mothers, estimates varied from 1000 in 2000, to 30,000 in 2003 (Huang and Yeoh 2005, 387). Study mothers face problems in the search for employment; many apparently leave China with the arrangement of a broker who promises them good jobs, only to realise once they get to Singapore that their professional and academic qualifications are not recognised and their lack of work experience in the country also counts against them. Many are relegated to manual jobs such as chambermaids and masseuses.[8] Although they are generally "sacrificial mothers" who have worked hard for the sake of a better future for their children, unfortunately, they have come to be generally portrayed in a negative light over time, affected by the presence of some opportunistic mothers among them who have exploited the study mother scheme[9] to enter the country for personal economic gain or to look for new husbands (Huang and Yeoh 2005). The negative connotation of the term "study mothers" has led to calls to change the term to a more neutral-sounding "study parents" instead.[10-] Huang and Yeoh (2011), in examining Chinese children's moves to Singapore for education, found the children to be mostly passive participants in the initial migration decision that was usually brought up by their mothers. As the children mature and become more independent and adapted to Singapore, ironically, some would suggest that their mothers return to China (Huang and Yeoh 2005).

2.6 Education migration and global householding

Discussions on Korean and Chinese children and their mothers' movements to Southeast Asia for the purpose of education suggests a simple objective of global householding as a strategy to enhance the future of their children – and in turn, the parents' well-being. However, the movement which is meant to be a search for better educational opportunities has shown to impact greatly on the lives and identities of their parents. For the Korean parents, where the mothers usually accompany the children, it means enduring long-term separation of the husbands from the wives, and the fathers from the children. Although this could be an emotional strain on the individuals, families also reveal resilience by maintaining strong family solidarity (Lee and Koo 2006). For the Chinese study mothers in Singapore, although some are in a similar situation of global householding with the Korean mothers, whose husbands remain in China to work and provide support, many are also more accurately referred to as "relocated" or "escaped" households where the mothers relocate with their children and seek employment in the hope of benefiting from the higher wages in the host countries. Anecdotal examples have also revealed that some mothers who are divorced or separated from their husbands further regard the transnational move as a way of escape to rebuild their household in a new country. Together, the children and their families reiterate the saliency of understanding the phenomenon from the broader context of the rising middle class in East Asia, the trend towards a lesser number of children per family and its implications and expectations on the only child – in the case of China's one-child policy, and the host countries' policies to attract foreign students, such as Singapore's policy of attracting international talent through the "Singapore Global Schoolhouse" ambition (Lee and Koo 2006).

3 Retirement migration: the flows of Japanese and Korean retirees to Southeast Asia

Retirement transnational migration, while a relatively new area of enquiry within the discourses on migration, is perceived in Western societies to have the potential to increase in substantial numbers with the ageing of the baby boomers (Sunil et al. 2007). Such have also been predicted by Southeast Asian countries in the recent decade regarding the migration of Japanese retirees to their respective countries, as shown in the various long-stay policies and programmes in countries such as Malaysia, Thailand and the Philippines, and healthcare business plans in Southeast Asia for long-term care facilities and retirement villages to woo retirees from Japan and other countries (Toyota and Xiang 2012). While Japanese retirees tend to dominate in the flow of retirees from East Asia to Southeast Asia, in this chapter we also examine the emerging trend of Korean retirees in the region. The discussion of Japanese and Korean retirees shows interesting subtle differences between the two, while they also highlight similar specificities in motivation and expectations of trans-border crossings that are impacted by the larger structural differences characterising work and retirement – such as the adequacy of pensions in both societies.

3.1 Japanese retirees to Southeast Asia

The idea of retiring overseas among the Japanese is relatively new, first mooted in the form of self-contained "Silver Towns" for Japanese overseas in the United States, Australia, Spain, New Zealand and the Philippines by the former Ministry of International Trade and Industry in 1986 under the "Silver Columbus Plan 92". However, the project was soon shelved under strong criticisms from both home and abroad condemning the government for the international exporting of unwanted unproductive members (Kitabatake 1986; Mizukami 2007). With the advent of super ageing in Japan, retirement overseas begins to be viewed in a different light. In 1992, with the launch of the Long-Stay Foundation where permanent migration was modified to a more flexible concept of long-term stay, retirement overseas soon emerged to become a viable option for older Japanese who were growing old with relatively better health, better income from pensions and their own savings and seeking post-work life as a time to enjoy a "second life". In the 1990s, the West was overwhelmingly the preferred choice among older Japanese. Surveys from the Japan Long-Stay Foundation shows that in 2000, among the top ten preferred destinations, Malaysia was the only Southeast Asian destination, taking tenth place. However, since 2006, Malaysia has consistently occupied first place; in 2010, besides Malaysia, Thailand (third), the Philippines (seventh) and Indonesia (ninth) have also become top destinations for older Japanese. The emerging retirement industry, fuelled by the state-industry nexus, is crucial in attracting Japanese retirees, as shown in Malaysia, the Philippines and Thailand (Toyota and Xiang 2012). On the whole, these Southeast Asian destinations are also receiving more East Asians, as evidenced in their retirement-related visa programmes. In the "Malaysia My Second Home Program" in 2010, Japan ranks first, followed by China. In the Philippines, the Philippine Retirement Authority launched a global initiative called Plan Metjack in 2008 targeting the Middle East, Europe, Taiwan, Japan, America, China and Korea (the plan is made up of the first letter of each country), among which retirees from East Asian countries have shown to be most responsive to the opportunity to retire in the Philippines, with Chinese at the top of the list, followed by Koreans, Taiwanese and Japanese.[11]

There are several reasons contributing to the shift in preferences to Southeast Asia as a retirement destination among the Japanese. Shimizu (2009), who expects a further acceleration of Japanese retirees moving to Southeast Asian destinations, lists the following reasons as attracting Japanese retirees to these countries:

1   the availability of special visas for a long stay;
2   warm climate during the winter season;
3   geographical nearness with little time difference;
4   the smiles, kindness and hospitality of the local people;
5   the reasonable prices of daily commodities and medical/care services (compared with Western countries).

Among these reasons, a lower cost of living inevitably features prominently among the retirees to Southeast Asia. In the study of Japanese retirees in Malaysia, Ono (2008, 2010) has attempted to showcase the varying patterns of retiree migration under three typologies: leisure migration, seasonal migration staying only during the winter months and economic migration. Economic affordability has shown to be of a general concern, where living in Malaysia is favoured for allowing pensioners to stretch their dollars by participating in a wide range of leisure activities such as golfing that would not be possible in Japan with a limited pension.

With the substantial increase in the proportion of Japanese aged 65 and over from 12 per cent in 1990 to 23.1 per cent in 2010, an increase of over 17 million in absolute numbers from 11.83 million to 29.58 million during the period (Statistics Bureau Japan 2011), coupled with Japan's economic doldrums, diminishing family support and the shortage of care workers in Japan, retirement migration to Southeast Asia is certainly deemed a viable strategy for those seeking financial sustainability and obtaining long-term care. Some of the migrants, such as those who were displaced and lost their jobs during the economic recession, even consider themselves "economic refugees"[12] and perceive themselves as being forced to live out of Japan due to economic necessity (Ono 2010). Furthermore, as Thailand and the Philippines tend to be dominated by Japanese older male migrants, compared with Malaysia, who tend to attract older couples, it also stereotyped these destinations as being preferred by older men who may have a desire to seek liaisons with local women. While there have sometimes been sensationalised media coverage of tragedies in such liaisons ending in death or the loss of one's life savings to local women, there have also been cases of happy endings such as family stability with new transnational families comprising young local wives and Japanese-Southeast Asian children, and even stories of older Japanese men in the Philippines being cared for by the whole village of the girlfriend/wife as one turns frail (Toyota 2006; Shimizu 2009). In examining how Japanese pensioners in Southeast Asia seek welfare security in old age, Toyota (2006) has identified four types of global householding strategies where the above examples could be classified, namely, (1) transnationalised households where the retirees lead "pendulum lives" by spending the winter in Southeast Asia and the rest of the year in Japan; (2) relocated households where the retirees move together with their aged parents for a more affordable aged care in Southeast Asia; (3) escaped households where those most likely to refer to themselves as "economic refugees" resort to moving overseas as an escape from household pressures in Japan, and (4) remade households where the retirees make new "families" with local women in Southeast Asia. The strategies adopted differentiated by economic status and demographic characteristics reflect diversities among what we refer unanimously as retirees or pensioners.

With the expectation that retirement transnational migration will increase in substantial numbers from Japan and other ageing East Asian countries to Southeast Asia, besides the attention on the push and pull factors affecting such migratory flows, there will be a further need to study the impact of this form of migration on local society. While there are concerns of conflict and unequal exchanges that may occur as Japanese retirement enclaves are formed in the destinations affecting local lives (Ono 2010), we can also expect positive impacts on local society. Other than economic benefits as retiree migrants expand local consumption of goods and services, the inter-cultural exchanges and volunteer efforts among philanthropic-minded and active retirees and older persons to engage with the local residents have the potential to enrich the local society and promote social cohesion. In Thailand, the Japanese are among the foreigners who are playing an active role in non-profit work for local communities, and they include older Japanese who have left Japan seeking meaningful engagements through helping others. One prominent example is the setting up of Ban Rom Sai, an orphanage for children with HIV by a Japanese woman called Miwa Natori when she was in her 50s. From an initial 12 orphans when it started in 1999, the number of children has since been more than doubled, and the orphanage has also expanded to include a cottage industry on handicraft and art work, a small-scale restaurant and a guest house business. It is the wish of Miwa that the orphans who have now become adults are willing to return to help manage the orphanage and benefit more unfortunate children.[13]

3.2 Korean retirees to Southeast Asia

In Korea, elderly parents were traditionally taken care of by their children. The rapid transformation of Korean society has weakened the traditional bond between parents and children, creating the problem of how elderly retirees should cope with the period after retirement. While society was looking for new models of behaviour for retirees, the concept of retirement migration appeared in the mid-2000s, attracting immediate public attention. Southeast Asia has been the region receiving the media focus, especially the Philippines and Malaysia. The major reasons Southeast Asia was proposed as the best destination provide an opportunity to compare the similarities and differences between Korean and Japanese cases.

As in Japan, geographical proximity and a low cost of living were stressed as major advantages. However, compared with Japan, the low living cost in Southeast Asia was made in an exaggerated fashion in the Korean media, which explains why the idea of retiring to Southeast Asia has attracted enormous media and public attention. The title of a book by Dongu Cheong (2005) demonstrates how life in Southeast Asia was erroneously reported and at the same time romanticised: "*Living like a Noble Abroad: With Two Million Korean Won*".[14]

In addition to the low expenses, two other economic factors were highlighted as the main attraction: the chances of earning money, either by working or by investment, and of the provision of English education to children and grandchildren. A guidebook to retirement migration refers to the case of a Korean retiree to the Philippines to illustrate these advantages (Hong 2008, 208):

> Kang, who retired to the Philippines in 2006, purchased a house for investment. Earning regular incomes from this property, he pursued real-estate study and received a brokerage license ... He now earns a substantial income as a consultant advising on real estate and investment for Koreans coming to the Philippines.

The major purpose of Kang's migration was to continue his economic activity after retirement. For him, the Philippines is described as the place for a second economic opportunity rather than for rest and enjoyment. Economic motivation is also visible among Koreans who view migration as an educational opportunity. For them, the favourite destinations are thus the Philippines and Malaysia where English is used, as a guidebook explains (Hong 2008, 245–5):

The international schools in the Philippines provide high-quality educational environment with relatively low educational and living expenses. By bringing their children or grandchildren, retirees kill "two birds with one stone".

Interest in retirement migration as a new economic opportunity reflects a different economic condition of Korean elders from their Japanese counterparts. First, Korean elders' economic condition after retirement is not stable. The Korean national pension scheme began only in 1988, thus unlike their Japanese counterparts, the monthly benefit pensioners receive is not large enough to cover their living expenses.[15] Second, it is a norm among Koreans to save to own a house as the major form of preparation for retirement. Consequently, many are asset-rich but lack cash flows, which are traditionally provided by their children. Third, as government policy for the elderly is not well developed, there is little provision on job opportunities for the elderly. Instead, older employees are faced with expectations to retire early in times of harsh economic situations which drastically affect their savings for retirement (Shin 2011). In sum, for many Koreans, instead of viewing post-retirement life as a period for relaxing retirement living, it is more realistically a period to embark on a second economic activity to sustain their daily living.

Under these circumstances, the media report portraying retirement migration as an opportunity to maintain a luxurious life and to earn a reasonable income drew keen public attention. The lack of data makes it difficult to examine whether the interest in retirement migration has actually triggered retirees' migration to Southeast Asia. There is, however, indirect evidence showing an increase of Korean retirees in Malaysia and the Philippines. The report on "Malaysia My Second Home Program" provides the list of nationalities of people applying for retirement visas and the rankings of Korean and Japanese retirees are in Table 3.2.

The rankings of Japanese applicants rise gradually, from fourth in 2006 to first in 2011. In the case of Koreans, it is more up and down. They are ranked as third and fifth in 2007 and 2008, respectively, but as tenth in 2010 and 2011.

In the Philippines, the dominance of Koreans in retirement visa applications is noticeable. Korean applicants numbered 692, compared to 113 Japanese applicants in 2008 (Kim 2009, 244). The trend of the dominance of Koreans over Japanese continues, as shown in the cumulative data between 2000 and 2010 (Figure 3.3) where Koreans are ranked as second and Japanese ranked as fourth in the Philippines.

Table 3.2 Ranks of Korean and Japanese in retirement visa application to Malaysia

	2006	2007	2008	2009	2010	2011	Overall (2001–11)
Korean	7th	3rd	5th	9th	10th	10th	10th
Japanese	4th	2nd	2nd	2nd	2nd	1st	3rd

Source: Malaysia My Second Home Program, www.mm2h.gov.my/statistic.php.

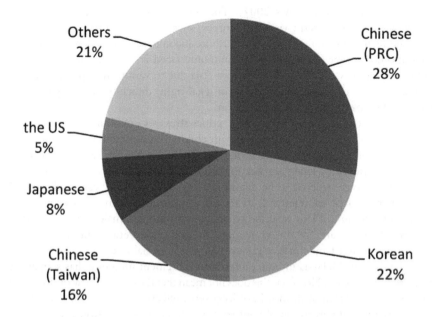

Figure 3.3 Origin of foreigners applying for retirement visas to the Philippines
Source: Philippine Retirement Authority, www.pra.gov.ph/dl_form/file_name/128/
PRNews_for_Web_1st_Issue.pdf.

The reversal to Malaysia in the Philippines case may be partly explained by the relatively low cost for applying for retirement visas.[16] For most Koreans, whose economic condition is not as good as the Japanese, the lower cost in applying for retirement visas in the Philippines makes the lodging of applications more attractive. Another factor is the human flow of Koreans into both countries: more Koreans visit the Philippines than Malaysia. In 2010, for example, about three times more Koreans visited the Philippines (740,622) than Malaysia (264,052) (Korean Tourism Organization 2010, 26). The larger flow of Koreans into the Philippines makes it possible for Korean retirees to have more economic opportunities there. Indeed, it has been noted that there is a tendency among Korean retirees to open small businesses in the Philippines, catering mostly to Korean residents living there (Kim 2013).

However, there is an increasing realisation of the obstacles in fulfilling their desire to be economically stable overseas. Many are disappointed with the realisation that the cost of living in Southeast Asia is not as cheap as was envisaged. Living expenses can be kept cheap only when one is willing to maintain a basic lifestyle. The cost jumps dramatically if one wishes to enjoy the same lifestyle as he or she is used to in Korea. "Two million Korean won is certainly insufficient for one to live like a noble", a critic puts forward his sceptical view, "with the same two million Korean won, retirees can live a comfortable, though not luxurious, life even in Korea" (Nocut News 2007). The host government's financial require-ments to obtain long-term visas for retirees, such as Malaysia's requirement for one-time financial proof and constant offshore income, serve as a deterrent to visa application. Another disappointment commonly faced is the difficulty in opening and managing new businesses in Southeast Asia due to various unexpected barriers including a lack of transparency, a lack of legal right, difficulty in managing local persons, the possibility of fraud and so on.

In addition to the economic problem, critics stress socio-cultural and emotional hardships such as the severance of ties with children, relatives and friends and dif-ficulty in adapting to a foreign environment. For most Korean retirees who have not had experience of living abroad, initiating and maintaining relationships with local people are considered to be daunting tasks. This difficulty can be illustrated indirectly by a lack of reference to romantic relationships in the discourse on retirement migration. This reflects the difficulty of Korean male retirees to make such relationships and at the same time suggests that retirement migration is viewed mainly as a family matter rather than as a personal one.

As the data on Malaysia indicate, interest in retirement migration has somewhat decreased for Koreans. However, this does not mean that the ebb and flow of discourse on retirement migration do not have long-term effects. The most notable one is that a new form of perception of Southeast Asia has emerged in Korea. Previously, Koreans' interactions with Southeast Asia have been confined mainly to business and tourism, so that, for many Koreans, the region is just viewed as a place for fortune, temporary rest and recreation. The popularity of the Korean discourse on migration adds a new dimension to how the region is perceived. The prospect of living in the region as permanent residents has become plausible for more Kor-eans, and this may prompt casual Korean visitors, whose number reached more than 3 million in 2011, to consider the region more attentively and empathically.

What will the future development of retirement migration be among the Koreans? When Koreans currently in their 30s and 40s reach retirement age, they will have a substantial amount of pension benefits and, coupled with the likelihood of Kor-eans in this age group to have more contact with foreign culture compared with present retirees, migration to Southeast Asian countries will likely be transformed from hope to a practical option.

3.3 Retirement migration and global householding

Discussions on the transnational movement of retirees from Japan and Korea to Southeast Asia highlight such moves in householding as strategies in search of security in welfare and ultimately a quest for a better later life. Whether they are – in Toyota's (2006) terms – for relocation, pendulum-like, escape or the remaking of households, for the purpose of living a life of leisure or to seek a second opportunity through small entrepreneurialism (Kim 2013), they contribute to global connections among households and the generations in different intensities.

Although education and retirement migration appear to be separate phenom-ena, as noted, they are sometimes intertwined and mutually influential, where the migration of one may impact on the other. Earlier examples of Korean retirees in the Philippines and Malaysia have shown that retirees may migrate with more objectives than for their own retirement needs, and perceive their move to benefit the younger generation, such as setting the path for the migration of their children and/or grandchildren for education. Fieldwork on Japanese retirees in Southeast Asia has also shown that although the retirees moved individually or as couples, they could change the perceived distance and image of Southeast Asia among their children and grandchildren, interest them to learn more about Southeast Asia through more frequent travel to visit their family members and may eventually also trigger their migration to Southeast Asia. In this way, retirement migration could intersect in an intergenerational manner, enriching the possibilities of different dimensions in global householding as they contribute to interdependency in the extended family, and providing the opportunity for grandparents and grandchildren to connect more intimately than they would have in their own countries.

4 Migratory students and retirees in a regional perspective

Analyses on trans-regional movement have rarely remarked on teenage students and elders, in that they do not belong to the typical form of migration. The foregoing discussion, however, shows that this new form of migration has been taking place and has a potential to increase in the near future. As teenagers and elders are relative newcomers to transnational mobility, and their characters and positions are novel to their host countries, their impact on the host and home countries and the security issues they pose are required to receive more attention from scholars of international migration.

This new form of migratory flow is also neglected in the discourse of politicians and policy makers trying to promote the East Asian community. The institutional framework for this regional community, namely ASEAN Plus Three, was established with the recognition that "the growing interaction within the region has helped increase opportunities for cooperation and collaboration with each other" and that the building of the East Asian community will strengthen "the elements essential for the promotion of peace, stability and prosperity in the region" (ASEAN 1999). In spite of this recognition, however, the new form of migration has not been considered as a factor to facilitate the growing interaction within the region. Unlike migrant workers who are incorporated as a part of "ASEAN Plus Three Cooperation Work Plan 2013–2017" (see 4.6.1) and unlike such non-traditional security issues as human trafficking and cybercrimes (see 1.3.11 and 1.3.12), the new form of migration is not mentioned (Ministry of Foreign Affairs in Korea 2013).

Lack of interest in the new form of migratory flows makes it difficult to appreciate whether it will increase "opportunities for cooperation and collaboration" in East Asia or will become a new threat to regional integration and security. If migrants continue to stay in enclaves and establish most of their everyday interactions within their own ethnic/national circle, the potential for misunderstanding is a real threat. However, both retiree and student migrants move to new host countries to stay for significant periods of time. Foreign students have to interact with locals in the classroom and in other school extra-curricular activities like sports and school-based activities and over time are likely to develop close ties with local peer groups. Likewise, elderly retirees encounter a range of locals in their everyday lives: shopkeepers, caregivers, volunteers and other senior citizens. The potential for positive contact, though somewhat limited by age, health and language, is good. As teenagers and elders are newcomers to regional migratory flows, their characters and situations are peculiar, and they are expected to grow in number, we need to evaluate the impact of their presence on the process of regionalisation. When more attention is given to and more discussions are made on this new migratory form, we will incorporate the new migratory flow as an agenda for regional integration and identity building in East Asia.

5 Concluding remarks

The migration of non-working-age population – school children and seniors – from East Asia to Southeast Asia is often perceived as a reverse flow, differentiated from the common norm of migrating to Western destinations for retirement and education. These developments show the Asian region to be increasingly serving as both an origin and destination for varied forms of migration. Southeast Asia is attractive to retirees and the families of school-age children for similar pull factors, such as a lower cost of living (when compared with Western countries), relatively close proximity to East Asian countries and the availability of visas in facilitating the desired form of migration. As noted in this chapter, the policy directions by destination countries to promote these forms of in-migration, together with industrial initiatives, play a crucial role in the continuity of such movements.

Increasing competition among some of the Southeast Asian countries to woo retirees and/or students from East Asia has been observed in the recent decade. Malaysia, for example, in its aspiration to develop into a regional education hub, has stepped up publicity to increase international student enrolment through the emphasis of Malaysia as a relatively low-cost country (with half the total education cost compared with Singapore). It will eventually liberalise private higher education to increase the options available for higher education among international (and local) students. Malaysia's "Malaysia My Second Home Program" launched in 2002, as a revamp from the earlier "Silver Hair Program" established in 1996, has also been welcomed as a "hassle-free retirement scheme" which reduces anxiety and contributes to positive experiences for retiree migration programme applicants (Wong and Musa 2014, 148). Despite general expectations that retirement migration would expand with more retirees in the near future, there has been caution against its sustainability in the long run as the consumption capacity of retirees will be affected if governments reduce pension pay-outs in the future (Toyota and Xiang 2012). Similarly, the recent financial crisis has affected the ability of children and mothers to continue to afford to keep transnational households, living and receiving an education in Southeast Asia. As some Southeast Asian countries have moved ahead faster than the rest in attracting these forms of migration, the challenges experienced by these head-start countries will serve as valuable lessons for those embarking on the same journey.

While education and retirement migration can generally be regarded as transient migration, where retirees are expected to eventually return back to their country of origin, both are at the same time likely to turn into permanent migration for the migrants. Among the retiree migrants, the availability of adequate care services affects one's decision to whether they will stay permanently at the destination. In Thailand, Malaysia, the Philippines and Indonesia, the care service business for "foreign" seniors has emerged, including specific training for care staff to be able to speak Japanese so as to better serve Japanese migrants. These initiatives could be government funded, for example, there have been various Japanese–Thai joint ventures supported by both governments in locales such as Bangkok and Ayut-thaya.[17] The Japanese government has also been considering using the Japanese Official Development Aid to pay for nursing homes for Japanese in the Philippines to achieve the twin objectives of easing the strain on the Japanese medical system while at the same time providing employment for Filipino nurses to work in their own country (Toyota 2006).

Education migration is another form of migration that may turn permanent over time, when graduates eventually seek employment in the destination country and opt to settle down. In Singapore, efforts to attract international students have been part of a broader policy to attract international talent for sustainable global competition of the small nation-state, supported by policies which require foreign tertiary students who have received tuition grants from the Singapore government to be contractually obliged to work in Singapore for a minimum period of three years upon graduation.[18] Such a scheme has been successful in harnessing talent, as students who have built their social networks in Singapore and started their career in the same destination country have a higher likelihood of getting married and settling down there. Compared with the retirees, younger people in education migration who mingle with the local population through schooling are more likely to integrate cohesively with the local host society, and may further strengthen their networks and ties through friendship and marriages. Migration, in shaping one's life trajectories and contributing to global householding, also plays an important role in shaping the nature and enriching the economic, social and multi-cultural outlook of the East and Southeast Asian societies.

In this chapter, we have chosen to examine the *reverse* phenomenon of educa-tion and retirement migration separately, however, as discussed earlier, we should not ignore the potential of the interaction of the two phenomena in giving rise to more forms of global households, where intergenerational relationships within the family could be emphasised and strengthened.

Finally, we should recognise that beyond the individual and the family, these forms of migratory flows from East Asia to Southeast Asia should be under-stood within the broader frameworks of globalisation processes and socio-political and patriarchal structural dimensions which have brought about the decisions and consequences of the move. As newcomers to migratory mobility, students and retirees have a potential to bring different impacts on the process of regionalisation, thus they bring attention to the need to examine the implications of such flows in facilitating or hampering the process of regional cooperation and identity building in the East Asian community.

In this sense, we see a potential regional commons being built from various migrant flows which criss-cross the ASEAN Plus Three region. Thus, while there is an institutional structure built to promote understanding and cooperation among governments, migrant flows will promote the grassroots equivalent in everyday life, as such flows create numerous potential for habitual encounters which may turn into enduring positive associations between hosts and guests.

Notes

1 Data presented in the chapter are drawn largely from secondary sources as well as empirical field studies by the authors where appropriate.
2 Data for this section comprises mainly of secondary materials, empirical observations and text analysis of advertisements and internet materials. In the next section on retiree migration, data on Japan also include multi-sited ethnographic research carried out in 2008–10.
3 See www.uhak.com/MotherPage.asp?SI_KeyCode=UH0466 (accessed 12 August 2012).
4 The quotes are respectively from www.studyservice.net/cat1.php?dmy=2012830160223;www.worldedu.co.kr/Nation/m_sub_main.php?j_type=20&tmcode=1106&tscode=1106001&modetype=tscode; and www.asiaok.net/subpage_02_04.htm (accessed 12 August 2012).
5 The third quote discussing the advantages of studying in Malaysia reflects the recent shift in Korea, namely, the extension of studying abroad to primary and secondary school students. As more of them go abroad for study, the media have disseminated stories of their deviational behaviour. Consequently, parents prefer a place which offers less exposure to alcohol and other entertainment facilities, and Malaysia is the place to satisfy this need.
6 The effort to develop Singapore as an international education hub started in 1997 with the Economic Development Board. To promote the aspiration of "Singapore: The Global Schoolhouse", the Education Services Strategic Tourism Unit was established by the Singapore Tourism Board to embark on overseas marketing (refer to www.singaporeedu.gov.sg, www.stb.gov.sg).
7 The term "study mother" is translated literally from the Chinese *pei du mama*, said to be coined by the Chinese media in Singapore (*Straits Times*, 24 August 2003).
8 Stories about the unfortunate experiences of these study mothers can be found in internet news and blogs in the Chinese language.
9 The so-called study mother scheme is basically a special long-term social visit pass for "Female visitors whose child or grandchild is studying in Singapore on a Student's Pass" (http://www.ica.gov.sg/page.aspx?pageid=174, accessed 25 April 2012). Until the end of 2003, these pass holders are allowed to seek employment in Singapore, but from November 2003, the regulation changes to ban working during the first year of their stay (Agence France Presse, Singapore bans mothers of Chinese students from working: report, 1 December 2003. www.singapore-window.org/sw03/031203af.htm, accessed 25 April 2012).
10 See http://mrbuffalo.blog.hexun.com/5129761_d.html.
11 The data are taken from the 2012 Long-Stay survey report conducted by the Long-Stay Foundation in Japan, www.longstay.or.jp/english/tc_1.html.
12 Compared to the Japanese born in the 1920s and 1930s who worked through the Japanese economic boom era, and mostly worked till retirement age receiving full

retirement benefits, those born later in the 1940s were less fortunate. This younger cohort of retirees are hit by economic doldrums, with some getting retrenched before retirement age, and finding themselves economically displaced (Toyota, 2006).

13 Fieldwork was done at Ban Rom Sai in August 2010. See the website of Ban Rom Sai at www.banromsai.org/about_banromsai/?mode=miwa_natori.

14 Two million Korean won was approximately USD 1,800 in 2005.

15 The average benefit of pensioners having paid his duties for 20 years is approximately USD 600 in 2012 (Park 2012).

16 In the case of the Philippines, people above the age of 50 years may obtain a visa with USD 10,000. To apply for a Malaysia visa, applicants aged 50 and above may comply with the financial proof of RM 350,000 in liquid assets and an offshore income of RM10,000 per month. For most Koreans who do not receive a monthly pension benefit of more than RM 10,000, the financial requirement of Malaysia is hard to be satisfied.

17 The two examples in Thailand are Riei Lumpini Residence Senior Service Apartment in Bangkok and Bansai Hospice House in Bangsai, Ayutthaya (Toyota 2006).

18 See http://tgolnline.moe.gov.sg/tigs/normal/index.action (accessed 28 April 2012).

References

ASEAN. 1999. "Joint Statement on East Asia Cooperation". Available at: www.asean.org/news/item/joint-statement-on-east-asia-cooperation-28-november-1999 (accessed on 25 August 2014).

Cheng, Miu Yu, Amir Mahmood and Peik Foong Yeap. 2013. "Malaysia as a Regional Education Hub: A Demand-Side Analysis". *Journal of Higher Education Policy and Management*, 35(5): 523–536.

Cheong, Dongu. 2005. *Gwijogeuro Sanen Beob: Handale 200 Manwoneuro Haeweeseo* [Living Like a Noble Abroad: With Two Million Korean Won in a Month]. Seoul: Ijibuk.

Douglass, Michael. 2006. "Global Householding in Pacific Asia". *International Development Planning Review*, 28(4): 421–445.

Douglass, Michael. 2012. *Global Households and Social Reproduction: Migration Research, Dynamics and Public Policy in East and Southeast Asia*. Asia Research Institute working paper series no. 188. Singapore: National University of Singapore.

Hong, Seokjun. 2009. "The Study of Motivations and Socio-Cultural Backgrounds of Korean Parents for Their Children to Study in Southeast Asia: The Case Study of Malaysia" (in Korean). *Sahwugwahak Yeongu* [Social Science Research], 20(4): 239–262.

Hong, Younggyu. 2008. *Eunteuimin Tteonagi Jeone Ggog Arayahal 50 Gaji* [50 Items You Have to Know Before Beginning Retirement Migration]. Seoul: Wonenwon Buks.

Huang, Shirlena and Brenda S. A. Yeoh. 2005. "Transnational Families and Their Children's Education: China's 'Study Mothers' in Singapore". *Global Networks* (special issue on "Asian Transnational Families"), 5(4): 379–400.

Huang, Shirlena and Brenda S. A. Yeoh. 2011. "Navigating the Terrains of Transnational Education: Children of Chinese 'Study Mothers' in Singapore". *Geoforum*, 42(3): 394–403.

Hugo, Graeme. 1996. "Asia on the Move: Research Challenges for Population Geography". *International Journal of Population Geography*, 2(2): 95–118.

Kachru, Braj. 1985. "Standards, Codification and Sociolinguistic Realism: The English Language in the Outer Circle", in Randolph Quirk and Henry Widdowson (eds), *English in the World: Teaching and Learning the Language and Literatures*. Cambridge: Cambridge University Press, 11–30.

Kim, Dohye. 2013. "South Koreans' Deferred Retirement in the Philippines". Paper presented at the Association of American Anthropology, 20–24 November, Chicago, IL.

Kim, Dong Yeob. 2009. "The Practice and Prospects of Korean Retirement Migration to Southeast Asia: The Philippine Case" (in Korean). *Donga Yeongu*, 57(2): 233–267.

Kitabatake, Takao. 1986. "Shiruba-Koronbia-Keikaku Sonogo" [Silver Colombia Plan – Further Report]. *Tsusan Journal*, 21(1): 58–61.

Korean Ministry of Education, Science and Technology. Each year (a). *Chojunggo Yuhagseng Chulgug mit Guigug Tonggye* [Statistics on Primary and Secondary Students Departing for and Returning from Studying Abroad]. Seoul: Ministry of Education, Science and Technology.

Korean Ministry of Education, Science and Technology. Each year (b). *Gugeu Hangugin Yuhakseng Tonggye* [Statistics on Tertiary-Level Students Studying Abroad]. Seoul: Ministry of Education, Science and Technology.

Korean Tourism Organization. Each year. *Hangugu Gwangwang Yeonbo* [Statistics on Korean Tourism]. Seoul: Korean Tourism Organization.

Lam, Lawrence. 1994. "Searching for a Safe Haven: The Migration and Settlement of Hong Kong Chinese Immigrants in Toronto", in Ronald Skeldon (ed.), *Reluctant Exiles? Migration from Hong Kong and the New Overseas Chinese*. New York: M. E. Sharpe, 163–79.

Lee, Jon Tong. 2008. "S. Koreans Sold on an Education in Singapore". *Straits Times*, 23 January.

Lee, Yean-Ju and Hagen Koo. 2006. "Wild Geese Fathers and a Globalized Family Strategy for Education in Korea", in Mike Douglass (ed.), Special Issue on Global Householding in East and Southeast Asia, *International Development Planning Review*, 28(4): 533–553.

Ministry of Foreign Affairs in Korea. 2013. *ASEAN Plus Three Cooperation Work Plan 2013–2017*, www.mofa.go.kr/mofat/htm/issue/2013a.doc (accessed on 25 August 2014).

Miralao, Virgina A. 2007. "Understanding the Korean Diaspora to the Philippines", in Virgina A. Miralao and Lorna P. Makil (eds), *Exploring Transnational Communities in the Philippines*. Manila: Philippine Social Science Council, 24–39.

Mizukami, Tetsuo. 2007. *The Sojourner Community: Japanese Migration and Residency in Australia*. Leiden and Boston, MA: Brill.

Moon, Hyun-Hee. 2009. "Positions, Functions and Meanings of English in South Korea". PhD thesis. Victoria: La Trobe University.

Nocut News. 2007. "Dongnama Eunteuimin, Wol 200 Manwoneuro Hwangjeseanghwal Eorimeobjyo" [You Cannot Live like an Emperor with Two Million Korean Won]. *Nocut News*, 10 April.

Ogawa, Reiko. 2010. "Migration of Indonesian Care Workers under the Japan-Indonesia Economic Partnership Agreement". *Urban Policy Studies*, 4: 61–75.

Ono, Mayumi. 2008. "Long-Stay Tourism and International Retirement Migration: Japanese Retirees in Malaysia", in S. Yamashita, M. Minami, D. W. Haines and J. Eades (eds), *Transnational Migration in East Asia: Japan in a Comparative Focus* (Senri Ethnological Reports 77). Osaka: National Museum of Ethnology, 151–63.

Ono, Mayumi. 2010. "Long-Stay Tourism: Elder Japanese Tourists in the Cameron Highlands, Malaysia", in M. Han and N. Graburn (eds), *Tourism and Glocalization: Perspectives on East Asian Societies* (Senri Ethnological Reports 76). Osaka: National Museum of Ethnology, 95–109.

Palaubsanon, Mitchelle L. 2010. "Koreans Top List of Tourists, Foreign Students in Cebu". *Philippine Star*, 11 July. Available at: www.philstar.com/Article.aspx?articleId=592317&publicationSubCategoryId=107 (accessed on 27 April 2012).

Park, Jongho. 2012. "Boheomryo Julinen Bangbeob Eueuro Syibsebnida" [Ways of Saving Insurance Fee Are Easy]. *Ohmynews*, 25 August.

Shimizu, Hiromu. 2009 "Paradise in Dream or in Reality? Japanese Retirees Migrating to the Philippines". Paper presented at Transnational Mobilities for Care: State, Market and Family Dynamics in Asia, Asia Research Institute, National University of Singapore, 10–11 September.

Shin, Kwang-Young. 2011. "Globalization and Social Inequality in South Korea", in Jesook Song (ed.), *New Millennium South Korea: Neoliberal Capitalism and Transnational Movements*. New York: Routledge, 11–28.

Statistics Bureau Japan. 2011. "Total Population, Table 2.2: Trends in Population". Available at: www.stat.go.jp/english/data/handbook/c02cont.htm#cha2_2 (accessed 27 April 2012).

Sunil, Thankam S., Viviana Rojas and Don Bradley. 2007. "United States' International Retirement Migration: The Reasons for Retiring to the Environs of Lake Chapala, Mexico". *Ageing and Society*, 27: 489–510.

Toyota, Mika. 2006. "Ageing and Transnational Householding: Japanese Retirees in Southeast Asia". *International Development Planning Review*, 28(4): 515–532.

Toyota, Mika and Xiang, Biao. 2012. "The Emerging Transnational 'Retirement Industry' in Southeast Asia". *International Journal of Sociology and Social Policy*, 32(11/12): 708–719.

Waters, Johanna L. 2005. "Transnational Family Strategies and Education in the Contemporary Chinese Diaspora". *Global Networks*, 5(4): 359–378.

Wong, Kee Mun and Ghazali Musa. 2014. "Retirement Motivation among 'Malaysia My Second Home' Participants". *Tourism Management*, 40: 141–154.

Yeoh, Brenda S. A. and Katie Willis. 2005. "Singaporeans in China: Transnational Women Elites and the Negotiation of Gendered Identities". *Geoforum*, 36(2): 211–222.

4 Transnational migration in East Asia

The evolving migration policy in South Korea and its implications

Pan Suk Kim and Heung Ju Kim

1 Introduction

Generally speaking, transnational migration is increasing around the world and East Asia, including South Korea (hereafter Korea), is not an exception. The number of incoming migrant workers is increasing in Korea and a large number of South Koreans are also living in Southeast Asia. Historically, many Koreans have been living in China and Japan, while Koreans living in the Association of Southeast Asian Nations (ASEAN) member countries have also been increasing over the years due to improving bilateral and multilateral relationships between Korea and ASEAN. Since the ASEAN Plus Three (APT) process began in 1997, APT cooperation has deepened and broadened greatly. Before 1997, there was little active policy cooperation, but, as APT structures developed, policy cooperation between ASEAN and Korea has rapidly increased. It includes cooperation in the areas of politics and security; trade and investment; tourism; agriculture, fishery and forestry; minerals; energy; education, science and technology; environment; migration; and culture and people-to-people contact. Many Koreans are now living in the Philippines, followed by Vietnam, Indonesia, Thailand, Singapore and others (Overseas Koreans Foundation 2011).

This chapter reviews public policy responses to the increase in Asian migrants in Korea. International labour migration is expected in the 21st century, not only because of liberal migration regulations, but also because of a shortage of labour in some countries with an ageing population, supply pressure, the domestic income gap between countries and the innovation of information technology (Kim 2008). The huge wave of migrants or foreign workers in the neo-liberal economic system is aggravated by poverty in developing countries. The Migration Policy Institute of the International Organization for Migration (IOM) estimates that the world population as of 2010 is 6.5 billion, and 213 million people are international migrants (about 3.1 per cent). This means that one out of 30 people is an international migrant (Lim and Jin 2011).

Accordingly, the population structures in sending and receiving countries change rapidly as a result of global migration. Just as people working and living outside their own home countries increase, the types and routes of migrants also become more diverse. There are some countries that have existing migrants from long-term colonial occupation and a general public acceptance of migrants. However, some countries that have begun to receive migrants were previously a source of migrants to other countries (Han and Seol 2007). For Korea, agricultural labour migration to Hawaii started in 1902, and the overseas migration policy of the Korean government began with the Overseas Migration Act in 1962. In 1963, Korea sent agricultural migrants to Latin America and economic migrants to Germany for mining work and nursing services and the Middle East for construction in the 1960s and 1970s. At that time, Korea was typically a sending country as it was developing its domestic industries and local jobs were still in short supply. However, this changed in the mid-1980s with Korea becoming a receiving country. Due to continuous economic growth, the "3D (difficult, dangerous and dirty) job avoidance phenomenon" appeared for the first time (Shim 2007) and a severe shortage of labour in manufacturing, construction and agricultural areas arose. Thus, immigrants to Korea outnumbered emigrants.

Policy measures on foreign migration began in the 1980s but the adoption of the industrial technical "trainee" system (Taiwan used a similar system to recruit migrant workers) from 1993 onward is the starting point of migration policy development in Korea. However, the industrial technical trainee system led to many problems in Korea and Taiwan because it regarded many incoming migrant workers as trainees and was a short-term programme. To resolve problems, a work permit system was adopted in 2004, and a social integration policy for foreign migrants was introduced in 2006 along with the widespread expansion of policies to develop a multiracial and multinational society (Won 2011).[1] Consequently, the increase of foreign migrants influenced change in the labour market, economic structure, cultural opening, expansion of ethnic diversity, and socio-political concerns about increasing ethnic groups (Kang 2006; Hwang et al. 2007; Won 2008; Jeon 2008; Choi 2008; Won 2011). In particular, the increase of female migrants particularly for marriage is a special characteristic as it challenges the premise of "one nation, one culture".[2] Such an increase in migration and multicultural families raised the need for policy intervention, and the corresponding endeavours of the government are embodied in its diverse policies.

It could be said that Korea is on its way to becoming a multiracial and multicultural society as foreign migrants exceed 2 per cent of the total population. A low birth rate and an ageing society has accelerated the shortage of labour, attracting a diverse range of foreigners residing in Korea with an increasing rate of permanent residence (Kim 2007). While the rapid progress of a multiracial society requires multicultural coexistence, a bias against migrant women and migrant labour causes various social conflicts (Kang 2007). The situation constitutes a serious problem of socio-cultural adaptation at the individual and social levels (Park and Yi 2009). For Korean society to achieve sound social integration and become a multicultural society without conflict, the socio-cultural adaptation of migrants has become one of the most important objectives of the country (Choi and Kim 2011). Korea is an important case study in which to understand how a host society can reshape its attitudes, enact new policies and mobilise the different organisations and society segments to create a more supportive environment for migrants. In this way, a country's domestic policies can go a significant way in supporting not just a regional market for migration but a supportive one.

The ageing society is a recent phenomenon that the human race has not experienced before, which is the result of an improved average life expectancy and a decrease in the birth rate in the 20th century (Laslett 1995). The ageing of society relates to a change in the composition (or pyramid) of the age levels which closely relates to population transition. Such a transition has appeared in different forms in advanced countries and developing countries (Choi and Kim 2011). While the population transition in advanced countries has been achieved over a long period, developing countries have experienced a rapid population transition in the late 20th century. Such an ageing process is experienced in different ways in different countries, thus policy making in Korea is problematic as it is based on advanced countries' experience of multiculturalism.

This chapter has two major research questions: (1) how did the transnational migration policy evolve in Korea over the years in both central and local governments; and (2) what kinds of policy models did the Korean government utilise? The chapter will first discuss theoretical issues on foreign migration, followed by a discussion on the status of the foreign population in Korea. Then, changes in the migration and social integration policies of the central and local governments will be discussed.

2 The regionalisation of foreign migration and structural model of policy on foreigners

2.1 Migration transition and the increase of foreign migrants in Korea

Since the migration to the cane farms in Hawaii in the early 20th century, many Koreans have migrated overseas, including to the North and South Americas. After Korea's liberation in 1945, many migrants returned to Korea while many others remained overseas. The majority of Koreans currently in China, the former USSR (Russia and Central Asia) and Japan are their descendants. In the early 1960s, a new type of migration appeared. Nurses and miners moved to West Germany and military workers went to Vietnam during the Vietnam War. After the 1960s, many were employed as deep-sea fishing crews. In the 1970s, construction workers moved to the Middle East and North Africa. As a result, Korea became an established labour-providing country. Money remittance played an important role in accumulating capital for the industrialisation of the country. However, this situation changed dramatically in the mid-1980s due to rapid economic growth in Korea. From 1987, the incoming migrants began to outnumber the outgoing migrants in a process called migration transition. Under the influence of globalisation and regionalisation in Asia, various types of population mobilisation took place worldwide, and the domestic human resource structure underwent rapid transition. As of 2012, the number of foreigners residing in Korea is over 1.4 million due to globalisation and the need for labour caused by a low birth rate and an ageing society. The types of migrants have diversified and include Koreans with foreign nationality, migrant women, foreign workers and refugees. Table 4.1 shows the migration status in Korea by nationality.

Recent East Asian migrants show a new pattern. The main migration trend has changed from "movement between the regions" in the 1980s for Europe, America and the Middle East to "movement within the East Asian region". As for labour migration, the unskilled have moved from South East Asia to North East Asia, and skilled workers have moved from North East Asia to South East Asia (Moon 2006). Figure 4.1 shows the number of migrated foreigners with acquisition of nationality as of 2012, and foreigners without Korean nationality, which includes foreign workers, female migrants, students, Koreans with foreign nationality and others. Foreigners with Korean nationality include marriage-naturalised Koreans, children of foreign residents and other holders.

As a result, Korea, Japan, Taiwan, Malaysia and Singapore have become a part of the "receiving country group"; Thailand has the medium position and China, Indonesia, Vietnam, the Philippines, Cambodia and Laos have become the "sending country group". The status of migrant workers in Korea and Japan shows the close relationship among East Asian countries (Miura 2011). Figure 4.2 shows the number of foreigners by country as of 2012 in Korea as a receiving country. Korean-Chinese are the largest in number followed by Chinese (*Han*) and Vietnamese.[3] Overall, the Asian rate is far higher than the non-Asian in Korea.

2.2 *Foreign migration and social integration policies*

2.2.1 *Changes in migration and multicultural policies in Korea*

In the midst of globalisation, migration has increased around the world. According to the 2010 international migration statistics, the amount of migration increased from 150 million in 1990 to 214 million in 2010 (UN 2009).[4] Such international migration not only influences the economy of providing and receiving countries, but also brings with it political and social implications, and cultural shock. In

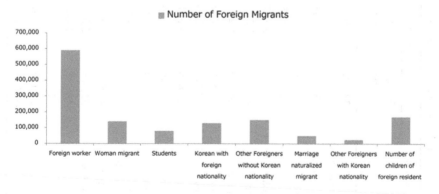

Figure 4.1 Number of foreigners with and without Korean nationality as of 2012
Source: Korean Immigration Service of the Ministry of Justice 2012.

Table 4.1 Status of foreigners in South Korea by nationality as of 2012

Classification	Foreigners without Korean nationality					Foreigners with Korean nationality			Total
	Foreign worker	Female migrant	Student	Korean with foreign nationality	Others	Marriage-naturalised migrant	Others	Children of foreign residents	
China (non-Korean)	22,992	34,906	62,289	0	27,114	19,764	11,162	33,231	211,458
China (Korean)	295,604	29,184	2,205	72,870	62,405	37,226	31,386	39,278	570,158
Taiwan	155	514	568	43	20,144	801	1,075	1,615	24,915
Japan	1,604	11,145	2,059	637	6,318	230	330	16,237	38,560
Mongolia	11,047	2,387	4,880	0	2,964	506	175	2,468	24,427
Vietnam	64,407	37,302	3,027	0	5,828	10,083	369	41,238	162,254
Philippines	26,855	8,292	522	12	2,697	5,134	403	15,820	59,735
Thailand	22,518	2,593	401	4	465	268	57	2,427	28,733
Indonesia	27,914	506	609	72	544	103	22	624	30,394
Cambodia	11,649	4,561	301	0	273	729	26	4,690	22,229
Myanmar	4,940	76	262	0	328	51	4	131	5,792
Malaysia	154	94	579	2	328	8	6	106	1,277
Others in Southeast Asia	771	257	472	42	396	13	10	215	2,176
South Asia	45,915	2,405	2,902	10	8,781	650	175	2,024	62,862
Central Asia	22,965	2,508	1,057	1,929	1,178	392	99	2,791	32,919
USA	13,796	2,408	919	40,421	9,343	9	330	1,422	68,648
Russia	2,483	1,315	495	978	1,705	170	458	1,139	8,743
Others	13,175	3,761	3,674	18,000	11,271	336	953	3,127	54,297
Total	588,944	144,214	87,221	135,020	162,082	76,473	47,040	168,583	1,409,577

Source: Korean Immigration Service of the Ministry of Justice 2012, www.immigration.go.kr/HP/TIMM/index.do?strOrgGbnCd=104000.

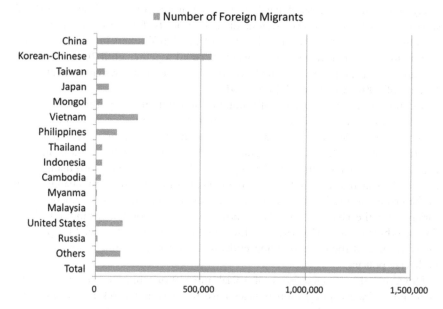

Figure 4.2 Number of foreign migrants in Korea by country as of 2012
Source: Korean Immigration Service of the Ministry of Justice 2012.

particular, problems relating to border control and migrants' relationship to the statute, as well as the problem of the social integration of migrant groups, arose. Since Korea's national diplomatic relations with China were normalised in 1992, the number of Chinese migrant women has increased due to the active involvement of local governments and an industrial training system, which stimulated the inflow of foreign migrants in Korea. Since then, related policies have been changed along with increasing concerns about social integration in Korea.

The Korean government's immigration policy is largely divided into two parts: immigration control and immigrant integration. Immigration policy is governed by two important laws: (1) the Act on the Employment of Foreign Workers for immigration control; and (2) the Basic Act on the Treatment of Foreigners Living in Korea and the Multicultural Family Support Act for immigrant integration.

In terms of immigration control, legislation targeting foreign workers started to appear in the early 1990s. While experiencing migrant transition, Korea suffers from a shortage of labour in some unskilled manufacturing industries due to the wage gap and high level of education since the end of the 1980s. Accordingly, the Korean Ministry of Justice introduced the Trainee System for Companies Investing Overseas in 1991, and received many foreign workers for training in Korea. However, the trainee system for companies invested overseas did not solve the labour shortage problem in Korea so a revised system called the Industrial Trainee System was introduced in November 1993 (Lee 2011). However, the systematic defect of the system created many illegal residents (who stayed in Korea after the expiration of the initial contract) and human rights problems (lack of occupational safety, insurance and related legal protection) arose from the foreign workers' situation, which led to a more serious discussion on the foreign worker policy. By promulgating the Act on the Employment of Foreign Workers in 2003, the work permit and industrial trainee system were executed together until 2006, when the foreign worker policy was unified to the "work permit" system (effective in January of 2007) which is still in use today.

Second, from the perspective of immigrant integration policy, the then Korean president Roh Moo-Hyun's remark in April 2006, "entrance to a multi-racial society is inevitable", led to the active establishment of a socially integrated multicultural policy in Korea. As a result, the Migrant's Social Integration Support Plan and Migrant Women's Social Integration Plan were adopted with many other policies.[5] As such, the migration of foreigners indicates various social changes such as the change in the labour market and economic structure, cultural opening and variety, and the change in the socio-political concerns or understandings about diverse ethnic groups. Moreover, multicultural families raised the need for political intervention and the corresponding endeavours of the government are embodied in diverse policies.

However, the characteristics of social integration support measures at the beginning of social integration policies have resulted in a quick policy response; rather as a tinkering phenomenon than a significant turn to target comprehensive national policy like immigration or social integration policy. The follow-up measures for supporting social integration which emerged as a legal device, that is, the Basic Act on the Treatment of Foreigners Living in Korea (2007) and the Multi-Cultural Families Support Act (2008) also appear prominently and this effort can be inferred through the Act for Management of Marriage Brokerage (2007) to protect the rights of immigrant women. The concept of social integration in Korean society can be seen as the cause of a fundamental change in policy, such as the work visa (work permit) system, the large influx of overseas Koreans work visa that allows up to five years to stay legally, increased sedentary workers according to the foreign work permit evidence. Table 4.2 shows policies on migration and their features.

2.2.2 Structural model of policy on foreigners and foreign migrants

The government policy direction creates different policies and programmes such as the government intervention philosophy on migration and settlement. In the process, the regulatory structure governing the status and treatment of migrants is progressively transformed. The focus of migration policy in Korea is in three areas: discrimination and exclusion, assimilation, and multiculturalism. Many different measures and means could be used for the policy, and different policies can be applied to different types of migrants. For example, discrimination and exclusion are applied to migrant workers; assimilation is applied to migrant women; and multiculturalism is applied to foreign students. Such a tendency may be applied differently by the local government.

Table 4.2 Policies and actions on migration and their features, 1991–2008

Period	Main policy	Key features
November 1991	Introduced the Trainee System for Companies Invested Overseas	Training system introduced for foreign workers
November 1993	Introduced the industrial trainee system	Foreign workers to come not as workers but trainees Actual management assigned to the Korean Federation of Small and Medium Business Illegal work and human rights problems arose later
January 1994–January 1995	The Korean government is under pressure due to foreign worker demonstrations including the Myeongdong Cathedral sit-in	Human rights of foreign workers raised as a social issue
July 1995	Foreign worker association is formed	Government organised action on foreign worker problem
September 1997	Transfer to training employment system	System revised to cope with criticism on trainee system
August 2003	Act on Employment of Foreign Workers promulgated in the National Assembly	Dual system for work permit and industrial trainee Started to seek social integration policy with foreigners/migrants
April 2006	Migrant women's social integration plan and migrant support plan announced	Promoted social integration policy with foreigners/migrants
May 2006	Basic planning of foreign policy and promotion system announced	Foreigner Policy Committee under the prime minister
January 2007	Work permit system unified	Unskilled foreign worker policy unified
May 2007	Basic Act on the Treatment of Foreigners Living in Korea enacted	Long-term basic plan for foreigner policy
March 2008	Multicultural Family Support Act promulgated	Basic framework for migrant women and family

Source: Lee 2011.

As such, the policy tendency may vary. In particular, as it is often called the multicultural(ism) policy, it is important to secure human rights, and social and cultural rights, by respecting the migrant workers' culture and values, and by providing social welfare services so that Korean society can be transformed into a sound multicultural society in a globalised era. However, foreign migrant policy in a capitalist economy and modern nation-state is a means of achieving a national purpose by accepting migrants. Thus, instead of providing them with the necessary qualifications, status or services, it tends to marginalise them socially to minimise social costs. Even in advanced countries stressing multiculturalism, their policies tend to have assimilating or exclusive characters to the extent of marginalising migrants (Choi and Kim 2011). Aside from the discriminating and excluding model on the labour force, the assimilating model and the multicultural model are widely accepted to accommodate multicultural society more positively. Table 4.3 shows three structural models of policy on foreigners and foreign migrants.

Foreign migrant workers and marriage immigrants are the main part of Korean foreign immigrant policy and they are two of the causes of social problems in Korean society that can be understood in terms of the occurrence of demographic change and social events. Because the proportion of foreigners has sharply increased through the inflow of immigrant marriage and foreign workers, social issues such as sexual problems and race discrimination have occurred since the early 2000s. For a short period of time, Korea enacted a variety of policies and legislation which tried to respond to immigration issues between the sending

Table 4.3 Structural models of policy on foreigners and foreign migrants

	Discrimination and exclusion model	Assimilation model	Multicultural model
Basic model	Prevent permanent residence which the mainstream does not want, and keep discriminating treatment	Support rapid assimilation based on "nationalised" and equal treatment in formality (system)	Recognise equal value of minority, support the maintenance of minor culture and give preference to some degree
Objective	Remove or minimise racial minority	Assimilation to mainstream	Social integration by recognising variety and coexistence
State role	Active regulation	Restricted support	Active support
View on migrant	Stranger and threatening	Partial recognition based on assimilation of mainstream society	Mutual respect and tolerance
View on equality	Stress justification for discrimination	Social security and equal opportunity	Secure an equal result beyond equal opportunity
Legal measure	Detection and deportation	Institutionalisation of non-discrimination	Permit all rights
Condition for granting nationality	Nationality principle, strict condition	Territorial principle, less strict condition	Territorial principle, permit double nationality
Identity	Differentiation	Assimilation	Coexistence

Source: Kymlicka 1996; Han and Seol 2007; Won 2012.

country and the receiving country. The policy of industrial trainees was established for foreign workers at first and that began to appear in the centre of a strong regulatory policy by the central government.

Trade unions for foreign workers were launched in the early 2000s to protect their rights along with reformative discussions of foreign worker policy through the employment permit system. Accordingly, the negative perception of foreign workers has been reduced and such development has led to modify the formation of a distorted social image. Such policies include: legalisation for the children of illegal foreign workers to receive primary education for a period of time, a large-scale multicultural festival held by the Ministry of Culture and Tourism for foreign workers, the establishment of international schools to learn the Korean language and culture for their children and so on. This kind of policy transition could provide useful lessons for neighbouring countries such as China and Japan.

2.2.3 Confusion of the legal system on foreigner support policy

There was no agreed philosophical ground on foreign migration policy in Korea for many years. Without social consensus, different policies have been carried out relative to the situation of government departments. The applied theories were different and operations also were mixed. The Ministry of Employment and Labour, the Ministry of Justice and the Foreigner Policy Committee under the prime minister took a discrimination model based on foreign worker policy, and as for international marriage, the assimilation model was adopted to sustain the "pure blood" ideology. On the other hand, the Ministry of Culture, Sports and Tourism, the Ministry of Health and Welfare, the Ministry of Women and Family and the National Human Rights Commission supported efforts to help foreign migrants to adapt to Korean society. Foreign migrants can be naturalised according to the Nationality Act. However, most foreign residents in Korea are under almost the same legal jurisdiction with Koreans including childbirth, childcare, education, employment, labour, housing purchase, medical and social insurance. Accordingly, there are many cases where new legal provisions have been added or revised to existing laws. For example, the National Pension Act, the National Health Insurance Act, the Employment Insurance Act, the National Basic Life Assurance Act, the Single Parent Family Support Act and the Act on Prevention of Family Violence and Protection of Victims all have regulations on foreigners. The Act on the Employment of Foreign Workers (enacted in August 2003), the Act on the Management of Marriage Brokerage (enacted in December 2007) and the Multi-Cultural Family Support Act (enacted in March 2008) have all been enacted. Table 4.4 outlines the basic policy responsibilities of departments in the central government.

As such, there is no integrated government measure and policy on foreigners but some policies overlap between departments and no priority is set (Ji et al. 2009). This is because the discussion of a multicultural society has been carried out without serious consideration for the existence of migrant groups, their status in Korean society, their imminent problems and the structural environment

Table 4.4 Basic policy responsibilities of central government departments on foreign migrants

Division	Legal system	Target	Focus
Prime Minister	Basic plan for foreigner policy and promotion system – in preparation	All foreigners and general people	Foreign policy committee Paradigm change of foreigner policy
Ministry of Justice	Basic Act on the Treatment of Foreigners Living in Korea (May 2007)		Basic plan of foreigner policy Migrant social adaptation support Preparation for multiculturalism
	Ministry of Justice Immigration (entrance and exit) Management Act (March 1963)		Foreigner control (protection), resident order
	Ministry of Justice Nationality Act		Nationality granting, etc.
Ministry of Security and Public Administration	Foreign resident support ordinance	Migrant	Migrant settlement support
Ministry of Gender Equality and Family	Multicultural Family Support Act (March 2008)	Multicultural family	Social adaptation for female migrants, welfare of multicultural family
Ministry of Education, Science and Technology	Educational support measure for children from multicultural families	Migrant children	Educational support for children from multicultural families
Ministry of Employment and Labour	Act on Foreigner Employment (August 2003)	Foreign workers	Foreign workers' work permit and social adaptation
Ministry of Unification	North Korean Refugee Protection and Settlement Support Act (January 1997)	North Korean refugees	North Korean refugee protection and settlement support

Source: Kim 2010.

in Korea. Furthermore, without serious consideration of the nature of social and cultural change, simply fragmented suggestions and allopathic alternatives are rampant, causing much confusion and limitation (Kim 2010). Various organisations developed policies for foreign migrants and such policies have been implemented for foreign migrants so that confusion and policy failures have occurred.

3 Local governments' response to increasing number of foreign migrants

Local governments also began to build up health clinics and welfare centres for foreign workers in the early 2000s. At this time, the most important event was integrated into the work permit system because, in 2007, the Constitutional Court ruled that the industrial trainee system is unconstitutional. Moreover, the Basic Act for the Treatment of Foreigners Living in Korea (2007) was enacted as a law to protect the rights of foreigners including foreign workers along with the improvement of the minimum wage system, the retirement system, health insurance and others. Table 4.5 shows features and changes of policy for foreign workers.

In the case of marriage migrants, the numbers increased to over 10,000 people each year in the early 2000s, but the absolute number of marriage migrants is not many and media covering events directly related to them is rarely seen. It was not recognised as a social issue until 2003. However, the social movement for the support of the marriage migrants began in 2004. With this movement, the Act for Management of Marriage Brokerage was enacted in 2007 to prevent human rights violations in the process of marriage. Even at the local government level, quantitative or qualitative policy design for marriage migrants was actively made. For example, several provincial-level governments (Southern Gyeongsang province, Northern Gyeongsang province, Southern Jeolla province, Gwangju metropolitan city, Gyeonggi province and Northern Gyeongsang province) developed various policies for the welfare of foreign migrants. At the local level, Sin-an county, Gangjin county and autonomous districts in Seoul also designed various policies for marriage migrants. Table 4.6 shows features and changes of policy for marriage migrants in local governments.

In this way, the main target of the migration policy is the foreign workers and marriage migrants in Korea. In the design of policies for foreign immigrants, discrimination and exclusion models initially appeared mainly through strong

Table 4.5 Features and changes of policy for foreign workers

	Step 1	*Step 2*	*Step 3*	*Step 4*
Time	Until 1993	1994–2003	2004–2006	2007–present
Special feature	Absence of policy	Industrial trainee system	Industrial trainee system, work permit system	Work permit system
Contents	Undocumented workers sideline	Exclusion of citizenship for foreign trainees Produced many illegal workers	Enforcement of work permit system Industrial trainee system that partially protects foreign workers	Unified work permit system

Source: Han and Park 2011.

Table 4.6 Features and changes of policy for marriage migrants

	Step 1	*Step 2*	*Step 3*
Time	Until 2004	2005–2007	2008–present
Special feature	Absence of policy	Enforcement of pilot support projects	The Multicultural Family Support Act
Contents	Marriage migrants sidelines	Diversification policy for the settlement Central and local governments participated	Transition to independent policy Actively support employment

Source: Han and Park 2011.

regulatory policies. However, the protection of the rights of foreign migrants was raised gradually in Korean society so that the control model was changed to the integrated model as the perception of foreign immigrants in Korean society changed due to the gradual increase of foreign workers and marriage migrants in Korea. Historically, Korean society had a fear of multiculturalism, particularly after the Japanese colonial rule. However, the Korean economy grew substantially at the same time as the shortage of labourers became serious in the manufacturing sector, and many Koreans understood that a substantial inflow of foreign migrants into Korea was inevitable. Moreover, local men in rural areas faced difficulties finding spouses and increasingly began to marry foreign women from Southeast Asia.

From the perspective of localism, the percentage of resident foreigners in the population is considerably low although foreigners are densely populated in some cities (see Figure 4.3). In such a situation, the demand for policy and its effects may vary according to the density of the foreign population, which indicates that at the local level there may be a problem with East Asian labour migration. Furthermore, each dense area, large cities, agricultural and industrial areas and traditionally foreign resident areas have different attributes and backgrounds. Thus, it is inevitable that a flexible migration policy is required (Miura 2011).

As for the number of migrants in local government areas, Seoul shows the greatest increase of foreign residents with 406,293 as of 2012, followed by Gyeonggi Province, Southern Gyeongsang Province, Incheon and Southern Chungcheong Province. Table 4.7 shows the migration status by provincial-level government.

Since the 1990s, as the number of foreign migrants and their social influence has expanded, the central government, local governments and non-governmental organisations (NGOs) prepared laws, policies and support programmes for the migration and settlement of foreign migrants. Thus, foreign migrants are granted some resident rights and the status of a legitimate social member of Korean society, receiving regulation and support required for their local settlement directly and indirectly. Such policies and activities aim to achieve the national and local objectives of the government by proper control of their settlement and to minimise social and cultural shock caused by them (Ko 2009).

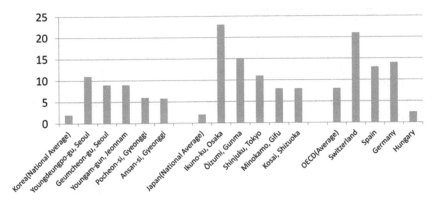

Figure 4.3 Percentage of foreign residents by localities and countries
Source: Miura 2011.

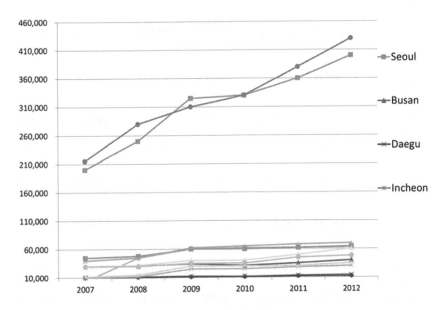

Figure 4.4 The increasing trend of foreigners by localities
Source: Korean Statistical Information Service 2012.

The increase of foreign migrants in each local government has required support policies and regulations. Although social integration policies on migrants are carried out by local governments, the Ministry of Security Public Administration is also involved in the enactment of a regulation that supervises the ordinance of local governments. On 31 October 2007, the then Ministry of Government Administration and Home Affairs (currently the Ministry of Security and Public Administration) prepared the Residing Foreigner Support Ordinance for stable and continual support and recommended local governments enact such

Table 4.7 Migration status by provincial-level governments

	2007	2008	2009	2010	2011	2012
Total	722,686	891,341	1,106,884	1,139,283	1,265,006	1,409,577
Seoul Capital City	207,417	260,019	334,910	336,221	366,279	406,293
Busan Metropolitan City	28,591	33,192	40,913	41,365	44,726	49,329
Daegu Metropolitan City	20,731	22,822	25,424	26,002	28,153	31,231
Incheon Metropolitan City	43,093	49,253	61,522	63,575	69,350	73,588
Gwangju Metropolitan City	10,784	13,077	15,659	16,632	18,824	20,649
Daejeon Metropolitan City	12,044	14,682	18,834	19,699	21,360	22,499
Ulsan Metropolitan City	12,034	14,667	18,914	19,354	21,400	25,163
Gyeonggi Province	214,727	277,991	323,964	337,821	380,606	424,946
Gwangwon Province	13,238	15,236	18,908	19,041	21,940	22,731
Northern Chungcheong Province	19,274	22,669	28,311	30,138	34,083	37,653
Southern Chungcheong Province	30,337	36,591	45,920	48,874	57,869	67,157
Northern Jeolla Province	14,903	18,423	27,223	28,450	31,515	35,281
Southern Jeolla Province	16,312	20,551	30,309	31,305	35,077	39,006
Northern Gyeongsang Province	34,579	36,685	44,831	46,658	50,808	56,250
Southern Gyeongsang Province	40,607	50,431	64,298	66,800	74,517	87,395
Jeju Special Self-Governing Province	4,015	5,052	6,944	7,348	8,499	10,406

Source: Korean Statistical Information Service 2012, http://www.kosis.kr.

ordinances. Thus, each local government enacted the Residing Foreigner Support Ordinance. However, the need of ordinances for an increasing number of multi-cultural families requiring support and systematic management was raised. In April 2007, Cheongju city in Northern Chungcheong Province enacted the Multi-cultural Family Support Ordinance for the first time. This ordinance has spread to other local areas along with the Multicultural Family Support Act[6] initiated by the Ministry of Gender Equality and Family. The Multicultural Family Support Act aims to integrate members of multicultural families into Korean society smoothly and it aims to promote: family counselling, educational services (for husbands and wives, parents and children), language training (writing, speaking, listening), legal advice and administrative support when they suffer from social maladjustment, family conflict and various hardships.

In addition, the Multicultural Family Support Ordinance at the local level includes support for families with regard to international marriage, adoption and transnational migration. Thus, the scope of the multicultural family has been expanded beyond that specified in law. Diverse ordinances, including an ordinance on the Multicultural Family Support Centre, and the Family Health Support Centre pursuant to Article 35 of the Basic Act on Family Health, the Social Welfare Centre, the Foreign Worker Support Centre, the Foreign Work and Migrant Women's Support Groups, pursuant to Article 34 of the Social Welfare Business Act, specify the appointment of organisations or groups for support within the available budget.

As of 2012, the Multicultural Family Support Ordinances are enacted in 16 provinces and 153 municipalities, and multicultural family support policies are operated mainly through the existing social welfare departments of municipalities and provinces. The enactment of ordinances increases along with the increased number of foreigners. Table 4.8 shows the status of the Multicultural Family Support Ordinance by local governments that are similar to the law in the Social Integrated Support System (in Table 4.8, the number outside the brackets is the number of autonomous district or municipality in the region, and the number inside the brackets is the number of autonomous district or municipality-enacted multicultural family support ordinances).

Table 4.8 Ordinances of multicultural family support in Korean provincial-level governments

Seoul	25 (20)	Gwangju	5(5)	Gangwon	18(13)	Southern Jeolla	22 (19)
Busan	16 (11)	Daejeon	5(3)	Northern Chungcheong	12(9)	Northern Gyeongsang	23 (16)
Daegu	8(5)	Ulsan	5(3)	Southern Chungcheong	16(7)	Southern Gyeongsang	20 (10)
Incheon	10 (8)	Gyeonggi	31 (16)	Northern Jeolla	14(8)	Jeju	N.A

Source: National Legislation Information Centre 2012, www.law.go.kr.

4 Conclusion

Historically, Korea has been a homogeneous society, but its population composition has changed substantially as its economy has grown over the years. Consequently, it is apparent that a multicultural society is an inevitable reality in Korea as a result of the increasing number of foreign migrants, a low birth rate and an ageing society, a shortage of labour and the wave of globalisation. As a reflection of the expansion of the social and spatial influence of foreign migrants, the central government, local governments and NGOs provide direct and indirect support for migrants and their settlement through laws and regulations on their resident qualifications and social status as members of Korean society. Such policies and activities aim to achieve the national and local objectives of the government by proper service of their settlement, and to minimise the social and cultural shock that migrants may bring. The central and local governments have executed various policies and events to engender social integration according to the need for the social support programme for the increasing number of multicultural families.

The government policy direction creates different policies and programmes, such as the government intervention philosophy on migration and settlement. The migration policy trend is divided into three areas: discrimination and exclusion, assimilation, and multiculturalism. In fact, the Korean government learned costly lessons from policy transitions: from a discrimination and exclusion model to an assimilation model, and an assimilation model to a multicultural model over the years, which may be labelled as the "Northeast policy models of policy transformation for migrant workers". This kind of policy transition and the Korean experience could provide further policy implications for China, Japan and other neighbouring countries.

Consequently, it is fair to say that such policy transitions still have many problems even though they seek social integration. There are many criticisms on different policy objectives, and sporadic and temporary policies by the responsible agencies and/or departments responsible. Therefore, it is time to complement the legal system to secure the comprehensiveness in this global era for the ever increasing number of foreign residents in Korea and to promote a coherent and systematic integration policy for ensuring a harmonious and inclusive society.

In this sense, a country's domestic migration policy can have a significant impact on shaping the regional migration market. It is easy for countries to treat migrants as a resource which can be exploited and returned once their use ends. However, migrant flows in a globalised world should be considered as enduring, involving networks of family and friends, often circular as well as multi-sited. Domestic policies among member countries within a common region can reduce the costs and problems associated with movement enabling a more supportive inter-state system to emerge which preserves shared human capital. The benefits of such human capital accrues to both sending and receiving countries, in the form of the fruits of labour, powering industry, sustaining innovations, allowing for elderly care as well as new family formation. Like many countries in ASEAN Plus Three, Korea sends and receives migrants. As regional migration becomes increasingly important in the APT region, Korean migration policies in the last ten years have made an important difference in the way migrants are accepted and integrated in Korea. It can be suggested that Korea's example may inspire other countries to adopt similar policies. In the process, a regional market for migrants may be transformed to a regional community for people from a common region.

The interdisciplinary study on multicultural society and the understanding of multicultural society are essential to reduce social conflict and to achieve social integration and harmony. Perhaps it is necessary to organise a joint-policy study group for the study of transnational migration in the ASEAN Plus Three countries. To respect other cultures equally, to give equal significance to such cultures and then to adopt such values to Korean culture are desirable ways to achieve real multiculturalism. Accordingly, it is required to change public awareness on multiculturalism through education and to modify the legal system so that members of multicultural families play an important role in Korean society as significant human resources.

Notes

1 In the first half of 2010, the number of foreign residents in Korea was recorded at 1,208,544, which exceeded 1.2 million for the first time. Migrant workers are the largest at 556,948, of which female migrants constitute 136,556 (11.3 per cent of the number of foreign residents in Korea). The legal system has been renovated to secure their human rights for social integration as Korea is on the way to being a multicultural society.
2 South Korea has been regarded as a somewhat homogeneous society for many years. As the number of international marriages and female migrant workers increased, the number of multicultural families has also increased substantially over the years. Accordingly, the premise of "one nation, one culture" does not work in South Korea anymore.
3 China has over 50 distinct ethnic groups and the largest ethnic group is the *Han* Chinese (over 90 per cent of the total population). Ethnic minorities account for about 8–9 per cent of the population of China. Ethnic minorities are the non-*Han* Chinese population. Among ethnic minorities in China, the proportion of the Korean-Chinese population is 0.1374 per cent (1,830,929 persons), according to the 2010 census in China.
4 Such number increases are not restricted to Europe or North America any more. Fifty three million global migrants (28 per cent) live in Asia. Thus, migration is now an international phenomenon.
5 It is unclear why the government considers migrant women as a separate category from migrant workers.
6 The Multicultural Family Support Act originated in the 17th Parliament together with the Mixed-Blood Family Support Plan (17 November 2006), the Migrant Family Protection and Support Plan (8 March 2007) and the Multicultural Family Support Plan (2 May 2007). Among these, the Migration Family Protection and Support Act and the Multicultural Family Support Acts are integrated and enacted as the Multicultural Family Support Act (21 March 2008, Act No. 8937, Enactment Date 22 September 2008) as an alternative to the Women and Family Committee on 19 February 2008.

References

Cho, Min Kyung and Kim, Yul. 2011. "A Study on the Relationship between Bicultural Identity and Socio-Cultural Adaptation of Immigrants in Korea". *Korean Journal of Political Science*, 18(2): 263–291.

Choi, Moo Hyun. 2008. "A Study of Anti-Discriminating Policy Instruments for Minority Groups in Multi-Cultural Society: Focusing on the 'Multi-Cultural Policy' of Participatory Government". *Korean Public Administration Review*, 42(3): 51–77.

Choi, Byung Doo and Kim, Yeung Keung. 2011. "Foreign Immigrants' Recognition on Related Policies and Supporting Activities". *Journal of Korean Regional Geography*, 17(4): 357–380.

Han, Geon Soo and Dong Hoon Seol. 2007. *The Policy and Institution in Korea from a Migrant Perspective*. Korean Women's Development Institute research paper.

Han, Seung Jun and Chi Sung Park. 2011. "The Impact of Public Policy on Social Construction of Foreigners: Comparative Case Study of Foreign Workers and Marriage Immigrants". *Korean Policy Studies Review*, 20(1): 51–82.

Hwang, Jung Mee, Yi Seon, Kim Myung Jin Lee, Hyun Choi and Tong Lee Joo. 2007. *The Research on Multi-Ethnic and Multi-Cultural Orientation of the Korean Society*. Korean Women's Development Institute research paper.

Jeon, Hyung Kwon. 2008. "Rethinking International Migration: Theoretical Perspectives on Diaspora Phenomenon". *Journal of North-East Asian Studies*, 49: 259–284.

Ji, Jong Wha, Myung Joo Jung, Hoon Cha Chang and Do Kyung Kim. 2009. "The Investing Inquiry on the Establishment of Multi-Cultural Policy Theory in Korea". *Social Welfare Policy*, 36(2): 471–501.

Kang, Hwi Won. 2006. "Integration of Korean Multicultural Society: Factors and Policy Directions". *Chung-Ang Public Administration Review*, 20(2): 5–34.

Kang, Hwi Won. 2007. "The Formation of a Multicultural Society and Local Governments in Korea". *Korean Public Administration Review*, Spring Academic Conference paper, 1–20.

Kim, Jung Sun. 2010. *Legal Research on Citizenship and Residence of Foreigners*. Seoul: Korea Legislation Research Institute.

Kim, Nam Il. 2007. "Foreign Policy Direction for the Implementation of an Open Society". *Korean Journal of Sociology*, 147–179.

Kim, Yi Seon. 2010. "Multiculturalization of Korean Society and 'Multicultural' Policy's Approach on Cultural Agenda". *Journal of Social Science Research*, 34(1): 167–192.

Kim, Young Lan. 2008. "A Study on the Socio-Cultural Adaptation of Immigrant Workers in Korea". *Discourse 201*, 11(2): 103–138.

Ko, Suk Hee. 2009. "The Policy Change and Prospect of Multi-Cultural Family in Korea". *Korean Public Administration Review*, 99–116.

Kymlicka, Will. 1996. *Multicultural Citizenship: A Liberal Theory of Minority Right*. Oxford: Oxford University Press.

Laslett, Peter. 1995. "Necessary Knowledge: Age and Aging in the Societies of the Past", in David I. Kertzer and Peter Laslett, eds, *Aging in the Past: Demography, Society, and Old Age*. Berkeley, CA: University of California Press, 4–79.

Lee, Byeong Ha. 2011. "The Legislative Impact of Immigration Policy in Korea". *Journal of Legislative Studies*, 32: 71–104.

Lim, Chae Wan and Hong Mei Jin. 2011. "An Analysis of Outflux and Influx Policy of International Labor Force in Korea". *Journal of North-East Asian Studies*, 59: 189–208.

Miura, Hiroki. 2011. "Foreign Migrant Workers and Multilevel Governance in East Asia: Analysis and Implications from a Soft Law Perspective". *Korean Journal of International Relations*, 51(3): 153–185.

Moon, Nam Cheol. 2006. "Mutation of Flows of FDI and Labour within East Asia". *Journal of the Korean Association of Regional Geography*, 12(2): 215–228.

Overseas Koreans Foundation. 2011. *The Present Status of Koreans in Overseas*. Seoul: Overseas Koreans Foundation.

Park, Eun Mi and Kon Su Yi. 2009. "Multicultural Society and Adoption to Local Society: Case of Migrant Women". *Korean Public Administration Quarterly*, 21(2): 407–431.

Shim, Bo Seon. 2007. "Formation and Transformation of Migrant Worker Policy: Analysis of Multiculturalist Policy in Korea". *Discourse 201*, 10(2): 41–76.

UN. 2009. *International Migration*. New York: Population Division of the UN Department of Economic and Social Affairs.

Won, Sook Yeon. 2008. "Inclusion or Exclusion? Discriminating Policy Orientations for Minority Groups under Multiculturalism". *Korean Public Administration Review*, 42(3): 29–49.

Won, Sook Yeon. 2011. "Antecedents of Attitude toward State Policy for Racial Minorities: Focusing on the American Experience of Affirmative Action and Illegal Immigrant Policies". *Korean Public Administration Review*, 45(4): 327–352.

Won, Sook Yeon. 2012. "The Impact of Public Policy on Perception of Public Servants in Seoul". *Korean Policy Studies Review*, 20(4): 561–589.

Websites

Korea Immigration Service of the Ministry of Justice. Available at: www.immigration.go.kr.
Korean Statistical Information Service. Available at: www.kosis.kr.
Ministry of Justice. Available at: www.moj.go.kr.
National Legislation Information Center. Available at: www.law.go.kr.

5 Regional cooperation in education in ASEAN and East Asia

Past, present and future

Azmi Mat Akhir

This chapter is devoted to informing on cooperation in higher education in the Southeast Asian and the wider East Asian regions which have been implemented and are being implemented and planned under the ASEAN and the ASEAN Plus Three (China, Republic of Korea and Japan) collaborative frameworks, as well as under the wider East Asia Summit (EAS) framework which includes Australia, New Zealand and India (ASEAN Secretariat 2005a) and the US and Russia (ASEAN+3+3+2 or ASEAN+8) (ASEAN Secretariat 2011). It is to be noted that, while there have been and there are bilateral and multilateral cooperation programmes and activities in education being implemented under other cooperation platforms or mechanisms between countries in Southeast Asia and the wider East Asia, the cooperation programmes and activities described here are essentially confined to those which are and will be implemented under the collaborative frameworks initiated by ASEAN at the time of writing this chapter.

1 The need to rethink education development at a regional scale

Education is central to development. A literate and educated population would result in productive and cohesive societies. Education, scientific research and labour are increasingly becoming borderless. For education, interest in and the practice of cross-border cooperation among universities and institutions of higher learning is gradually spreading across the ASEAN region and beyond as stakeholders grasp that sharing ideas about educational strategies adds value to and supports the mutual growth of educational institutions. Mobility of students, graduates, professors and researchers is increasing as they seek enrolment and job opportunities in institutions in countries other than their own. This reflects the need to cultivate a regional perspective on curricula, instructional quality and institutional standards.

The issue of cross-border education has emerged as a growing area of concern and opportunity. Cross-border education will play an important and growing role in strengthening a region's capability and participation in the global economy, and in the transfer of ideas, technologies and understanding of people and cultures. It will benefit from improved transparency of regulations, qualifications recognition and quality improvements for both national systems and regional interaction.

Cooperation on cross-border education among countries in Southeast and Northeast Asia will benefit the overall ASEAN and East Asian region.

ASEAN has committed itself towards building an ASEAN Community by 2015 on three closely intertwined pillars, namely the ASEAN Political-Security Community (APSC), the ASEAN Economic Community (AEC) and the ASEAN Socio-Cultural Community (ASCC) (ASEAN Secretariat, 2004 and 2007a). In principle, the APSC pillar is about *peace*, the AEC pillar is about *prosperity*, while the ASCC pillar is about *people* (Azmi Mat Akhir, 2007). These three elements of *peace, prosperity* and *people* are at the core of a strong ASEAN community. The APSC and the AEC are the means through which ASEAN would secure a brighter future for its younger generation, while the ASCC, with its focus on people, is about grooming them to inherit this future. And *people* and *prosperity*, in union, reflect *progress*. Thus, the ASEAN Community, ultimately, is about achieving a sustained environment of peace and progress in the region.

The issue of education is one of the priorities to be addressed under the ASCC pillar. Schools and their teachers and universities and their faculties all have a key role in building a successful and resilient ASCC. Through formal education, schools and universities ensure that the students have the knowledge and skills to be productive members of society. They also instil the shared values of the community in the students, fostering a bond to the community, so that they grow up and come out to become responsible and caring members of society.

Human development through education lies at the very core of a strong and resilient ASCC. A concrete human development strategy is essential in order to build a strong socio-cultural community, and a concerted cooperation in education among ASEAN member states, particularly higher education, is indispensable. Although education is ultimately a national responsibility and the bulk of policy planning will be done at the member states' respective ministries of education, ASEAN, as well as ASEAN Plus Three, cooperation can help facilitate the exchange of best practice and the acquisition of new techniques at the regional level. In this regard, ASEAN has embarked on many "capacity building" activities, which include training workshops, knowledge sharing and the promotion of life-long learning. Capacity building is about helping the region's people gain the different types and levels of expertise needed to contribute to its economy and society.

Regional cooperation in education would help increase linkages between universities and promote collaboration, networking, and research and development among institutions and authorities involved in education. Promoting improved standards and access to education through networking and institutional collaboration in the region, as well as between this region and the outside world, is one of the concerns being addressed under the ASCC Plan of Action 2009–2015 (ASEAN Secretariat 2010a). ASEAN established the ASEAN University Network (AUN) in November 1995 for the purpose of further enhancing this regional cooperation (ASEAN Secretariat 1995). Along the same lines, a Community of East Asian Scholars (CEAS) has been established as the implementing body for the project on the promotion of ASEAN and East Asian Studies in ASEAN Plus Three countries, which was financed by the ASEAN Plus Three Fund and coordinated by the Faculty of Political Science, Thammasat University, Bangkok. Essentially, the AUN programme, together with that of CEAS, would work towards the cultivation of an East Asian identity.

2 ASEAN, ASEAN Plus Three and East Asia cooperation mechanisms and activities in education

2.1 *Cooperation mechanisms*

In order to ensure effective planning and implementation of cooperation programmes and activities in education, cooperation mechanisms have been established at respective ASEAN, ASEAN Plus Three and EAS levels. ASEAN has established relevant bodies at the ministerial, senior officials and expert levels, while under the ASEAN Plus Three framework these ASEAN bodies have been expanded to include representation from the respective ministerial, senior officials and expert bodies from the Plus Three countries. Further, at the EAS framework level, these bodies have been joined by representatives from other ASEAN Dialogue Partner countries which are participating countries of the EAS.

Cooperation in education among ASEAN member states falls under the policy guidance of the ASEAN Education Ministers Meeting (ASED) which is assisted by its Senior Officials Meeting on Education (SOM-ED). The ASED meets once a year and the SOM-ED meets prior to and back-to-back with each annual ASED. The ASED was convened for the first time only in March 2006 (ASEAN Secretariat 2006). The first meeting of the ASEAN Ministers of Education was actually held in 1977 (ASEAN Secretariat 1988a). However, there has been no follow-up meeting since then. Cooperation in education then was planned and implemented by the ASEAN Sub-Committee on Education of the ASEAN Committee on Social Development. When this was dissolved in 1999 the Sub-Committee was later transformed into the Senior Officials Meeting for the ASED, the SOM-ED.

At the ASEAN Plus Three level, cooperation in education at the policy level (ministerial and senior official levels) involves the ASED+3 and the SOMED+3, while cooperation activities under the EAS Education Ministers Meeting (EAS-EMM) are handled by special task forces established on a task-oriented basis, as and when needed, and are responsible to the EAS-EMM. The ASEAN Plus Three Education Ministers Meeting (APT-EMM) and the EAS-EMM are convened once every two years back-to-back with the ASED and with each other. The first APT-EMM and the first EAS-EMM were held on 4 July 2012 in Yogyakarta, Indonesia, in conjunction with the 7th ASED (ASEAN Secretariat 2012a).

2.2 *ASEAN's policies and priorities on cooperation in education*

Mandates on the direction for cooperation in education in ASEAN came from the Bangkok Declaration 1967 (ASEAN Secretariat 1988b), the declarations of the

4th ASEAN Summit 1992 (ASEAN Secretariat, 1992) and the 9th ASEAN Summit 2003 (ASEAN Secretariat 2004) and the ASEAN Charter 2008 (ASEAN Secretariat 2009a). The Bangkok or ASEAN Declaration of 1967 stated that one of the aims and purposes of the establishment of ASEAN was to promote Southeast Asian Studies; the 4th ASEAN Summit held on 27–8 January 1992 in Singapore, declared that:

> The ASEAN Member Countries shall continue to enhance awareness of ASEAN among the people in the region through expansion of ASEAN studies as part of Southeast Asian Studies in the school and university curricula and the introduction of ASEAN student exchange programmes at the secondary and tertiary levels of education.
>
> (ASEAN Secretariat 1992)

This was subsequently re-emphasised by the 9th ASEAN Summit held in Bali, Indonesia in October 2003 in its Declaration of the ASEAN Concord II, or the Bali Concord II, for the ASCC, that:

> ASEAN shall ensure that its work force shall be prepared for, and benefit from, economic integration by investing more resources for basic and higher education, training, science and technology development, job creation, and social protection. The development and enhancement of human resources is a key strategy for employment generation, alleviating poverty and socio-economic disparities, and ensuring economic growth with equity. ASEAN shall continue existing efforts to promote regional mobility and mutual recognition of professional credentials, talents, and skills development.
>
> (ASEAN Secretariat 2004)

Eventually the ASEAN Charter stipulates that one of the purposes of ASEAN is:

> to develop human resources through closer cooperation in education and life-long learning, and in science and technology, for the empowerment of the peoples of ASEAN and for the strengthening of the ASEAN Community.
>
> (ASEAN Secretariat 2009a)

Consequently, the important role of the education sector in political and security, economic and socio-cultural pillars of the ASEAN Community was confirmed in the Cha-Am Hua Hin Declaration of the 15th ASEAN Summit in October 2009 (ASEAN Secretariat 2009b). The education sector is therefore central to ASEAN's commitment to build the ASEAN Community by 2015.

The Vientiane Action Programme, which was adopted at the 10th ASEAN Summit in Vientiane in 2003 (ASEAN Secretariat 2005b), and subsequently the ASCC Blueprint adopted in 2008 (ASEAN Secretariat 2009c and 2010a), focused on the facilitation of universal access to education and the promotion of high standards in education. Before the adoption of the blueprints on the three ASEAN

Community pillars, as contained in the Roadmap for an ASEAN Community 2015 (ASEAN Secretariat 2010a), the Vientiane Action Programme was ASEAN's work programme towards realising the ASEAN Community. The priorities for ASCC on education are to (ASEAN Secretariat, 2009a and 2010a):

1   facilitate access by differently advantaged groups (youth, women, physically disadvantaged) to education to obtain the skills and knowledge necessary for gainful employment and meaningful participation in society;
2   create enabling environments to prepare the youth for their future role as ASEAN citizens equipped with the necessary skills in leadership, entrepreneurship and technical and vocational abilities;
3   promote environmental education through formal and non-formal education systems, capacity building and networking; and
4   promote ASEAN language learning through scholarships and exchanges of linguists.

2.3 Cooperation plans and activities in education at the ASEAN level

Pursuant to the above-mentioned declarations of the 4th and 9th ASEAN Summits, a number of cooperation initiatives in the primary and secondary education sub-sectors were undertaken by the then ASEAN Sub-Committee on Education toward integrating ASEAN studies in primary and secondary school curricula, implementing student-exchange programmes at secondary school level, and the implementation of the ASEAN Primary School Mathematics and Science Olympiad (implemented during October 2004–December 2004 and hosted by Indonesia) among others (ASEAN Secretariat 2000).

ASED has set out its broad goals and objectives for 2009–15 in the ASCC Blueprint as part of the Roadmap for an ASEAN Community 2015 (ASEAN Secretariat 2010a), and these goals and objectives have been transformed into a concrete and implementable plan of action that will also take into account the efforts of other regional bodies which are related to education, particularly the Southeast Asian Ministers of Education Organisation. The Blueprint includes a section on *Advancing and Prioritizing Education* as part of the larger effort on human development. The education activities would be implemented by the SOM-ED through its respective subsidiary bodies. The Blueprint sets out four objectives for the work on education, namely:

1   Ensuring the integration of education priorities into ASEAN's development agenda and creating a knowledge-based society.
2   Achieving universal access to primary education.
3   Promoting early childcare and development.
4   Enhancing awareness of ASEAN to youths through education and activities to build an ASEAN identity based on friendship and cooperation.

In order to meet these objectives, 21 activities have been identified that should be implemented by ASEAN either independently or through close cooperation and collaboration with other entities, including its dialogue partners.

Education also figures in the AEC Blueprint which, in the section on facilitating the free flow of skilled labour, calls for ASEAN to harmonise and standardise related services as follows (ASEAN Secretariat 2010b):

1 Enhance cooperation among the AUN member universities to increase the regional mobility of students and faculty.
2 Develop core competencies and qualifications for job/occupational and trainer skills required in priority and other service sectors.
3 Strengthen the research capabilities of each member state by promoting skills, job placement and information networks among member states.

3 Advancing and prioritising education: *ASEAN 5-Year Work Plan on Education – 2011–2015*

For the socio-cultural pillar of the ASEAN Community, the education sector is expected to contribute to the establishment of a socially responsible ASEAN Community, one in which citizens share a common identity and dwell in a society that enhances the well-being, livelihood and welfare of all people (ASEAN Secretariat 2009c). Education is also expected to enhance the competitiveness of individual member states and ASEAN, as a whole, by developing human resources, which is a common attribute of all the three pillars of the ASEAN Community. ASEAN is also committed to foster technical cooperation and capacity-building activities in the region, promote tripartite and public-sector cooperation, enhance the quality of skills of workers in all ASEAN member states and promote life-long learning (ASEAN Secretariat 2010c).

An ASEAN 5-Year Work Plan on Education 2011–2015 was developed following the decision of the 4th Meeting of ASED held 5–8 April 2009, Phuket, Thailand, which considered it as important to have a work plan to guide the work of the SOM-ED in an integrated manner towards the building of an ASEAN Community by 2015 (ASEAN Secretariat 2009d). The Work Plan on Education clarifies ASEAN's role as a regional partner in the education sector, and serves as the framework to strengthen, deepen and widen educational cooperation within ASEAN and with the Plus Three countries, the EAS participating countries and other ASEAN dialogue partner countries.

Within ASEAN, the Work Plan on Education supports ASEAN programmes that raise awareness of regional identity; promote access to and improve the quality of basic (primary and secondary) and higher (tertiary) education; support regional mobility programmes for students, teachers and faculty and strategies for the internationalisation of education; and support for other ASEAN sectoral bodies with an interest in education, including the ASEAN Senior Officials on the Environment, the ASEAN Committee on Disaster Management, the ASEAN

Senior Officers' Meeting for Social Welfare and Development, the ASEAN Task Force on AIDS and the ASEAN Intergovernmental Commission on Human Rights. The AUN and the Southeast Asian Ministers of Education Organisation would be the key partners in the implementation of these programmes. Therefore, the overall objective and priority of the Work Plan on Education 2011–2015 is to build towards the vision of an ASEAN education sector in which individual member states' education sectors offer progressive, systematic and organisational capacities, practices and programmes that support and promote ASEAN's education access and quality, as well as the region's competitiveness in the global market (ASEAN Secretariat 2009d).

Before the end of 2015, the ASED, with the assistance of SOM-ED, would evaluate the achievements of the Work Plan 2011–2015 and would decide on a new plan of action to carry on regional cooperation in education with specified duration beyond 2015. Cooperation activities may include new initiatives and the extension of former ongoing activities.

3.1 ASEAN University Network

3.1.1 AUN's institutional framework

The 4th ASEAN Summit's declaration in 1992 also led to the establishment of the AUN in November 1995 through a charter (ASEAN Secretariat 2009e) and an agreement (ASEAN Secretariat 2009f), with the main purpose of spearheading regional cooperation activities in higher education among ASEAN member states. The general objective of the AUN is to strengthen the existing network of cooperation among universities in ASEAN by promoting collaborative studies and research programmes on the priority areas identified by ASEAN, while the specific objectives are to promote cooperation and solidarity among scientists in ASEAN, to develop academic and professional human resources in the region and to produce and transmit scientific and scholarly knowledge and information to achieve ASEAN's goals.

Structurally, the AUN is composed of participating or member universities, the Board of Trustees (BOT) and a Secretariat (ASEAN Secretariat 2009e). Initially, AUN started with 11 members. The membership then gradually increased to 17 when Vietnam, Laos, Myanmar and Cambodia joined ASEAN in 1995, 1997 and 1999, respectively. Membership was then opened to other universities in the ASEAN member states every three years. At the time of writing, the membership had expanded to 30 universities (ASEAN Secretariat 2009e; AUN Secretariat 2006, 2012b and 2013). In order to maintain quality membership and fruitful collaborations, the AUN-BOT has adopted nine admission criteria for AUN membership enlargement (AUN Secretariat 2012b).

The AUN-BOT is comprised of one representative from each ASEAN member state, who is the Vice-Chancellor/President/Rector of the university representing other member universities from a particular member state, with the Secretary-General of ASEAN and the Executive Director of the AUN Secretariat as ex-officio members. The BOT formulates policies for the operation of the network, approves proposals for projects, including budget allocation, work programmes and implementation activities, and conducts periodic reviews and evaluation of ongoing projects and activities. The chairmanship of AUN-BOT has been assumed by Thailand ever since the establishment of the network in the person of the Commissioner of Higher Education of Thailand. The BOT used to meet twice a year, but reduced to only once a year from 2010 (AUN Secretariat 2008).

The AUN Secretariat is located at Chulalongkorn University, Bangkok and headed by an executive director appointed by the AUN-BOT for a fixed term of four years, renewable for another term. The Secretariat plans and organises, coordinates, monitors and evaluates the programmes, projects and activities of the AUN; proposes and develops ideas, innovations or mechanisms for sourcing and generating funds for the operation of a self-reliant and self-sustaining AUN; and assesses and reviews periodically the accomplishments of the AUN and reports to every AUN-BOT meeting. With the institutionalisation of the ASED and its SOM-ED in March 2006, the AUN Secretariat also informs on the progress of AUN's programmes and activities to the ASED through the SOM-ED.

3.1.2 Programmes and activities of AUN

The establishment of the AUN has contributed greatly towards promoting a regional identity through the development of human resources in the region. The various collaborative projects that are ongoing among AUN participating universities, as well as those between them and institutions of higher education from ASEAN dialogue partner countries such as China, the European Union, Japan and the Republic of Korea, are reflections of ASEAN's policy of internationalising its higher education. Programmes of AUN include Course and Programme Development, Academic Exchange Programme, Cultural or Non-Academic Programme, Training and Capacity-Building Programme, Academic Conferences and Collaborative Research Programme, Systems and Mechanisms of Higher Education, Sub-Networking Programmes, Policy Dialogues, and a Database and Knowledge Centre. Some of these programmes, which are being implemented on a regular basis, are described briefly below.

3.1.3 Course and programme development

3.1.3.1 ASEAN STUDIES PROGRAMME UNDERGRADUATE LEVEL

The ASEAN Studies Programme (ASP) was the first prioritised activity of the AUN from the very first year of its establishment. The AUN ASP was first introduced at the University of Malaya as a number of undergraduate courses at the Department of Southeast Asian Studies of its Faculty of Arts and Social Sciences in 2000 (AUN Secretariat 2007). The ASP courses were also offered to other University of Malaya undergraduate students as electives. During those years, students who participated in this programme came from several universities in ASEAN countries and also from Japan. These undergraduate-level courses on ASEAN studies are still being offered at the University of Malaya.

In order to ensure that the ASP would truly serve as a mechanism for fostering the awareness of regional identity and a sense of *ASEANness* among students in ASEAN countries, AUN developed initial foundation courses for an undergraduate ASEAN Studies Development Programme in a regional and global context meant for students of its members and other interested universities in the ASEAN region (AUN Secretariat 2009). Interested AUN and non-AUN member universities would be free to start their own ASEAN studies programme as and whenever they wished. As a first step forward, an AUN ASEAN Studies Training Programme, under funding support by the Asian Development Bank, would be implemented for academic staff in Cambodia, Laos and Myanmar in 2014, aimed at building intellectual capital for the teaching and learning of ASEAN integration and Asian regionalism. In addition, an AUN ASEAN Studies Academy was launched in 2013 to provide technical and personnel support towards the development of this undergraduate ASEAN Studies Programme. The Academy, co-hosted by AUN member universities, comprises of ASEAN Studies study companions of 21 topics embedded in the knowledge and perspective of ASEAN in the socio-cultural, political-security and economic pillars of the ASEAN Community; a pool of academic multinational experts in ASEAN Studies; and the Academy Service which includes training programmes, summer schools (non-credit) and a lecture tour.

3.1.3.2 POSTGRADUATE LEVEL

AUN's postgraduate ASEAN Studies Programme is being offered as the *International Masters in ASEAN Studies* at the Asia-Europe Institute, University of Malaya (AEI-UM) from the academic session September 2006–August 2007, with full financial support from the Government of Malaysia through its then Ministry of Higher Education (currently the Ministry of Education). This constitutes Malaysia's contribution towards the fulfilment of AUN's obligation to the core aspiration of the 4th ASEAN Summit's declaration on education, specifically on enhancing awareness of ASEAN among the peoples of this region.

The Masters is a one-year programme (September–August) of full coursework consisting of five programme core courses and three AEI-UM core courses, with each course given in a two-week module. Students are also required to undertake a two-month internship and write a project paper of 15,000–20,000 words as partial fulfilments for the Master's degree (Anonymous 2011). The lecturers comprise of experts from ASEAN countries and Europe, while students taking the Masters programme come from within and outside the ASEAN region as well.

The programme provides an advanced level of understanding of the political, economic, social and cultural forces which shape ASEAN, as well as the attendant policy process. It aims to critically assess the significance of ASEAN as a regional organisation. In terms of job opportunities for its graduates, this programme has been designed for students for whom a Master's degree will be a prelude to careers in fields related to business, international, regional, governmental and non-governmental organisations, or any career where an advanced knowledge of ASEAN, regional integration and globalisation is required.

In an effort to further enhance ASEAN awareness in higher education at the research level, the AUN-BOT has also approved the implementation of an International PhD Programme in ASEAN Studies (AUN Secretariat 2007 and 2008), also at the AEI-UM. Opportunities are opened for candidates to enrol for PhD research in the various areas of ASEAN regional cooperation. The aims of the PhD programme, among others, are to strengthen students' research abilities within the areas of ASEAN studies and ultimately provide them with the skills and ideas towards a better understanding of ASEAN as an institution and a process, as well as a region; to provide students with theories, methodologies, practice and applications in order to keep pace with current developments in research and have the opportunities to work in different ASEAN settings; and to foster a stronger cooperation among universities in the region through networking, exchanges of expertise, joint research, joint supervision and the sharing of curricula and experiences.

3.1.3.3 ACADEMIC EXCHANGE PROGRAMME

The Academic Exchange Programme among AUN member universities aims to enhance academic mobility among students and faculty members in ASEAN countries, provide an opportunity for students and faculty members to exchange knowledge and expertise and promote cooperation and solidarity among scholars, academics and students in ASEAN member states (AUN Secretariat 2007). Annually, a number of full and partial scholarships are being provided by AUN member universities for students and faculty members in the fields of language, religion, cross-cultural studies, etc. (AUN Secretariat 2012a and 2013). AUN is also coordinating academic exchange programmes between its member universities and universities in China, Japan and the Republic of Korea under the ASEAN+1 framework (AUN Secretariat 2012a and 2013).

3.1.3.4 CULTURAL OR NON-ACADEMIC PROGRAMME

AUN Educational Forum and Young Speakers Contest

This programme was started in 1998 to provide opportunities for ASEAN students to share and acquire knowledge, values and attitudes from each other; to provide a platform for ASEAN youth to express their ideas and opinions on ASEAN issues; and to create a network of friendship. It is participated by students and lecturers from ASEAN and the Plus Three countries. Activities of the programme include a speakers' contest, an education forum, guest lecture, a workshop and presentation on ASEAN issues, an educational trip and a cultural programme. Hosting of the programme is rotated annually among ASEAN member states and member universities take turns to host the programme.

ASEAN Youth Cultural Forum

This programme was started in 2003 to share each of the ASEAN countries' cultures and traditions, which are composed of music, song and dance; enhancing and strengthening mutual understanding, friendship and cooperation in order to maintain, preserve and enrich the cultures of each ASEAN country and promote better understanding of cultural variations among ASEAN countries. The activities, which are participated by students and lecturers, include lectures on music, song and dance; a consolidating workshop; cultural performances; and a cultural visit. Since November 2013, the forum had also included students from the Plus Three countries and has been transformed into the ASEAN+3 Youth Cultural Forum.

ASEAN Student Leaders' Forum

This yearly programme, started in 2012, serves as a platform to bring together student leaders, as well as the Vice Presidents/Vice Rectors/Deputy Vice-Chancellors for Student Affairs from AUN member and non-member universities in South East Asia to discuss the various issues relevant for further cooperation. The ultimate objective of this forum is to create a better understanding between the student unions and high-level university administrators in the ASEAN region. The 2nd forum was hosted by Chulalongkorn University in June 2013 which gathered 62 student leaders and 28 Vice-Presidents/Executives for Student Affairs from 25 AUN member universities (AUN Secretariat 2013).

3.1.3.5 DEVELOPMENT OF SYSTEMS AND MECHANISMS IN HIGHER EDUCATION

AUN quality assurance system

Quality improvement is significant in leading universities in ASEAN to ensure a high-quality standard of education towards harmonisation. An AUN quality assurance (AUN-QA) system was initiated to promote the development of a quality assurance system as an instrument for maintaining, improving and enhancing teaching, research and the overall academic standards of AUN member universities. A manual for the implementation of the AUN-QA Guidelines was published for use as reference by member universities and revised from time to time (AUN Secretariat 2006b, 2012b). The application of the AUN-QA assessment was programme-based and conducted on a voluntary basis. The Guideline for AUN Quality Assessment and Assessors and Framework for AUN-QA Strategic Action Plan for 2012–2015 was published in 2013 to set the outline of a strategic plan, including key activities, in order to further develop the AUN-QA system through the enhancement of QA assessment and capacity building among the AUN member universities (AUN Secretariat 2013).

The AUN-QA system will also be extended to non-AUN member universities in the ASEAN region with the ultimate aim of acquiring regional and international recognition. The AUN was also involved with the Asian Development Bank in a three-year project on Strengthening Capacity of University Quality Assurance System towards Uplifting Higher Education Quality in the Greater Mekong Sub-Region (GMS) Countries (AUN Secretariat 2013).

ASEAN credit transfer system

The AUN has developed guidelines on an ASEAN Credit Transfer System (ACTS) in the form of a manual each for students and for university administrators which were published in 2011 to ensure common understanding and implementation, i.e. to apply the ACTS grading scale as a common practice for the exchange of students under ACTS application (AUN Secretariat 2011). The first phase of ACTS was implemented among AUN member universities in 2011 to 2012. As of end of the 2012–13 implementation period, a total of 12,369 courses were available on offer for student exchange and 14 AUN member universities had participated both as host and home universities (AUN Secretariat 2013). AUN would expand the ACTS scheme to non-AUN member universities in 2014 in collaboration with ASEAN International Mobility for Students and be opened to all universities in ASEAN by 2017. The scheme is coordinated by Universitas Indonesia and the AUN-ACTS website can be accessed at http://acts.ui.ac.id.

3.1.3.6 SUB-NETWORKING PROGRAMMES

AUN Southeast Asia Engineering Education Development Network

The Southeast Asia Engineering Education Development Network (SEED-Net) project was established as an autonomous sub-network of the AUN in April 2001 as an initiative of the ASEAN-Japan Summit Meeting in 1997 and the ASEAN Plus Three Summit Meeting in 1999. The project aimed at promoting human resources development in engineering in ASEAN through the establishment of a network of 19 leading member institutions from ten ASEAN countries with the support of 11 leading Japanese universities. Funding support for the project was mainly by the Japanese government through the Japan International Cooperation Agency and partially through the ASEAN Foundation (AUN/SEED-Net Secretariat 2008).

Besides promoting human resource development in engineering in ASEAN countries, the basic objectives of the network are to activate internationally competitive personnel in leading engineering educational institutions in the ASEAN region for advancing academic cooperation and for providing educational and technical assistance to less advanced engineering institutions, and to promote collaboration and solidarity between academics and professionals in the region through the cross-border and region-wise development of engineering education and research capabilities. Activities of the sub-network included support for graduate programmes through the granting of scholarships, collaborative research, thesis research support, special equipment support, a Japanese professors dispatch programme, a short-term study programme in Japan, a short-term visit programme to Japan and to ASEAN member countries, field-wise seminars and promotional trips. The member institutions were responsible for training young graduates and teaching staff from other members to acquire Masters and Doctoral/PhD degrees in a Sandwich Programme with Japanese support universities (AUN/SEED-Net Secretariat 2008). Details of AUN/SEED-Net activities, scholarships and grants are accessible at www.seed-net.org.

ASEAN Graduate Business and Economics Programme Network

This network began in September 2000 with the aim of promoting and strengthening the relationship among academics, scholars and students in the areas of business and economics; to lift the quality level of graduate programmes related to business and economics of the AUN member universities; and to internationalise the graduate business economics programmes of AUN member universities at regional and global levels. Its activities include student and faculty exchange programmes, joint research, the publication of the *Journal of ASEAN Business and Economic Research* and annual meetings. Each annual meeting of the network has three main activities, namely: Dean's Conference, Academic Seminar and ASEAN Strategic Business Game Competition. The network also developed an online faculty database for use as primary information to facilitate faculty research collaboration, faculty exchanges and external thesis examination; developed case studies among different network countries on the theme "Sustainable Community Ecopreneurship: Business Model Innovation for Optimizing Potentials of SMEs in ASEAN" under the leadership of Universiti Sains Malaysia; and organised PhD Colloquia to provide platforms for PhD students to exchange and discuss their research topics with other students and academic faculties around the region.

The network is run by a Secretariat which is hosted in rotation among AUN member universities on a five-yearly basis. The network has been extended to include collaboration with Chinese business schools through the establishment of the ASEAN-China Business School Network under the framework of ASEAN-China cooperation. The ASEAN-China network was launched on 2 April 2013 at Universitas Gadjah Mada, Yogyakarta, Indonesia with funding support from the ASEAN Foundation.

Information networking: AUN inter-library online

The purpose of this programme is to enhance information networking among member universities in order to facilitate information dissemination and collaboration among members and to establish and develop an online information exchange system in the member universities. It resulted in the establishment of the AUN Inter-Library Online (AUNILO), including the AUN homepage, with links to the homepages of member universities. The AUNILO portal has also been established at the University of Malaya at http://www.aunilo.um.edu.my. Other AUNILO online platforms include a photo gallery via FlickPro, fully accessible at www.flickr.com/photos/aunilo and the AUNILO Community via Facebook at http://www.facebook.com/AUNILO. Through AUNILO, member libraries have been exchanging information on current trends of the usage of digital information and the implications for libraries and the utilisation of new technology, including exchanging experiences and ideas on moving library services from an *e*-library towards an *m*-library utilising mobile technology.

3.1.3.7 TRAINING AND CAPACITY-BUILDING PROGRAMME

AUN internship programme

The AUN Secretariat offers internship placement for students from AUN member universities and partner universities from the ASEAN, Plus Three and EAS countries. During the internship, interns conduct research work in the areas of higher education cooperation, mobility and youth. At the same time, they are also trained on programme development and management skills.

3.1.3.8 ACADEMIC CONFERENCES AND COLLABORATIVE RESEARCH PROGRAMME

This programme aims to share efforts, expertise and technology among researchers of various fields in ASEAN through the promotion of research collaboration, as well as to enhance regional cooperation which would lead to better solutions to regional problems and sustainable development. Activities so far have included a Sustainable Energy and Environmental Forum, organised jointly by member universities and non-AUN members in conjunction with another event on energy and the environment, the AUN-Kyoto University Symposium 2012 (AUN Secretariat 2012a) and the ASEAN-Korea Academic Conference 2013 (AUN Secretariat 2013). However, several activities on research collaboration proposed earlier have not materialised due to funding and other implementation constraints.

3.1.3.9 DATABASE AND KNOWLEDGE CENTRE

An AUN Academic Directory has been developed by the AUN Secretariat which serves as the database and information hub of resources under the AUN framework of cooperation, namely: human rights, ASEAN Studies, human security development, ICT, economics and business, energy, intellectual property rights, university social responsibility, etc. The directory will facilitate possible cooperation in these areas and the database is freely accessible on the AUN website (www.aunsec.org).

3.1.3.10 POLICY DIALOGUES

From time to time the AUN has been consistently organising policy dialogues at the ASEAN as well as ASEAN Plus Three levels to review ongoing programmes and activities with a view to come up with recommendations for improving the implementation of those programmes and activities. Dialogues which had been conducted include, among others: (1) ASEAN+3 Heads of International Relations Offices' Meetings; (2) ASEAN Cyber University (for Cambodia, Laos, Myanmar and Vietnam); (3) Asia-Europe Meeting Rectors' Conferences; (4) ASEAN+3 Rectors' Conferences; (5) Project on AUN-Kyoto University Student Mobility towards Human Security Development; and (6) AUN-SUN/SixERS Vice Presidents' Meeting (AUN Secretariat 2013).

3.1.4 Future role of AUN

The AUN will continue to be the sole regional mechanism for networking among institutions of higher education in ASEAN (and ASEAN Plus Three) cooperation frameworks. All the above mentioned programmes and activities of the AUN have benefited the students and faculty members of its member universities in the respective areas of cooperation involved. As indicated in some of the above, some of these collaborative programmes have also been opened to participation by non-AUN member universities. The 5th AUN Rectors' Meeting, held on 3 July 2013 in Yangon, discussed the future direction of the network in terms of expansion with the combination of a "Quality-Excellence Model" and "Network of Networks" with a regional orientation practice. This combined model, with a strong orientation on regional integration, would bring about the expansion of higher education development to non-AUN member universities. The youths had also been involved in AUN activities which had been a good way to promote understanding amongst the people of ASEAN, especially in realising the vision of an ASEAN Community (AUN Secretariat 2013).

4 ASEAN Plus Three cooperation in education

Besides several activities between ASEAN and members of the Plus Three countries being implemented on an ASEAN+1 basis under the AUN collaborative programme as mentioned earlier, there are also activities planned specifically for the ASEAN Plus Three framework in education, as described below.

4.1 ASEAN Plus Three Plan of Action on Education for 2010–2017

Since its initiation in November 1999, the ASEAN Plus Three cooperation is being pursued in several areas including education (ASEAN Secretariat 2007b and 2007c). An *ASEAN Plus Three Plan of Action on Education for 2010–2017* was adopted by the first Meeting of the ASEAN Plus Three Senior Officials Meeting on Education (SOM-ED+3) held on 25 November 2010 in Brunei Darussalam (ASEAN Secretariat 2010d). The general objective of the plan is to encourage the ASEAN Plus Three member countries to expand their efforts in implementing the plan at the national and bilateral levels to the regional level; while the specific objectives are to urge the ASEAN Plus Three members to: (1) develop a more cohesive, regional strategy aimed at promoting comprehensive education programmes among them for the timeframe 2010–17; (2) enhance awareness of community building to youth through education and activities to foster an East Asian identity based on friendship and cooperation; (3) enhance coordination among ASEAN bodies dealing with education; and (4) ensure the integration of education priorities into ASEAN Plus Three's development agenda.

In order to achieve the above-mentioned general and specific objectives, the plan identified the following six areas of cooperation:

1   Encourage investments in education and training to accelerate learning opportunities for out-of-school children and youth and to upgrade the quality of educational institutions, including human resources development for teachers, lecturers and administrative personnel.

2   Promote collaboration, networking and research and development among institutions and authorities involved in education.

3   Promote higher education cooperation, increase linkages between universities through the AUN and encourage credit transfers between universities in ASEAN Plus Three countries.

4   Support research activities and exchanges of ASEAN Plus Three scholars and professionals interested in the ASEAN Plus Three relationship.

5   Continue to make efforts to expedite visa-application procedures for students and intellectuals of ASEAN member countries who travel to the Plus Three countries for academic purposes, in accordance with existing national regulations.

6   Cultivate an East Asian identity through the promotion of ASEAN Studies and East Asian Studies in the region.

Each of these areas of cooperation or strategies is accompanied by a list of the actions and tentative implementation schedules (ASEAN Secretariat 2007c), the details of which shall not be described here.

4.2 ASEAN Plus Three University Network

The ASEAN Plus Three University Network was established through a memorandum of understanding between AUN and Plus Three member universities at the inaugural ASEAN+3 Rectors' Conference held on 1 November 2012 in Beijing. The initiative was taken to further intensify the mechanism of ASEAN Plus Three cooperation in university networking and East Asia community building. The mission of the network is to facilitate closer collaboration and cooperation between higher education institutions in ASEAN Plus Three countries, and to further deliberate, prepare and propose recommendations to the SOMED+3 and the ASED+3 (ASEAN Secretariat 2012c).

The network is composed of presidents, rectors and vice-chancellors of designated representatives of the AUN member universities and universities from the Plus Three countries and the Executive Director of the AUN Secretariat. The network meets under the ASEAN+3 Rectors' Conference that is being convened biannually in ASEAN Plus Three countries, unless the meeting agrees otherwise. The chairmanship of the network is held by the President, Rector or Vice-Chancellor of the country hosting the meeting, and the tenure of chairmanship is for two years, beginning at the end of each ASEAN+3 Rectors' Conference. The AUN Secretariat serves as the permanent secretariat of the network and is assisted by a focal point from each country in the preparation for the ASEAN+3 Rectors' Conference and related activities. Admission of new members is conducted in accordance with the recommendation of the governments/authorised agencies responsible for higher education of the ASEAN Plus Three countries, in consultation with the AUN Secretariat, unless otherwise agreed upon by the participating universities.

The network's scope of activity includes the following priorities for higher education cooperation in the East Asian region:

1 Develop and recommend collaborative strategies and programmes/projects for ASEAN Plus Three cooperation on higher education developments.
2 Review progress of the implementation of projects and activities in the network, recommend measures for improvement and identify priority areas for ASEAN Plus Three cooperation in higher education.
3 Intensify the ASEAN+3 universities' networking among AUN member universities and participating universities from China, Japan and the Republic of Korea.
4 Deliberate and recommend common positions, where appropriate, especially in preparation for regional and international meetings relevant to educational development.
5 Jointly collaborate with regional and international agencies and other relevant agencies and co sponsors in implementing programmes under the network scheme.

4.2.1 Mobility of higher education and ensuring quality assurance of higher education among ASEAN Plus Three countries

Pursuant to the decision of the first ASEAN Plus Three Education Ministers Meeting (APT EMM) in July 2012, and upon Japan's initiative, a working group on Mobility of Higher Education and Ensuring Quality Assurance of Higher Education among ASEAN Plus Three countries was established to strengthen and facilitate policy dialogue, coordination, collaboration and promotion of quality assurance and mobility of higher education. The working group is tasked to look into, amongst other things, strategies and activities related to the development of the credit transfer system and harmonisation of academic standards in the ASEAN Plus Three Plan of Action on Education: 2010–2017 (M. Kamal and P. K. J. Budidarmo, personal communication, 2013).[1]

The working group convened its first meeting in Tokyo on 30 September 2013 in which representatives from ASEAN Plus Three countries shared information on ongoing initiatives related to mobility in higher education, and emphasised the need to develop a systematic and holistic approach to promote mobility in higher education and strengthen cooperation in the quality assurance of higher education (ASEAN Secretariat 2013). They also exchanged ideas on strengthening and facilitating policy dialogue, coordination, collaboration and the promotion of mobility and quality assurance of higher education. The working group also discussed its future directions, including developing "ASEAN Plus Three guidelines for the promotion of student exchange with quality assurance" by 2017, and facilitating a setting in 2014 where quality assurance agencies and, as needed, government officials from ASEAN Plus Three countries would meet on a regular basis.

4.2.2 Community of East Asian scholars and the project on the promotion of ASEAN and East Asian studies in ASEAN Plus Three countries

This project, for which this book forms an output, was launched on 11 December 2010 and was supported by the ASEAN Plus Three Fund, initially over a period of three years (December 2010–December 2013) and later extended to August 2015. It was spearheaded and coordinated by Thammasat University. For the purpose of continuity of relationships between the universities in this effort, CEAS was established to proceed with the implementation of the Project, with its website at www.ceas-edu.org/.

The main objectives of the project, which were also CEAS's objectives, were three-fold, viz: to create a four-volume (later reduced to three volumes) edited collection that analyses East Asian regionalism which is designed for use in university classrooms at both undergraduate and graduate levels to provide academic knowledge about the geography, religions, cultures, legal and political systems, societies and economies of ASEAN and East Asian countries (especially the Plus Three countries – China, Japan and South Korea); to stimulate discussion and research on regional heritage and common values in ASEAN Plus Three countries, which would be fostered through a series of workshops at which scholars would develop and comment on the project's teaching contents; and CEAS workshops would provide a forum in which negotiations about faculty and student exchanges among participating universities could take place (Wajjwalku 2013).

At the time of writing, 17 universities from ASEAN Plus Three countries have participated in the project, ten from ASEAN, one from China, four from Japan and two from South Korea.

4.3 East Asia Summit cooperation in education

At the second EAS meeting held in 2007, the leaders of the 16 participating countries agreed to strengthen regional cooperation in education (ASEAN Secretariat 2007d). As a follow-up action, the ASEAN Secretariat commissioned a project, under the ASEAN-Australia Development Cooperation Program, Regional Economic Policy Support Facility – Phase II with funding from the Australian Agency for International Development, to develop strategies for EAS participants to enhance regional economic competitiveness and strengthen community building in a balanced and sustainable manner through cooperation in education. The project's scope encompassed regional cooperation in basic education (primary and secondary), technical and vocational education and training and higher education. Thirteen projects had been proposed to the East Asian Summit through the EAS Education Ministers Meeting in 2011 (Nugroho and McKenzie 2010), out of which five were for primary and secondary education, three for technical and vocational education and training and three for the higher education sub-sector.

The three projects for the higher education sub-sector are: (1) Regional Credit Transfer System Harmonisation; (2) EAS Regional Leadership Fellow Programme; and (3) Promotion of the UNESCO Convention on Qualification Recognition in Asia and the Pacific. These projects were already at the various stages of implementation at the time of writing.

5 Future outlook

The ultimate objective of cooperation in education among universities and countries is to enhance internationalisation of the education sector. Enhancement of quality assurance and recognition, so as to facilitate credit transfer, and collaborative research among universities are important approaches which should be undertaken in order to further realise the internationalisation of education from the aspect of increased mobility of students, faculty members and researchers in the ASEAN Plus Three region.

Mutual recognition of qualifications and quality assurance are crucial for mobility and cooperation. Good quality of institutions and study programmes will create trust between higher education institutions and strengthen mobility within this region. External quality assurance of study programmes should be in place and, fortunately, this has been so in many countries in this region. Alongside quality assurance, an effective system of academic credit transfer has long been recognised as a key element in promoting student and staff mobility and cross-border educational cooperation. Several systems of credit transfer have either been operated or under development among different sub-groups of countries and higher education institutions in the EAS region. Although differences in approach to credit transfer are to be expected in a region as diverse as the EAS, there would be much to gain from harmonising existing systems for greater region-wide applicability.

Collaboration in research among universities would strengthen their abilities and ultimately provide them with skills and ideas towards a better understanding of the region; assist and enable students to achieve excellence in multidisciplinary research, postgraduate education and training to meet the growing demands of the worlds of academia, economics, politics, science and technology and the arts; provide them with theories, methodologies, practice and applications in order to keep pace with current developments in research and have the opportunities to work in different ASEAN, APT and EAS settings; and foster a stronger cooperation among universities in the region through networking, exchanges of expertise, joint research, joint supervision and the sharing of experiences and curricula.

This research could also include studies by PhD candidates. Such an effort would be in tandem with the rapid development of a globalised world and the culture of seeking knowledge globally. Collaborative research activities will provide a fulfilling and stimulating research and educational experience with a comprehensive range of research areas in all fields of natural sciences as well as social sciences and humanities in East Asia that are rigorous, challenging and innovative. In other words, both depth and breadth of knowledge would be catered for. Depth of knowledge is assured through the exploration of interdisciplinary approaches and exchange of ideas and development of research, while breadth is undertaken through the comparative exploration of other kinds of knowledge in other related areas. Collaborative research among universities would help to foresee the changes of societal and industry standards, trends and behavioural patterns and, most importantly, strengthen cooperation and exchanges in tertiary education.

The East Asia region, especially the ASEAN region, is continually in need of new knowledge and data to formulate future strategies and plans of action for cooperation in the various political and security, economic and socio-cultural sectors. The collaborative research activities should be structured to serve the above-mentioned purposes. In-depth research conducted by faculty members and students under the collaboration can provide more and up-to-date information on the various areas of regional sectoral cooperation under the ASEAN, ASEAN Plus Three and EAS frameworks. Therefore, collaborative research among universities in the wider East Asia region will provide new knowledge and enhance a better understanding that can serve policy guidelines and recommendations for member governments to pursue as well.

With the ever emerging educational challenges and opportunities in a global world, countries in the region need to further collaborate toward the development of a more coordinated, cohesive and coherent ASEAN and East Asian position and their contribution to global education issues. At the same time, there is also the need for greater interaction and dialogue between ASEAN, APT and EAS bodies in charge of education with other sectoral bodies of these three cooperation frameworks which have an interest in education, as well as with regional and international educational organisations, ASEAN dialogue partners, the private sector and other parties to ensure synergy, minimise any overlapping areas of cooperation and to maximise efficiency in the allocation of resources. Member states should put more effort to avail national resources to implement programmes and activities of the respective education work plans. In addition, the ASEAN-help-ASEAN approach should always be adopted and strengthened to help the lesser-developed ASEAN member states.

Where and when opportunities exist, joint initiatives and activities between universities or a "Network of Networks" should be undertaken by ASEAN and its Plus Three members to sustain the noble ventures of educating the next generation and strengthening the region's competitiveness. An immediate example at hand would be a networking between the AUN and CEAS and those in other regions of the world. Needless to say, the various cooperation frameworks in ASEAN, ASEAN Plus Three and EAS should be fully utilised for all these endeavours to enhance the internationalisation of education, regionally and globally.

Note

1 Kamal Mamat was Senior Officer and Budidarmo P. Kuntjoro Jakti was Technical Officer of the Education, Youth and Training Division, ASEAN Socio-Cultural Community Department, ASEAN Secretariat.

References

Akhir, Azmi Mat. 2007. "Keynote Address on 'ASEAN Higher Education Policy': Towards Internationalisation". In *Report of the Second ASEAN-China Rectors' Conference, 15–16 March, Hanoi, "Towards an Enhanced ASEAN-China Academic Partnership"*, ASEAN University Network.

Anonymous. 2011. *Graduate Study at AEI*. Kuala Lumpur: University of Malaya, Asia-Europe Institute.

ASEAN Secretariat. 1988a. "Joint Communique of the First Meeting of the ASEAN Education Ministers, Manila, 8–9 December 1977". In *ASEAN Document Series 1967–1988*, 3rd Edition. Jakarta: ASEAN, 369–70.

ASEAN Secretariat. 1988b. "The ASEAN Declaration (Bangkok Declaration)". In *ASEAN Document Series 1967–1988*, 3rd Edition. Jakarta: ASEAN, 27–8.

ASEAN Secretariat. 1992. "Declaration of the 4th ASEAN Summit (Singapore Declaration of 1992), 27–28 January 1992, Singapore". In *ASEAN Document Series 1991–1992: Supplementary Edition*. Jakarta: ASEAN, 16–20.

ASEAN Secretariat. 1995. *Charter of the ASEAN University Network*. Jakarta: ASEAN.

ASEAN Secretariat. 2000. *ASEAN Awareness and Understanding through Education*. Press release: 8th Meeting of the ASEAN Sub-Committee on Education, Yangon, Myanmar, 25–6 September. Available at: www.aseansec.org/23178.htm.

ASEAN Secretariat. 2004. "Declaration of ASEAN Concord II, 9th ASEAN Summit, 6–7 October 2003 in Bali, Indonesia". In *ASEAN Document Series 2003*. Jakarta: ASEAN, 9–21.

ASEAN Secretariat. 2005a. "Kuala Lumpur Declaration on the East Asia Summit, Kuala Lumpur, 14 December 2005". Available at: www.aseansec.org/22765.htm.

ASEAN Secretariat. 2005b. "Vientiane Action Programme (VAP) 2004–2010". In *ASEAN Document Series 2004*. Jakarta: ASEAN, 20–49.

ASEAN Secretariat. 2006. "Joint Statement from the 1st ASEAN Education Ministers Meeting and the 41st SEAMEO Council Conference, Singapore, 23 March 2006". In *ASEAN Documents Series 2006*. Jakarta: ASEAN, 790–8.

ASEAN Secretariat. 2007a. "Cebu Declaration on the Acceleration of the Establishment of an ASEAN Community by 2015", Cebu, Philippines, 13 January. Available at: www.aseansec.org/19260.htm.

ASEAN Secretariat. 2007b. "Second Joint Statement on East Asia Cooperation and ASEAN-Plus-Three Cooperation Work Plan (2007–2017)". Available at: www.aseansec.org/22206.pdf.

ASEAN Secretariat. 2007c. "ASEAN Plus Three Cooperation Work Plan". Available at: www.aseansec.org/21104.pdf.

ASEAN Secretariat. 2007d. "Chairman's Statement of the Second East Asia Summit", Cebu, Philippines, 15 January. Available at: www.aseansec.org/19302.htm.

ASEAN Secretariat. 2009a. *Charter of the Association of Southeast Asian Nations*. Jakarta: ASEAN.

ASEAN Secretariat. 2009b. "Cha-Am Hua Hin Declaration on Strengthening Cooperation on Education to Achieve an ASEAN Caring and Sharing Community", adopted 24 October at the 15th ASEAN Summit in Cha-am Hua Hin, Thailand. Available at: www.aseansec.org/15thsummit/Declaration-Education.pdf.

ASEAN Secretariat. 2009c. *ASEAN Socio-Cultural Community Blueprint*. Jakarta: ASEAN.

ASEAN Secretariat. 2009d. "Joint Statement of the Fourth ASEAN Education Ministers Meeting, 5–8 April 2009", Phuket, Thailand.

ASEAN Secretariat. 2009e. *Charter of the ASEAN University Network*. Available at: www.aseansec.org/8724.htm.

ASEAN Secretariat. 2009f. *Agreement on the Establishment of the ASEAN University Network*. Available at: www.aseansec.org/8722/htm.

ASEAN Secretariat. 2010a. "ASEAN Socio-Cultural Community Blueprint". In *Roadmap for an ASEAN Community: 2009–2015*. Jakarta: ASEAN, 67–92.

ASEAN Secretariat. 2010b. "ASEAN Economic Community Blueprint". In *Roadmap for an ASEAN Community: 2009–2015*. Jakarta: ASEAN, 21–66.

ASEAN Secretariat. 2010c. "ASEAN Leaders' Statement on Human Resources and Skills Development for Economic Recovery and Sustainable Growth", adopted 28 October at the 17th ASEAN Summit in Ha Noi, Vietnam.

ASEAN Secretariat. 2010d. "ASEAN-Plus-Three Plan of Action on Education for 2010–2017". In *Report of the First Meeting of the ASEAN-Plus-Three Senior Officials Meeting on Education (APT-EMM), 25 November, Bandar Seri Begawan* (unpublished).

ASEAN Secretariat. 2011. "Bali Declaration on the Sixth East Asia Summit, Bali, Indonesia", 19 November. Available at: www.aseansec.org/22765.htm.

ASEAN Secretariat. 2012a. "Joint Statement of the First ASEAN Plus Three Education Ministers Meeting", Yogyakarta, Indonesia, 4 July. Available at: www.aseansec.org/documents/pdf.

ASEAN Secretariat. 2012b. "The Enhancement of AUN-QA System Implementation in Universities in ASEAN Countries". In *Report of the 7th SOM-ED, 29 November, Bangkok*.

ASEAN Secretariat. 2012c. "ASEAN University Network (AUN) Secretariat's Information Paper: Progress Report of the ASEAN University Network (AUN): Establishment of ASEAN+3 University Network and 1st ASEAN+3 Rectors' Conference". In *Report of the 7th SOM-ED, 29 November, Bangkok*.

ASEAN Secretariat. 2013. "Summary Record: The 1st ASEAN Plus Three Working Group on Mobility of Higher Education and Ensuring Quality Assurance of Higher Education among ASEAN Plus Three Countries", 30 September, Tokyo (unpublished).

AUN Secretariat. 2006a. "Report of the 20th Meeting of the Board of Trustees of the ASEAN University Network", November, Manila.

AUN Secretariat. 2006b. *ASEAN University Network Quality Assurance (AUN-QA): Manual for the Implementation of the Guidelines*. Available at: www.aunsec.org/site/upload/qa/QA_Manual.pdf.

AUN Secretariat. 2007. "Report of the 22nd AUN-BOT Meeting", 1–2 December, Pattaya, Thailand (unpublished).

AUN Secretariat. 2008. "Report of the 23rd Meeting of the Board of Trustees of the ASEAN University Network", 19–20 June, Hanoi (unpublished).

AUN Secretariat. 2009. "Report of the AUN-AEI-EWC ASEAN Studies Curriculum Development Workshop", 3–5 September, Kuala Lumpur (unpublished).

AUN Secretariat. 2011. *ASEAN Credit Transfer System (ACTS)*. Available at: http://acts.ui.ac.id/index.php/home.

AUN Secretariat. 2012a. "Report of 28th Meeting of the Board of Trustees of the ASEAN University Network AUN-BOT Meeting", 12–13 July, Putrajaya, Malaysia (unpublished).

AUN Secretariat. 2012b. "Operational Guidelines for the Membership Enlargement of the ASEAN University Network (AUN)", AUN.

AUN Secretariat. 2013. "Report of 29th Meeting of the Board of Trustees of the ASEAN University Network AUN-BOT Meeting", 3–5 July, Yangon, Myanmar (unpublished).

AUN/SEED-Net Secretariat. 2008. *The First Book of Achievements: Seeds of Hope*. Bangkok: Chulalongkorn University.

Nugroho, Tita and Philip McKenzie. 2010. "Regional Workshop 2 on Education Cooperation in East Asia Summit Countries for Regional Competitiveness and Community Building", 27–8 September, Phuket, Thailand (unpublished).

Wajjwalku, Siriporn. 2013. *Project Announcement*. CEAS Secretariat, Faculty of Political Science, Thammasat University (unpublished).

6 ASEAN and APT regionalisation and economic development

Hong Son Nguyen and Anh Thu Nguyen

1 Introduction

Over the past three decades, the Association of Southeast Asian Nations (ASEAN) has proved to be the most dynamic regional organisation in the developing world, with the growth rate twice as fast as the world economic growth. As a result, ASEAN has doubled its share in the world's total GDP (ERIA 2012). At a broader view, East Asian economies, including ASEAN, have grown rapidly over the last four decades, driven mainly by the great expansion of trade and foreign direct investment (FDI). The development of international production and distribution networks in East Asia is one key factor promoting remarkable trade and investment expansion in the region. The other important factor behind this expansion is the trade and investment liberalisation of member countries under a common regional framework.

From the early 1990s, the agenda of regional economic integration has become the priority of ASEAN. As stipulated in the vision for 2020, the objective of ASEAN's integration is "transforming ASEAN into a stable, prosperous, and highly competitive region with equitable economic development, and reduced poverty and socio-economic disparities" (Institute of Southeast Asian Studies 2009). With that objective, ASEAN's integration includes not only trade but also deeper integration in intra-regional and socio-economic ties. ASEAN member countries agreed on the establishment of an ASEAN Economic Community (AEC) in 2015, which will help ASEAN become a single market and production base, competitive economic region, a region of equitable economic development and integration into the global economy.

ASEAN's economic integration is also characterised by its free trade agreements (FTAs) with major partners, including Japan, South Korea, China, India, Australia and New Zealand, which have made ASEAN become the integration hub in East Asia. Recently, the launching of Regional Comprehensive Economic Partnership Agreement negotiation has further confirmed ASEAN commitment in fully integrating into the global economy. This agreement, involving the participation of ASEAN members and its six FTA partners, will have a broader and deeper integration with significant improvements over the existing ASEAN+1 FTAs.

According to economic theory, integration can promote economic growth, as long as it can create a good competitive environment. Thus, the important role of integration is to deal with different regulatory impediments to competition, including those that discriminate against foreign suppliers and those that discriminate against all new suppliers (Dee 2007). Empirical evidence of ASEAN and ASEAN Plus Three (APT) so far has proved that ASEAN's efforts to deepen integration has had certain positive impacts on the economic development of its members as well as the whole region. The gains include facilitating trade flows, investment, technology spill-over, finance and finally, accelerating growth and boosting development. One of the important achievements of ASEAN is the shared goal of poverty reduction, which is declining by nearly half in some ASEAN countries, compared to the 1990s. Rapid economic growth and poverty reduction are the results of sound macroeconomic management of member countries and are partly the benefits of deeper economic integration, which directly leads to the rapid growth of exports and high rates of investment.

This chapter will analyse the economic integration progress in ASEAN and APT through empirical evidences of trade, investment and finance in the region. It also analyses to what extent the recent formal policy initiatives through bilateral and regional FTAs have its impacts on this progress and on regional economic development.

2 Economic integration in ASEAN and APT

Balassa (1961) introduced a simple assessment of economic integration by different levels, which is widely accepted as basic integration theory. Economic integrationincludes the following levels: free-trade area, customs union, common market, economic union and complete economic integration. At the initial stage of free trade area, member nations, though abandoning tariffs for each other, maintain their own policy of tariff for non-member countries. The following level – customs union – requires the common tariff policy towards non-member nations. The level of common market then requires further free movements of other production factors, including labour and capital. The economic union takes economic integration a step further by requiring deeper integration with a common set of economic policies. Total economic integration is reached when the countries in a region adopt a set of integrated monetary, fiscal and other economic policies.

Based on this classification, any assessment of economic integration should include the analysis of trade, investment and financial cooperation of the region, as well as the related formal policies framework.

Economic integration in ASEAN and APT has both de facto and de jure aspects, since it is promoted by the development of the distribution and production network in the region and deepened further by the forming of bilateral and regional FTAs (ERIA 2009). Those integration efforts are illustrated by a wide range of treaties and agreements, including, among others, the ASEAN Trade in Goods Agreement (ATIGA), the ASEAN Framework Agreement on Services, and the ASEAN Comprehensive Agreement on Investment and other ASEAN+1

FTAs. To achieve the common target of establishing the AEC in 2015, ASEAN in particular has been undertaking a wide range of measures, including those to promote free flows of goods, services, investment and freer flow of capital.

The integration process in ASEAN and APT is characterised mainly by the expansion of trade and investment, as well as a formal FTA framework in the region. Although financial cooperation has yet to become the main area of integration in East Asia, it has also to be analysed here since it is related to a high level of economic integration.

2.1 Trade as a key factor of integration

Trade liberalisation is always the beginning of any economic integration process. The expansion of trade in ASEAN and APT has been considered the clear evidence of economic integration in the region. This part analyses the trade pattern of ASEAN and APT countries, concentrating on the intra-trade in ASEAN and trade between ASEAN and APT countries.

As stipulated in the blueprint for establishing the AEC, trade liberalisation is viewed as the key to the development of AEC and, especially, to the establishment of a single market and production base by allowing the free flow of goods within the region (Institute of Southeast Asian Studies 2009). Trade liberalisation and facilitation include both at-the-border and behind-the-border measures to make trade easier, less costly and more efficient (Hew 2005, 2007). For trade liberalisation, various important measures have been undertaken including tariff reduction under CEPT/ATIGA;[1] customs reforms; ASEAN Single Window and computerising other trade-related measures and other trade-facilitation measures.

One key instrument of trade liberalisation so far in ASEAN is the removal of tariffs and non-tariffs barriers under CEPT/ATIGA. In this agreement, the roadmap for tariff reduction to 0 per cent is 2015 for Thailand, Malaysia, the Philippines, Singapore, Brunei and Indonesia and 2020 for the rest of ASEAN. The implementation of the CEPT/ATIGA roadmap has revealed enormous efforts of ASEAN countries, with the present average tariff of 0.05 per cent for ASEAN-6 and 2.61 per cent for Cambodia, Laos, Myanmar and Vietnam (ASEAN statistics).

Total exports and imports of ASEAN were more than USD 1,252 billion in 2012, an increase of nearly three times compared to the figure for 2000. The relative growth rate of exports in the 2000–12 period in the agricultural sector was 12.82 per cent, while the figure for the oil and petroleum sector was 14.07 per cent, and that of the telecommunications equipment was 3.18 per cent. Export growth of all industries was 9.28 per cent on average, which contributes to a more open ASEAN market (UNcomtrade statistics). The following section analyses trade characteristics and some indicators to provide insight into the trade growth in different sectors and find out the impacts of integration on ASEAN comparative advantages as well as its trade potentials in the world market.

Although the intra-trade volume in ASEAN has witnessed an increasing trend over the past decade, its share in the total ASEAN trade is rather low. It reached a peak of nearly 25.5 per cent in 2010 and dropped to 24.5 per cent in 2012.

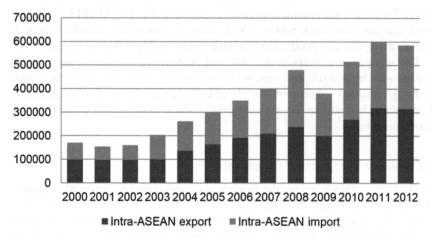

Figure 6.1 Intra-ASEAN trade (unit: USD million)
Source: ASEAN Secretariat.

This means that as a region, ASEAN trades more with non-member countries than within itself. ASEAN's major trading partners include China, Japan, the European Union, the US and South Korea. Specifically, trade volume with APT countries accounted for 28.8 per cent of ASEAN total trade. In 2012, trade volume between ASEAN and the Plus Three countries increased by 5 per cent compared to 2011, reaching USD 712 billion. Among them, Japan is one of the first countries to establish foreign relations with ASEAN in 1973. In recent years, cooperation between ASEAN and Japan is being actively implemented through the Action Plan on the ASEAN–Japan Strategic Partnership in the periods of 2005–10 and 2011–15. China, Japan and South Korea have always been the major trading partners with ASEAN. In 2012, the total ASEAN–China trade volume reached roughly USD 319 billion, while that of ASEAN–Japan reached more than USD 262 billion and ASEAN–South Korea was USD 131 billion (ASEAN statistics).

Comparative advantages of ASEAN countries

The reason why ASEAN countries tend to trade more with non-member countries lies in the similarity of the import-export structure of its members. The revealed comparative advantage index (RCA)[2] shows the level of comparative advantage of ASEAN compared to other countries. By using the trade data of 2000–12, this section analyses the RCA of six major exports of ASEAN, namely: office and telecommunication equipment, integrated circuits and electronic components, agricultural products, machinery and transport equipment, fuel and mining products and textiles.

The sectors that ASEAN as a whole have the highest RCA during the period 2000–12 were office and telecommunication equipment and integrated circuits and electronic components. High RCA in these sectors represents comparative advantage of ASEAN over other countries and regions. There are some reasons behind this fact. The first reason is the growth of these sectors in some ASEAN countries, especially Thailand and Singapore. The second reason is investment from China, Japan and South Korea in these sectors in ASEAN countries. This investment, in turn, is partially the result of investment facilitation and trade integration of ASEAN with its partner countries.

The ASEAN–Japan Comprehensive Partnership Agreement and ASEAN–China Free Trade Agreement, therefore, will have further impacts on these sectors along with the roadmap of trade liberalisation. In 2012 alone, total ASEAN export turnover of office and telecommunication equipment to these two markets reached nearly USD 60 billion, accounting for 18.64 per cent of total export.

Agricultural products and machinery and transport equipment are the sectors having relatively high RCA (Table 6.1). The agriculture sector shows the advantages of ASEAN countries in terms of natural resources. RCA in this sector has increased from 1.06 in 2000 to 1.47 in 2012. Fuel and mining products and textiles are two major traditional exports of ASEAN. However, RCA of those sectors are smaller than unity, representing comparative disadvantages.

Although some ASEAN countries are abundant in labour, which is favourable for labour-intensive sectors like textile and garment, these countries can only participate in the low value-added stage of the sector value chain, thus leading to low export value. Over the last decade, the RCA of textiles remained unchanged at the rate of approximately 0.8. The textile sector in ASEAN is losing its comparative advantage since advanced technology is crucial in this sector rather than low-skill labour. For fuel and mining products, the export volume is high but the value-added is comparatively low since the technology is not fully developed.

Trade liberalisation of ASEAN with its partners can have benefits to these sectors only if ASEAN can improve its competitiveness to participate in the higher value-added stage of the value chain. Regarding the RCA for individual countries in ASEAN, it can be seen that member countries tend to have similar comparative advantage in some sectors (Table 6.2). Comparative advantages of agricultural products and textiles are clearly expressed in Vietnam, Thailand, Indonesia and

Table 6.1 RCA of ASEAN

	2007	2008	2009	2010	2011	2012
Agricultural products	1.34	1.48	1.3	1.41	1.57	1.47
Fuel and mining products	0.92	0.94	0.99	0.94	0.96	0.91
Machinery and transport equipment	1.23	1.19	1.2	1.19	1.12	1.13
Office and telecom equipment	2.76	2.67	2.49	2.45	2.37	2.28
Integrated circuits and electronic components	4.97	4.84	4.68	4.33	4.33	4.14
Textiles	0.75	0.73	0.77	0.79	0.79	0.79

Source: Author's calculations based on UNComtrade statistics.

Table 6.2 Comparative advantages of ASEAN member countries

Sector	Country	2003	2004	2005	2006	2007	2008	2009	2010	2011	2012
Agricultural products	Vietnam	2.81	2.71	2.88	3	2.88	2.79	2.49	2.62	2.53	2.43
	Singapore	0.25	0.25	0.24	0.24	0.25	0.26	0.25	0.25	0.27	0.27
	Thailand	2.08	2.09	1.98	2.13	2.01	2.14	1.95	2.04	2.36	2.03
	Indonesia	1.65	2.02	1.99	2.22	2.49	2.83	2.24	2.55	2.65	2.65
	Malaysia	1.22	1.23	1.17	1.24	1.44	1.67	1.41	1.63	1.88	1.66
Textile and garment	Vietnam	1.03	1.15	1.16	1.47	1.6	1.61	2.09	2.57	2.42	2.32
	Singapore	0.26	0.23	0.21	0.19	0.19	0.17	0.16	0.14	0.13	0.13
	Thailand	1.18	1.26	1.29	1.23	1.19	1.17	1.17	1.18	1.14	0.99
	Indonesia	2	1.99	2	1.94	1.91	1.7	1.59	1.59	1.48	1.55
	Malaysia	0.43	0.46	0.5	0.5	0.49	0.5	0.51	0.51	0.55	0.51
Oil and petroleum products	Vietnam	1.65	1.7	1.53	1.31	1.13	0.96	0.86	0.61	0.55	0.48
	Singapore	0.75	0.79	0.77	0.76	0.81	0.91	0.91	0.88	0.94	0.86
	Thailand	0.28	0.33	0.32	0.34	0.33	0.35	0.34	0.32	0.32	0.34
	Indonesia	2.59	2.41	2.15	1.9	1.84	1.66	2.01	1.99	1.89	1.76
	Malaysia	0.86	0.89	0.85	0.79	0.84	0.91	0.9	0.9	0.9	1
Electronics products	Vietnam	0.1	0.21	0.23	0.16	0.16	0.15	0.14	0.21	0.31	0.67
	Singapore	6.3	6.83	7.16	7.75	7.99	8.29	8.1	7.75	7.55	7.61
	Thailand	2.14	1.84	1.8	1.99	2.05	1.78	1.71	1.53	1.54	1.27
	Indonesia	0.28	0.31	0.36	0.21	0.23	0.23	0.19	0.18	0.18	0.18
	Malaysia	5.82	5.2	5.16	4.93	5.43	5.24	5.94	4.84	5.7	5.51

Source: Author's calculations based on UNComtrade database.

Table 6.3 Comparative disadvantage of ASEAN member countries

Sector	Country	2003	2004	2005	2006	2007	2008	2009	2010	2011	2012
Steel	Vietnam	0.2	0.2	0.2	0.3	0.3	0.9	0.4	0.7	0.8	0.8
	Singapore	0.3	0.3	0.3	0.3	0.3	0.3	0.4	0.3	0.3	0.3
	Thailand	0.5	0.5	0.5	0.5	0.7	0.4	0.4	0.4	0.3	0.5
	Indonesia	0.3	0.4	0.4	0.5	0.4	0.4	0.4	0.4	0.4	0.3
	Malaysia	0.5	0.5	0.4	0.5	0.5	0.4	0.6	0.5	0.5	0.5
Chemicals	Vietnam	0.2	0.1	0.2	0.2	0.2	0.2	0.2	0.2	0.3	0.3
	Singapore	1.1	1.1	1.1	1.1	1.1	0.9	1.0	1.0	1.2	1.2
	Thailand	0.6	0.7	0.8	0.8	0.7	0.7	0.7	0.8	0.9	0.9
	Indonesia	0.5	0.5	0.5	0.5	0.5	0.5	0.4	0.5	0.5	0.5
	Malaysia	0.5	0.5	0.6	0.5	0.6	0.6	0.5	0.6	0.6	0.6

Source: Author's calculations based on UNComtrade database.

Malaysia, thanks to abundant labour resources and long-history agriculture. By 2012, Vietnam was the world's second-largest rice exporter with 7.7 million tons; Thailand was the third with 7.5 million tons of rice exported. So far, the agricultural sector is a source of strength to ASEAN countries; however, it needs to have a long-term sustainable development strategy to deal with the negative impacts of climate change, the impact of the shifting economic structure in ASEAN and the low competitiveness of the sector. Regarding the textile and garment industry, except for Vietnam, the remaining countries in ASEAN have RCA dropped; Indonesia has the biggest drop of this index, from 2 down to 1.5 in the last ten years. With such a declining trend, it can be projected that the textile industry is no longer an advantage of the ASEAN region.

The fuel and mining industry is not fully an advantage of all ASEAN countries. Indonesia is the only country that has an advantage in this sector; however, its index also decreased from 2.6 to nearly 1.8 in the period 2003–12. Before 2008, Vietnam had a large competitive advantage with RCA bigger than unity, but export has stopped growing in recent years. Conversely, imports increased significantly due to rising demand for petroleum products. Thailand, Malaysia and Singapore's indicators have not changed much (RCA is smaller than 1) because of natural resources constraints. For the above-mentioned industries, both Singapore and Malaysia do not have the advantage; however, these countries have a high RCA index with a continuous increase in the period of 2000–12 in the integrated circuit and computer components industry. RCA of computer components industry of Singapore was 5.3 in 2000 and 7.6 in 2012, and the figure for Malaysia was 4 in 2000 and 5.5 in 2012. In general, Indonesia, Thailand and Vietnam have more advantages in the labour-intensive industries such as agriculture and textiles, while Singapore and Malaysia have the advantages in the industries using high-quality labour such as electronics and computer components.

The sectors that ASEAN have comparative disadvantage in are industries requiring the use of high-level skills of mining and processing such as chemicals, steel, fuel and mining products (Table 6.3). Although ASEAN countries also have some potential in natural resources such as oil, coal and bauxite, but with ineffective extraction and processing, the competitiveness of these industries is relatively low in comparison with other countries. Regarding the iron, steel and chemical industries, RCA index fluctuations are erratic and always less than one, which means a low comparative advantage.

Trade complementarity

Table 6.4 indicates the extent to which exports of ASEAN countries commercially supplement import demand of each member of ASEAN in 2012 by TC indices.[3] Cambodia seems to have a low level of complementarity with other ASEAN members, whereas that of more developed countries like Singapore and Thailand are relatively high.

Based on complementary indicators, it can be seen that capacity on the market penetration of ASEAN countries' products into the markets of member states are

Table 6.4 Trade complementarity within ASEAN in 2012

	Brunei	Cambodia	Indonesia	Malaysia	Philippines	Singapore	Thailand	Partner Vietnam
Brunei	***	16.35	27.26	18.97	26.2	37,70	23.68	14.75
Cambodia	14.07	***	11.57	12.38	11.04	8.09	9.89	8.84
Indonesia	41.76	41.84	***	49.76	52.59	60.24	51.28	42.87
Malaysia	51.03	41.08	63.23	***	75.55	77.43	70.82	66.31
Philippines	43.65	29.31	47.43	66.38	***	59.06	56.74	54.46
Singapore	51.88	42.53	66.72	78.73	76.14	***	74.33	65.67
Thailand	62.23	45.65	64.85	64.4	60.72	56.48	***	60.99
Vietnam	51.43	39.5	48.72	58.19	56.23	53.07	52,85	***

Source: Author's calculations based on UNComtrade database.

gradually improved, but only focused on the more developed countries in ASEAN. The gap in the level of economic development as well as weak competitiveness are among the reasons of low penetration of less-developed countries in ASEAN to other members.

Figure 6.2 shows the TC index of ASEAN and its major partners, including ASEAN Plus Six, the US and European Union. In general, ASEAN has relatively high TC with these partners, which is more than 74. Among them, ASEAN+6 shows the highest TC, reaching 83 in 2012, which is the evidence of ASEAN economic integration with these partners.

Figure 6.2 clearly shows that ASEAN has the highest complementary index with Plus Six partners, including Japan, South Korea and China. This leads to the fact that "intra-regional trade" in East Asia is higher than that of NAFTA and nearly reaches the level of the European Union, whereas, as analysed earlier, the intra-regional trade of ASEAN is much lower. This asymmetry rooted from the nature of the production network in East Asia, with the lead of more developed countries like Japan, South Korea and China. Other evidence of the production network in East Asia is the growing international flows of intermediate goods in the region. Intermediate goods constitute for more than 60 per cent of Asian total imports and around 50 per cent of its total exports (WTO and IDE-JETRO 2011). Asia in general, ASEAN and APT in particular, have become the world's key player in the international production network, which will be further elaborated in the next section.

2.2 FDI in ASEAN

The expansion of FDI in ASEAN and APT has been the direct result of East Asian production networks, with the lead of Japan, China and also South Korea. Furthermore, the economic integration framework under FTAs in ASEAN and APT not only has an impact on trade but also has direct and indirect impacts on investment

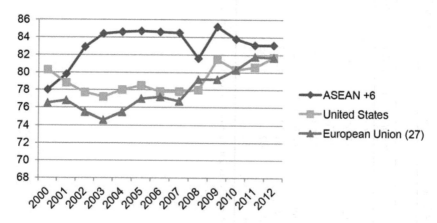

Figure 6.2 TC of ASEAN with its major partners
Source: Calculations based on World Trade Organization statistics.

in ASEAN. Free flows of investment are, therefore, considered an important pillar of AEC 2015, among other production factors of single market and production base. Free flows of investment help promote intra-regional investment and at the same time create favourable conditions for investment from other countries/ regions outside ASEAN. For ASEAN countries, FDI is valued as an important engine of economic development (Nazaroedin 2010). This section provides an overview of FDI into ASEAN and discusses the nature of the production network in ASEAN and APT.

Over the last decade, FDI flows into ASEAN has been increasing but with an unstable trend, which is the consequence of the financial crises in 1997–8, the economic recession in Japan in 2001 and in the United States and Europe in 2007–8. After the financial crisis of 1997–8, FDI into ASEAN decreased sharply, the FDI inflows share of ASEAN fell from 8.41 per cent in 1996 to 2.74 per cent in 2002. Asia in general and ASEAN in particular was no longer a "paradise" for FDI (Utama 2005).

However, economic reforms together with investment promotion has pulled FDI back to ASEAN, reaching USD 85.6 billion in 2007, which accounted for 4.95 global FDI (ASEAN Secretariat 2012). The economic recession of 2007–8 again had negative impacts on FDI inflows into ASEAN. In the last three years, however, in spite of the economic difficulties, FDI into ASEAN has been continuously increasing, reaching USD 111.4 billion in 2012 (Figure 6.3).

The main investors into ASEAN include the European Union, US and Japan. For years, the bilateral trade and economic links between ASEAN and APT have been strengthening. China, Japan and South Korea have become the largest trading partners and top FDI investors in ASEAN. Also, APT plays an important role in supporting the process of building the ASEAN community. To connect ASEAN, Japan has selected 33 priority projects of ASEAN economic corridor development. ASEAN and APT pledged to further promote cooperation and investment in various fields, namely environmental protection, climate change action, disaster management, education, science and technology. FDI inflows are distributed unevenly among ASEAN member countries (Figure 6.4). In 2012, FDI concentrated in ASEAN-6 countries, with the share of 88.8 per cent.

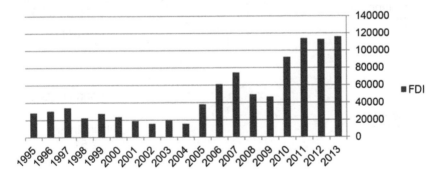

Figure 6.3 FDI inflows into ASEAN 1995–2013 (unit: million USD)
Source: ASEAN FDI database.

Through FDI, multinational corporations have formed their production net-works and supply chains in East Asia. Production has been divided into many processes and located in different countries based on their comparative advantages. Specifically, production networks in East Asia date back to the 1980s, when Japan used the region as an assembly base to meet world and regional demand. Later in the 1990s, the emergence of China gradually moved the centre of the produc-tion network. Over the past three decades, the creation and expansion of pro-duction networks in the region have created a new division of labour among countries (Ando and Kimura 2010). Large inflows of FDI to ASEAN and East Asia have, in turn, promoted the region's flows of trade.

It can also be said that FDI inflows into ASEAN have been flourishing partially thanks to the FDI policies of its member countries. The progress of investment liberalisation in ASEAN, however, is still rather slow. Investment liberalisation progress depends largely on domestic reforms and so-called behind-the-border policies. The FDI inflows into ASEAN still encounter enormous impediments from member countries. These include restrictions on areas of investment, foreign ownership, non-transparent screening and appraisal, among other things. ASEAN integration, while being progressive in trade liberalisation, fails to significantly phase out barriers to foreign investment.

Intra-ASEAN investment has risen, as ASEAN countries are moving toward a more integrated investment environment. Singapore and Indonesia are the two largest FDI recipient countries in the period of 1995–2011. Singapore accounted for over 30 per cent of total intra-ASEAN FDI since 1994, except for 2008 due to the world economic crisis. Thailand and Malaysia were respectively the third and

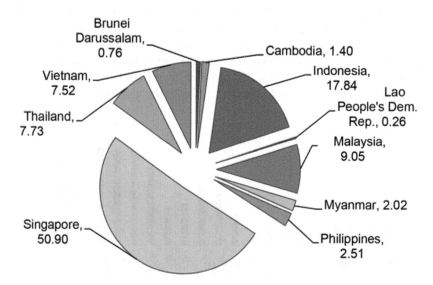

Figure 6.4 FDI inflows into ASEAN member countries 2012 (%)
Source: UNCTAD statistics.

fourth largest FDI recipients in the region, followed by Vietnam. These five ASEAN countries accounted for about 93 per cent of investment flows in the region in the same period.

Investment in the region is concentrated in three main areas, namely manufacturing, real estate and finance, which accounts for at least 65 per cent of total intra-ASEAN investment between 2002 and 2011. Companies from Singapore and Malaysia have dominated investment in the region, especially in the financial and real estate sectors. Most of the FDI inflows to Brunei are investment in mining and quarrying. The Philippines and Vietnam are mainly dependent on the manufacturing sector to attract FDI. As regards to Thailand, manufacturing, financial services and the insurance sector are those most attractive to investors.

Additionally, FDI in the services industry has continued to develop sustainably. In 2000–2, services accounted for over 50 per cent of total capital inflows, focusing on finance and telecommunications. FDI in services increased four-fold from an annual average of roughly USD 12 billion in 2000–2 to roughly USD 48 billion in the period 2009–11 (ASEAN FDI database). Intra-ASEAN FDI has also been the evidence of the changing production network in East Asia, with a more active participation of emerging ASEAN countries.

2.3 Financial integration in ASEAN and APT

Along with efforts to promote trade and investment in the region, cooperation in the financial sector is also focused by ASEAN countries toward the establishment of AEC in 2015. Under the AEC blueprint, ASEAN seeks to achieve a smooth

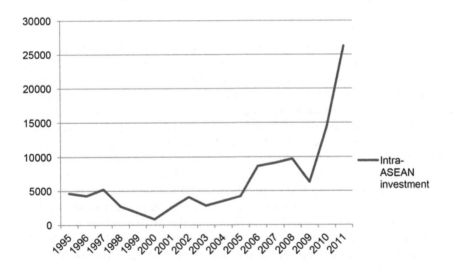

Figure 6.5 Intra-ASEAN investment 1995–2011 (unit: USD million)
Source: ASEAN Secretariat, ASEAN FDI database.

regional financial system with the liberalisation of capital accounts and inter-linked capital markets in order to further promote trade and investment. Financial cooperation has also been promoted beyond ASEAN to include APT countries. Accordingly, a number of cooperation agreements and series of joint initiatives and commitments in the field of finance have been born and are now under implementation.

The *Roadmap for Monetary and Financial Integration in ASEAN* adopted in 2003 has accelerated harmonisation with the objectives of the overall plan of the ASEAN Economic Community established in 2007. In 2011, the ASEAN Financial Integration Framework was adopted by the ASEAN Central Bank governors, providing a general approach for the liberalisation and integration process under the AEC. The Framework's objective is the "semi-integrated financial market of ASEAN by 2020". ASEAN Central Bank governors also endorsed the ASEAN Banking Integration Framework in 2011, with the banking sector as a key driver in the financial integration process.

Specifically, the financial integration framework of AEC comprises of: (i) *Financial Services Liberalisation*, including the gradual removal of restrictions on ASEAN banks, insurance companies or investment companies in providing financial services in other ASEAN countries; (ii) *Capital Account Liberalisation*, with the objective of freer flow of capital by gradually removing restrictions on foreign exchange transactions, including trade, foreign direct investments, portfolio investments and so on. The long-term goal of capital market development is the cross-border cooperation between capital markets in ASEAN; (iii) *Capital Market Development* in ASEAN focuses on developing and integrating regional capital market. This will be implemented by building capacity, infrastructure and harmonisation of domestic laws and regulations of the member countries; and (iv) *Harmonised Payments and Settlement Systems*, which will facilitate the linkages of financial sectors of ASEAN member countries (Institute of Southeast Asian Studies 2009).

Relating to APT integration, the Chiang Mai Initiative was launched at the Finance Minister Meeting of APT in 2000 as a currency swap mechanism in the region to address the temporary payment difficulties and supplement the current financial agreement of the international organisations. Then, in March 2010, the Chiang Mai Initiative Multilateralization officially took effect after five ASEAN member countries and the APT adopted and consolidated all of the mechanisms of bilateral currency swap that had been established previously. This initiative provided guidance on liquidity specifically mentioned in the ASEAN swap agreement and bilateral swap arrangements in ASEAN and APT. In the multilateral swap arrangement worth USD 120 billion, ASEAN countries contributed 20 per cent (equivalent to USD 24 billion); the remaining 80 per cent of the fund size (equivalent to USD 96 billion) is contributed by the APT contribution. So far, the scale of capital contributions to the fund by members has doubled to USD 240 billion in the Finance Ministers Meeting and central bank governors of ASEAN in 2012. In addition, the loan term has also increased, the dependence on International Monetary Fund policies has been reduced and loan programmes to prevent crises and support countries in crisis are also being proposed.

Also, other initiatives were launched in the framework of financial and monetary cooperation in the region such as the Asian Bond Market Initiative, launched in 2003 with the goal of developing the bond market by local currency, making regional bond markets more accessible and effective for both issuers and investors.

In order to achieve the financial liberalisation objective in 2015, significant efforts have been made by ASEAN to ease restrictions on foreign exchange transactions, payments and money transfers to proceed to the objective of removing capital controls and restrictions in ASEAN. Noted achievements include the linking of three ASEAN stock exchanges (Malaysia, Singapore and Thailand), the launching of the ASEAN corporate governance scorecard and the development of the Bond Market Development Scorecard for the assessment of ASEAN public-listed companies and measuring the state of ASEAN's bond market development, respectively. Additionally, training programmes enhancing the financial capacity for ASEAN countries and central bank officials on regional economic surveillance have been promoted to enhance the capacity of countries towards comprehensive integration by 2015. In Asia, financial links have been strengthened over time. According to the Asian Development Bank's Asian Bonds Monitor, from 2000 to 2012, the size of the Asian bond market (excluding Japan) grew from USD 600 billion to USD 6.5 trillion.

Overall, ASEAN and APT have achieved certain progress in financial and monetary cooperation through important collaborative initiatives; however, cooperation in this field is still at an early stage and the development is much slower than cooperation in the fields of trade and investment. Asia's role, particularly ASEAN, in international finance has not matched its rapid expansion of international trade and investment. According to the Asian Development Bank, the ratio of bank assets to GDP is projected to increase steadily every year, but it will be difficult to catch up with the current levels of Europe by 2030 if ASEAN do not make more effort in the integration of the banking sector between member countries. The level of cross-border banking in Asia, in general, is still three times lower than that of the Euro area (Pongsaparn and Unteroberdoerster 2011).

The low level of financial integration in ASEAN can be accounted for, to some extent, by financial restrictions in the member countries. In terms of the openness level of the capital market, most ASEAN countries still impose extensive controls for transactions on capital accounts. Policies are relatively open to attract capital inflows but control is tight on capital outflows including investment flows to countries in the region. According to Chinn and Ito (2008), Singapore is the only nation having almost completely open capital accounts, followed by Cambodia and Indonesia. The capital accounts of countries such as Thailand, Laos, Vietnam, Malaysia and Myanmar have low levels of openness, meaning more stringent state intervention on capital transactions in these countries. The liberalisation of capital flows is one of the major challenges for ASEAN countries since free movement of capital flows is a prerequisite for the creation of a unified ASEAN market. The liberalisation of the capital account comes with potential risks, which require ASEAN countries to take measures of risk monitoring and warning as well as strengthening cooperation and coordination in monetary policy. This will help

ASEAN member countries to stabilise intra-ASEAN exchange rates towards sustainable capital account liberalisation, which will significantly promote cooperation on trade and investment in the region.

The difference in the management of the banking sector among member countries is also a factor slowing down the integration process. A number of countries not only have strict control measures against offshore banks but also apply restrictions on the operation of foreign banks in the domestic market. Stock markets have developed in recent years; however, the scale and operation of this market in some member states is still limited. Intra-portfolio investment, despite an increase in absolute value over recent years, is still limited compared to investment outside the region. Concerning the APT countries, the ratio of portfolio investment flows in the region only accounts for 5–6 per cent of total portfolio investment across the regions.

The above analysis shows that ASEAN countries need to step up efforts to cooperate in the financial and monetary sector to achieve its objectives. Some of the difficulties ASEAN encountered stem from the problems pertaining to the development gap of financial systems, the lack of risk-minimising tools, weak financial potential and bank governance and an ineffective monitoring system. There are also other obstacles, namely the careful control of member states in the field of financial integration and a lack of close collaboration in the monetary and financial sector, which lead to the ineffectiveness of cooperation initiatives in this area. To overcome these difficulties, member states should strengthen cooperation and mutual assistance, especially in infrastructure development, to serve the administration and supervision of financial systems, cooperate in the construction of smooth economic and financial information systems and timely risk warnings, as well as strengthen the role of each country in the implementation of cooperation initiatives, in order to proceed to the integration target in 2015.

3 Economic integration and economic growth in ASEAN and APT

Economic integration, especially the comprehensive removal of the non-discriminatory restrictions to competition as analysed earlier, plays an important role in promoting economic growth in East Asia in general and in ASEAN in particular. During the last decade, ASEAN has grown at the average rate of 5 per cent annually. ASEAN is widely considered as the most dynamic regional organisation in the developing world, with the growth rate twice as fast as the world economic growth. ASEAN as a whole can be ranked the ninth biggest economy in the world.

After two decades of intra-regional and global integration, ASEAN economies have maintained a relatively high and stable economic growth rate. After joining ASEAN in the 1990s, Vietnam, Laos and Cambodia have witnessed significant GDP growth compared to the region and the world. Despite the slowdown of GDP growth due to the financial crisis of 1997–8, ASEAN member countries, namely Indonesia, Malaysia, Thailand and the Philippines, still maintained an impressive annual average growth rate of 7 per cent from the year 2000. The recovery of ASEAN after the recent world economic recession has proved to be one of the motivations for the recovery of the world economy.

GDP growth leads to the restructuring of ASEAN's economies. Most ASEAN countries developed from backward economies based mainly on agriculture and natural resources. Along with regional and global economic integration, the economic structure of ASEAN countries has changed significantly, marking their position in a global dynamic and modern service market. In 2012, compared to agriculture and manufacturing, the service sector accounted for the greatest share in most ASEAN economies. Service and industry are becoming a development base for ASEAN, contributing more than 80 per cent of its GDP.

GDP per capita is another criterion for measuring ASEAN's economic development. The continuous soar of GDP per capita in Southeast Asia contributes to higher living standards of people in the region (Table 6.5). Based on the classification criteria of the World Bank, ASEAN countries are divided into three groups of income: Singapore, Brunei and Malaysia are the countries having a high income; Thailand, Indonesia and the Philippines are the countries having a high-middle income; Vietnam, Laos, Cambodia and Myanmar belong to the low-middle-income group. GDP per capita in ASEAN is estimated to be growing at a high rate in the next 20 years.

Governments play an important role in the economic development in ASEAN. Along with integration progress, ASEAN countries' governments have created FDI-encouraging policies and implemented tariff reductions and other trade in goods and services. As analysed in the previous section, FDI can be considered the decisive factor of economic development in ASEAN. Integration creates favourable conditions for ASEAN countries to encourage great inflows of FDI, leading to the development of manufacturing and service sectors, technology spill-overs, boosting export and accelerating growth. Deeper integration in AEC is estimated to bring about further benefits to ASEAN countries in terms of trade, competitiveness and GDP growth (Petri et al. 2010; Plummer and Chia 2009).

The quantitative research of factors directly affecting the growth of ASEAN countries by Hussin and Saidin (2012) shows that governments are essential agents in promoting economic growth based on their power to shape the national economic environments through their policies. With the economic integration in ASEAN, ASEAN governments have created policies to encourage FDI and have committed to implement tax cuts and the conditions that promote the flows of commercial goods and services in the region. This move will reduce the cost of imports, increase trade exchanges between countries and create incentives for economic growth. Agbetsiafa (2010), in a study of the causal relationship between regional integration, trade openness and economic growth, proposed that the increase in commodity exports would improve production facilities and human resources, leading to an increase in real GDP per capita in the country and avoiding deficits. As discussed in the above section, through integration, ASEAN countries have created conditions in favour of attracting large FDI inflows, thereby absorbing the advanced technology in the region and around the world, leading to innovative domestic products.

Table 6.5 GDP per capita of ASEAN and APT (PPP$)

Countries	2005	2006	2007	2008	2009	2010	2011	2012
Brunei	48.998	51.803	52.816	52.262	51.116	52.208	54.357	55.405
Cambodia	1.450	1.632	1.809	2.114	2.030	2.157	2.308	2.516
Indonesia	3.199	3.447	3.716	3.986	4.174	4.354	4.664	4.971
Laos	3.185	1.755	2.052	2.213	2.350	2.522	4.664	2.904
Malaysia	12.035	12.925	13.814	14.523	14.165	14.813	16.028	16.976
Myanmar	788	894	1.055	942	1.099	1.195	1.406	1.490
Philippines	3.061	3.260	3.550	3.661	3.664	3.920	4.069	4.339
Singapore	45.369	49.120	52.735	52.329	50.812	58.063	61.068	61.461
Thailand	6.839	7.365	7.905	8.227	8.053	8.742	8.902	9.609
Vietnam	2.163	2.391	2.630	2.859	3.108	3.289	3.442	3.706
ASEAN	**3.917**	**4.230**	**4.581**	**4.822**	**4.901**	**5.221**	**5.520**	**5.869**
Japan	30.441	31.763	33.397	33.589	31.746	33.668	33.838	35.178
South Korea	22.783	24.247	26.101	26.689	26.680	28.613	29.786	30.801
China	4.115	4.753	5.543	6.162	6.747	7.503	8.322	9.083

Source: www.data.worldbank.org.

One important achievement of ASEAN is poverty reduction, which is declining by nearly half in some ASEAN countries, compared to the 1990s. Table 6.6 shows that the proportion of population at the poverty line in most of ASEAN countries has declined over time. This rapid growth and poverty reduction are the results of sound macroeconomic management of member countries and are partly the benefits of a deeper economic integration, which directly leads to a rapid growth of exports and high rates of investment.

Economic achievements contribute significantly to improving welfare, healthcare and education, increasing living standards for the people in the region. The concept of human development goes beyond the notion of growth in real per capita income and includes other non-material dimensions such as education, health, gender equality, etc. Regarding education, in general, the literacy and elementary education rate of ASEAN reached quite a high level (more than 90 per cent). Among ASEAN countries, Malaysia clearly is leading in expenditure on education, followed by Thailand, Brunei, the Philippines and Singapore. However, the number of people receiving higher education (high school, university level) is lower than the average of the countries in the Organisation for Economic Cooperation and Development. As education is considered the key for ASEAN's development, ASEAN countries have put much effort into promoting the quality of higher education. Between education and health, ASEAN countries apparently spent more on education. In general, health expenditure had a limited share in government expenditure and witnessed a minimal increase over the last decade (UNDP 2005, 2013).

The trend of the human development index has significantly improved for most countries in ASEAN. However, the human development index shows that ASEAN is a region of wide disparities across countries. Singapore and Brunei rank the highest and can be considered as having "high human development", comparable to developed countries in the world. Upper "medium human development" includes Malaysia, Thailand and the Philippines, whereas Vietnam and Indonesia belong to "medium human development". Lower "medium human development" includes Cambodia, Myanmar and Laos. These countries, at the same time, have a

Table 6.6 Poverty headcount ratio at the national poverty line of some ASEAN countries (percentage of population)

Country	2007	2008	2009	2010	2011	2012
Cambodia	45	34	23.9	22.1	20.5	–
Indonesia	–	–	14.2	13.3	12.5	12.0
Laos		27.6	–	–	–	–
Malaysia	3.6	–	3.8	–	–	1.7
Philippines	–	–	26.3	–	–	25.2
Thailand	20.9	20.5	19.1	16.9	13.2	–
Vietnam	–	–	20.7	–	17.2	–

Source: World Bank statistics.

higher level of human poverty index compared to other countries in ASEAN (Swaha and Sarika 2010).

4 Conclusion

Economic integration in East Asia has been promoted by the development of distribution and production networks in the region and strengthened further by the forming of bilateral and regional FTAs. Those economic integration efforts in ASEAN have brought about significant economic development for the member countries. Thanks to regional trade and investment liberalisation progress, trade growth of ASEAN countries has been impressive. In addition, FDI in the region increased significantly over the last decade, in spite of the global economic down-turn. Intra-ASEAN FDI rose even faster. Such trade and FDI performance reflects stronger economic ties between ASEAN member countries.

However, one important characteristic of ASEAN and APT countries is that ASEAN countries themselves are relatively similar in their comparative advantage, while ASEAN and APT countries are more complementary. Thus, ASEAN countries tend to be competitive both in expanding their export markets and in attracting foreign investment, including that from APT countries. With the ability to create connectivity and the single market in the region, AEC and integration within APT and the ASEAN+6 framework will create a single market and production base in ASEAN, limiting the competitive nature of ASEAN economies and enabling countries in the region to effectively participate in regional production networks.

Recently, the income gap between higher-income countries and lower-income countries in ASEAN has been reduced. However, there is still an apparently large disparity in the basic economic and human development indicators in Southeast Asia, which is a hindrance to more effective regional economic integration. ASEAN should, therefore, look for various policies – both at national and regional levels – to narrow this development gap and strengthen regional cooperation for the common final objective of economic and human development. Those policies would also ensure that countries reap the opportunities of economic integration and at the same time assure convergence among them.

Notes

1 Common Effective Preferential Tariff Scheme (CEPT) under ASEAN Free Trade Area/ ASEAN Trade in Goods Agreement (ATIGA)
2 $RCA_{ij} = (x_{ij}/X_{it})/(x_{wj}/X_{wt})$ where x_{ij} and x_{wj} are the values of country i's exports of product j and of world exports of product j; X_{it} and X_{wt} are the country's total exports and world total exports. $RCA>1$ reveals the comparative advantage of the sector.
3 The TC Index aims to reveal the prospects for trade by showing how well the structures of a country's imports and exports match. A value of zero indicates no goods that are exported by one country are imported by the other and a value of 100 indicates the export and import shares exactly match. $TC_{kj} = 100 - \Sigma abs(m_{ik} - x_{ij})/2$ where m_{ik} is the share (%) of good i in country k's imports and x_{ij} is the share (%) of good i in the exports of country j.

References

Agbetsiafa, D. K. 2010. "Regional Integration, Trade Openness, and Economic Growth: Causality Evidence from UEMOA Countries". *International Business and Economics Research Journal*, 9(10): 55.

Ando, M. and Kimura, F. 2010. "The Special Patterns of Production and Distribution Networks in East Asia". In P. Athukorala (ed.), *The Rise of Asia: Trade and Investment in Global Perspective*. London: Routledge, 61–88.

ASEAN Secretariat. 2012. *ASEAN Economic Community Chartbook 2012*. Jakarta: ASEAN.

Balassa, B. 1961. *The Theory of Economic Integration: An Introduction*. Santa Barbara, CA: Greenwood Publishing Group.

Chinn, M. and Ito, H. 2008. "A New Measure of Financial Openness". *Journal of Comparative Policy Analysis*, 10(3): 309–322.

Dee, P. 2007. "East Asian Economic Integration and Its Impact on Future Growth". *World Economy*, 30: 405–423.

ERIA. 2009. *Deepening East Asian Economic Integration*. Research Project No. 1. Jakarta: ERIA.

ERIA. 2012. *The Integrative Report of the ASEAN Economic Community Blueprint Mid Term Review Project*. Jakarta: ERIA.

Hew, D. 2005. *Roadmap to an ASEAN Economic Community*. Singapore: Institute of Southeast Asian Studies.

Hew, D. ed. 2007. *Brick by Brick: The Building of an ASEAN Economic Community*. Singapore: Institute of Southeast Asian Studies.

Hussin, F. and N. Saidin. 2012. "Economic Growth in ASEAN-4 Countries: A Panel Data Analysis". *International Journal of Economics and Finance*, 4(9): 119–129.

Institute of Southeast Asian Studies. 2009. *ASEAN Economic Community Blueprint*. Singapore: ISEAS Publishing.

Nazaroedin, R. I. 2010. *The ASEAN Comprehensive on Investment Agreement (ACIA): Possible Lesson Learned*. MENA-OECD Conferences: WG-1 on Investment Policies and Promotion, Paris, France.

Petri, P. A., M. G. Plummer and F. Zhai. 2010. "The Economics of the ASEAN Economic Community". *IDEAS: Economics and Finance Research*. Available at: https://ideas.rep ec.org/p/brd/wpaper/13.html.

Plummer, M. G. and S. Y. Chia. 2009. *Realizing the ASEAN Economic Community: A Comprehensive Assessment*. Singapore: Institute of Southeast Asia Studies.

Pongsaparn, R. and O. Unteroberdoerster. 2011. *Financial Integration and Rebalancing in Asia*. IMF Working Paper. WP/11/43. Washington, DC: IMF.

Swaha, S. and T. Sarika. 2010. "Balancing Human Development with Economic Growth: A Study of ASEAN 5". *Annals of the University of Petroşani, Economics*, 10(1): 335–348.

UNDP. 2005. *The State of Human Development in Southeast Asia*. New York: UNDP.

UNDP. 2013. *The Rise of the South: Human Progress in a Diverse World*. New York: UNDP.

Utama, N. 2005. *Foreign Direct Investment in ASEAN Countries: An Empirical Investigation*. Nantes: University of Nantes.

WTO and IDE-JETRO. 2011. *Trade Patterns and Global Value Chains in East Asia: From Trade in Goods to Trade in Tasks*. World Trade Organization.

7 Energy security in ASEAN and ASEAN Plus Three

Cooperation through the Trans-ASEAN Gas Pipeline

Harit Intakanok

1 Introduction

ASEAN as a regional network of member countries is home to some 600 million people. Through rapid economic development, the region is gradually rising in GDP resulting in a growing energy demand to run its economies and fulfil the needs of Southeast Asian populations. Today, out of those 600 million people, 219 million still lack access to electricity and another 100 million still have limited access to energy services (Sovacool 2009b). The prognosis looks yet more challenging with many analysts predicting that the overall demand for energy and fuels will increase by 200 percent in the upcoming two decades (Chang and Li 2012). As these energy demands are closely tied to economic development, one of the key questions in ASEAN countries is how to meet such growing demands.

According to the Japanese Institute of Energy Economics, energy demand such as electricity in the ASEAN region is expected to grow 6 to over 7 per cent per year – by 2030 this could be three to four times higher than the current level. This is an exceptionally high growth, if compared to the overall Asia-Pacific yearly increase of electricity demand of 3 to 4 per cent as reported by the Asian Development Bank. One of the main factors contributing to this is again reflected in the high economic growth within the ASEAN region (Chang and Li 2012). Despite the fact that many of the member countries are considered to be rich in energy resources (possessing 22 billion barrels of oil, 227 trillion cubic feet of natural gas, 46 billion tons of coal, 234 GW of hydropower potential as well as 20 GW of geothermal capacity), meeting such high growing demand is still a major challenge for a number of reasons. Energy is distributed in an uneven fashion. Hydropower, for example, is limited to the Greater Mekong sub-region (Thailand, Laos, Vietnam, Cambodia, Myanmar and China) (Institute of Southeast Asia Studies 2009), while coal, oil and gas are located mostly in Malaysia and Indonesia. The different pace of economic development among member countries also poses a challenge to the nature of regional power distribution. This in turn could put a crucial brake on the utilisation of region's resources as opposed to the fast-growing electricity demand (Chang and Li 2012).

Therefore, linking energy resource-rich countries with the energy poorer ones in ASEAN could be a key start to a more regional approach to energy security in

ASEAN (and ASEAN Plus Three). Through the process of integration of ASEAN 2015, it is no surprise to find that ASEAN members are now looking within the region to secure energy for both the short term and long term. Though this is the case, the ten member countries tend to adopt very different strategic energy security positions with regard to ASEAN, due mainly to their different stage of economic development. To put it simply, many view that while the more developed countries such as Thailand, Indonesia, Malaysia, Singapore or Brunei understand economic development in terms of rising GDP, for the less developed such as Myanmar, Laos and Cambodia, it is rather in terms of securing the basic needs of their still very poor populations. The Philippines and Vietnam find themselves "somewhere in-between". Thus, energy security means different things to different member countries. On the one hand, for Thailand, Malaysia, Indonesia and Singapore, energy security means fuelling their rapid economic growth and having enough reserves, either locally or imported, to sustain rising domestic consumption. On the other hand, for poorer member states such as Laos, Cambodia and even energy-rich Myanmar, energy security means not only fuelling economic growth, but mainly bringing the electricity and energy supply across their infrastructure-poor nations. Adding to this are two small countries at two extremes on the energy production spectrum, Brunei, who is self-sufficient and ready to export rich natural resources, and Singapore, who has no energy resources at all (ACE 2013c).

Looking forward to the ASEAN community, energy security is very much a subject of active discussion. From the beginning, the ASEAN Vision adopted in 1997 by the heads of member states at the second ASEAN Informal Summit in Kuala Lumpur agreed to create an energy-interconnected Southeast Asia network at two levels. One of the key projects was the creation of the ASEAN Power Grid (APG) which interconnects all member countries and facilitates cross-border power trade. This first-level project of APG could eventually provide a solution to the growing energy demand and lower the cost of energy transport amongst member countries. Within this energy integration framework the largest energy-integrating ASEAN project was the idea of the Trans-ASEAN Gas Pipeline (TAGP). Through these visions, since 2000 a working group was set up and has been exploring the possibilities defined by the ASEAN Interconnection Master Plan Study produced in 2003 (Chang and Li 2012).

This chapter will take a look at energy security in terms of its role in the economic development process in ASEAN (and ASEAN Plus Three) and its background in terms of regional energy needs with particular attention to different stakes of particular member countries. The main focus will be TAGP as a leading project through different stakeholders' activities aiming to investigate the prospects and remaining challenges of such a project. The energy outlook of individual members of ASEAN will also be discussed. The aim is to summarise the energy situation in ASEAN and point out its prospective development under tighter integration, while examining the choice to develop its first regional pipeline.

2 Energy in ASEAN

ASEAN is arguably one of the most dynamic regions of the world. Over the period of 1980 and 1999 the economy of the region grew annually by 5 per cent and energy consumption by 7.5 per cent. This rate is expected to continue until 2020 and the annual energy supply must increase by an estimated 4.2 per cent to sustain that level of growth. Through the combination of rich natural resources and developmentalist economic policies in this region that attract foreign investment, ASEAN has been one of the fastest-growing economies for the past few decades. As a result, high industrialisation patterns as well as the development of export-oriented technologies has intensified, in turn allowing high-energy consumption scenarios to arise across the region.

The increasing demand for energy in ASEAN has been contributed through various factors. Apart from production-driven energy demands Southeast Asia is rapidly urbanising, and this brings higher demand for energy. By 2025 more than 50 per cent of the region's population is estimated to live in urban areas (Sovacool 2010). These then become megacities and "extended metropolitan regions", which are especially prone to fast economic growth, industrialisation and higher energy demand.

Looking at the energy usages within the region, the main source pushing economic growth in recent history has been oil. Oil has been the ASEAN region's main commercial energy resource and is bound to stay dominant for the near future at least. The demand is currently at 4.4 mb/d, followed by natural gas at 141bcm, with coal use on the rise at double-digit rates since 1990 (now at 16 per cent of the overall demand). The call for renewable energy has recently been intensified compared to the global average reflecting heavy use of traditional biomass in rural areas with low incomes and lack of access to modern fuel (IEA 2013).

In terms of energy resources, Southeast Asia is well stocked compared to the rest of the world. The distribution of these is, however, uneven and often far from key areas of many member countries. In terms of export, ASEAN members ship out coal (220Mtoe), natural gas (62bcm) and bio-fuels in a volume that more than offsets net imports of oil (1.9 mb/d). Indonesia is the dominant producer and has been increasing its coal output and exports in the past ten years with nearly all of the coal resources of the region located in the country (83 per cent) (IEA 2013). On the other hand, natural gas and oil are to be found in member countries such as Brunei, Indonesia, Malaysia and Vietnam, whereas Indonesia and the Philippines possess reserves of geothermal energy – the second and fourth producers worldwide (ACE 2013a). As for liquefied natural gas and crude oil exporters, Brunei, Malaysia and Indonesia are dominant. Lastly, hydropower energy can be found in all of the countries except Brunei and Singapore with Singapore being the only country without actual natural resources, however, it does have the capacity to process them (Karki et al. 2005).

The rapid increase in energy consumption in the ASEAN region was evident during the 1980s with the annual growth rate doubled (compared to the 1970s). Energy consumption then grew by some 7 per cent in the 1990s and then gradually became 7.5 per cent by the end of the century. Currently, the annual energy consumption growth rate for the region is set to increase by 4.2 per cent over the next 15 years. In this, Indonesia, with the largest population of the ten member countries, is responsible for half of the primary energy consumption in the region (ACE 2013a). Although some progress has been made to tackle the extraordinary energy demand in the region, one of the main challenges concerns investment in energy infrastructure, particularly as a region. A reliable and extensive regional energy infrastructure has the direct effect of improvement in energy sufficiency and sustainability. Other major challenges that remain include energy policies and political backgrounds that tend to vary across the region, underlining differences in the way in which each country manages their energy supply and demand, also reflected in the level of their economic development. Given this, for a stable economic development as a region, some of the key goals for ASEAN members are affordability as well as improved efficiency (IEA 2013).

3 Energy consumption and production in ASEAN member countries

The early effort among the ASEAN member states to achieve energy security through regional cooperation was in the establishment of the ASEAN Center for Energy (ACE) on 4 January 1999 (at the new ACE headquarters in Kuningan, Jakarta, Indonesia). In this, the commitments, responsibilities, liabilities and assets of the ten-year long ASEAN-EC Energy Management Training and Research Center were handed over to ACE.

ACE together with the Institute of Energy Economics, Japan and the energy authorities in ASEAN member countries produce reports which look into the energy needs of each nation.

3.1 Brunei

Natural gas and oil are the main energy sources in Brunei Darussalam with the primary energy supply statistics in 2007 for these two sources of energy at 2.028 MTOE and 0.764 MTOE, respectively. For the generation of electricity, natural gas was mainly used until the production of methanol came into play in 2010 (3396 GWh was generated in 2007), with primarily fuel consumption on the other hand heavily reliant on oil (ACE 2011).

As Brunei Darussalam has sufficient reserves of gas and oil (producing 20.19 MTOE of gas and oil, of which 17.41 MTOE was exported in 2007), many therefore consider Brunei Darussalam to be the strongest energy producer in ASEAN (EIA 2013). In terms of regulation, the energy market in Brunei Darussalam is state regulated with energy prices subsidised. Although this is the case, to prevent the smuggling of fuels to neighbouring economies the state has increased considerably the price of motor gasoline and diesel for vehicles and vessels not registered in Brunei Darussalam.

3.2 Cambodia

The country's primary energy comes from fuel-wood and imported petroleum products with electricity widely used in the capital, provincial cities and urbanised areas. The current system of energy supply is structurally poor affecting domestic energy consumption massively, as only 35 per cent of the population has access to reliable electricity. Furthermore, the price of electricity in Cambodia is one of the highest in the world – most therefore use traditional sources of wood and charcoal. For development, the country relies on imported fossil fuel, mainly diesel and heavy oil. In this, the demand for energy is expected to increase five-fold in the near future, flagging the need for energy reform within the country.

Given the fact that the country has abundant renewable energy resources, with the potential of mini, micro and pico hydro being about 300 MW (only 1 MW has been utilised), it is not surprising to find that the government has been working hard to initiate the development and utilisation of new and renewable energy sources. Some of the projects include hydropower and coal power plants aiming to boost domestic energy production to provide electricity to 70 per cent of the population by 2030 (UN 2013). Despite this plan, development of such projects needs financial and technical assistance, which the Cambodian government is trying to open up for regional support.

3.3 Indonesia

Indonesia's total energy consumption increased dramatically by 50 per cent between 2001 and 2010. Based on fuel types, petroleum continues to dominate accounting for roughly 30 per cent, although this is slowly decreasing. Coal, on the other hand, tripled in consumption during the same period, surpassing natural gas as the second most consumed. The other types of energy mainly consist of biomass dominated mainly by wood, growing an average rate of 1 per cent annually. Despite constant shifts in the share of different types of energy in total energy consumption, oil more or less remained above 30 per cent with coal and natural gas following in second and third place, respectively (ACE 2013a).

Today, the country struggles to meet the growing demand for energy due to a lack of infrastructure, but also regulates to attract investment. Indonesia was still the world's largest exporter of coal by weight and eighth largest exporter of natural gas in 2011. The Indonesian government increasingly tries to shift the domestic production of energy from exports to secure energy for internal use. Currently, due to the natural decline of oil production, Indonesia plans to prioritise coal and gas consumption as the main energy mix to meet domestic requirements.

3.4 Laos

Laos strongly relies on imported fuels, as a landlocked country with no oil and gas reserves. As a result, it is prone to high energy prices and supply shortages. The country's primary energy demand mix consists of four types of energy, namely oil, hydro, coal and other energy which consists mostly of biomass and charcoal. Together with population growth, energy consumption in Laos has been rising steadily. In terms of resources, there are some reserves of coal, but mainly biomass and hydropower with good potential of solar, wind and geothermal in parts of the country.

As most Laotians live in the countryside and mountainous areas, energy consumption is dominated by wood and charcoal, accounting for almost 70 per cent of overall consumption. (in 2007, the biomass energy supply amounted to 1.3 MTOE and accounted for 61.4 per cent of the total) (ACE 2011). In this, fossil fuel follows with 17 per cent and coal accounts for only 3 per cent. Overall, energy consumption in Laos is generally very low compared to other developing countries, with most being for residential use. In terms of energy resources, many considered the country to have long-term potential in producing energy that came from Laos' rivers as the downstream of Mekong passed. In this respect, for the last few years the Lao government has been working closely with many agencies in planning 11 hydropower projects, some of which are already being pursued (Vongchanh 2013).

3.5 Malaysia

During the 1990s, the major proportion of primary energy consumption in Malaysia came from oil and gas, accounting for around 80 per cent of the overall total energy consumption. In 2011, oil and natural gas were still the two main primary energy sources with 39 per cent and 37 per cent consumed, respectively. As for other types of fuel, coal accounts for 18 per cent, biomass and waste for another 4 per cent, while hydropower makes up 2 per cent of total consumption. In the light of the fast economic growth, Malaysia has been heavily reliant on oil and natural gas. As a result, the government has been making encouraging investment in renewable energy to achieve more balance (ACE 2009).

For energy resources within the country, Malaysia has been encouraging oil and gas exploration and production projects in a series of incentives ever since 2010. The country is also set to become a regional oil storage, trading and development hub – although with potential disputes with China, Vietnam and the Philippines due to initiatives in the South China Sea (EIA 2013).

3.6 Myanmar

Myanmar's main energy use is biomass-energy centred with wood alone accounting for 70 per cent of all primary energy supply in 2009, which is almost four times the second most important source, natural gas. Despite Myanmar's relatively low levels of energy access, with only 22 per cent of its population being connected to electricity, the country does possess significant energy resources (UNDP 2013). Coupled with the fact that traditional biomass is used mostly, covering three quarters of total energy consumption, the recent "opening" of the country allowing new opportunities to the world (energy) market, there have been recent efforts to invest more in hydroelectric, gas and coal. In this, China is set to become a partner in two other planned natural gas projects, one of which is to construct twin oil and gas pipelines from the port of Kyaukphyu to Kumming in southwestern China (WEF et al. 2013).

In terms of oil, the country produces a minimal volume of crude oil from two basins (on and offshore). Thus, with limited production and refining capacity, the country relies heavily on net oil imports. Natural gas on the other hand has increased in production in recent years to 420 billion cubic feet in 2011 with exports to Thailand accounting for 75 per cent of Myanmar's natural gas output (SEE 2013).

3.7 The Philippines

The total primary energy consumption in the Philippines is dominated by oil at around 40 per cent of the total, with coal following at 20 per cent. The rest comes from biomass and waste making up 20 per cent, then natural gas and renewable sources adding up the final 20 per cent. Over the past few decades, the average annual growth rate of the country's primary energy consumption has moved beyond 2 per cent.

The Philippines is a net energy importer, which is interesting considering its low consumption relative to its neighbours. For the energy resource, while the archipelago produces a small volume of oil, natural gas and coal, geothermal, hydropower and other renewable sources constitute a significant share of electricity generation. The total oil production in 2012 reached 25,000 barrels a day and Shell and Petron are the two key players in oil exploration and production in the Philippines. The domestic production of (dry) natural gas reached 102 billion cubic feet in 2011 with all consumed domestically. In terms of coal, half of the production is used domestically and the rest is imported. In this, coal consumption in the Philippines is projected to rise due to domestic supply and calls for coal-fired power plants (KPMG 2013).

3.8 Singapore

Singapore's total energy consumption, including the energy use in the international aviation sector, grew at the rate of around 5 per cent annually from the early 1990s to the late 2000s. In this, the country is heavily dependent on petroleum use, mostly in the refining and petrochemical industries and it is key to its economy. The oil product was the most consumed product in the early 1990s which accounted for around 85 per cent of the total energy consumption, and then declined to around 80 per cent in the late 2000s (ACE 2011).

In terms of energy resources, Singapore has no coal and renewable resources. Largely, the country is dependent on Indonesia and Malaysia for its natural gas imports for power generation. As a result, the government has launched many energy-saving programmes such as the Energy Efficiency National Partnership programme (in 2010) to help companies create energy-management systems to improve energy efficiency (ACE 2009).

3.9 *Thailand*

Due to limited domestic resources, Thailand imports nearly 68 per cent of its crude oil and most of its coal supply. Thailand's primary energy consumption is mostly based on fossil fuels at around 80 per cent with oil accounting for around 40 per cent of total energy consumption (ACE 2011). This is, however, down nearly half since 2000 as natural gas is replacing oil with nearly a third share in total energy consumption. Despite having large proven natural gas reserves (especially in the gulf of Thailand), the country is still dependent on gas imports (around 28 per cent from its neighbouring country, Myanmar) due to heavy demand. Other types of fuel apart from oil are indigenous energy resources such as coal and biomass.

To meet growing energy demands domestically, the production of gas as an energy commodity has been speeding up in recent years. As a result of this, natural gas and coal are therefore projected to be the largest energy sources with the shares of oil and diesel power plants projected to decrease in the near future. Solid biomass and waste have always been and still are playing a strong role in the community, especially for those in the countryside.

3.10 *Vietnam*

As the third largest country in ASEAN after Indonesia and the Philippines in terms of population, Vietnam's energy demand has been increasing at a rapid rate to keep up with the fast economic growth, industrialisation and expansion of the export market. The remarkable economic development has been achieved in Vietnam through the adoption of the "Doi Moi" (Reform) policy employed in 1986. From this, Vietnam was also successful in domestic energy resource development through foreign investment. As a result, the country has remarkably moved from being an energy importer to an exporter in 1990 (ACE 2011).

The country is a net exporter of crude oil, but also a net importer of oil products with oil consumption doubling from 2000 to 2012. Although the majority of refined products are imported, Vietnam is quickly becoming a key oil and natural gas producer in the ASEAN region. The government boosted exploration by allowing more foreign investment in the oil and gas sectors resulting in greater market-oriented reforms – this allowed sustainable growth in the production of oil and gas. The proven crude oil reserves in Vietnam account for 4.4 billion barrels, which makes the country the 3rd largest holder of crude oil reserves in Asia – after China and India. Currently, Vietnam manages to produce 364,000 barrels a day – primarily in the Cuu Long Basin area where the only refinery in the country is located. In this, Petro-Vietnam is the key company in the oil and gas sector, having formed partnerships with ExxonMobil, Chevron and Zarubezhneft (IEA 2013). Despite the fact that Vietnam is currently considered to be an energy producer with the country holding large oil reserves and being gas self-sufficient, predictions foresee demand surpassing supply.

4 Regional cooperation on energy security

For the last few decades, high energy prices, especially soaring prices of oil (as the main energy source), has been the feature. Together with geopolitical events threatening oil fields, there is a certain level of vulnerability in the energy sector worldwide. In Southeast Asia, such instability and potential disruptions will slow the economic development of ASEAN at both the national and regional levels. Regional energy cooperation has been flagged by leaders of the region as the main issue for ASEAN, and leaders have been working together in recent years to identify energy security issues. Based on the visions to achieve energy security in the region, the regional energy structure plan can be summarised as follows (areas of cooperation):

- development and exploration of new energy sources and supplies;
- diversification of the energy variety and promotion of alternative fuel;
- facilitating energy efficiency and conservation (with an emphasis on demand side measures, energy savings and energy efficient technologies);
- promotion of renewable energy such as hydro, solar, wind power and bio-fuels from palm oil, sugar cane and coconut;
- strengthening emergency response coordination in case of energy supply disruption.

(ASEAN 2013)

ASEAN has also been drafting the ASEAN Plus Three Oil Stockpiling Roadmap as of August 2008, approved by the 5th AMEM Plus Three in Bangkok, Thailand. There were four principles to it: (1) voluntary and non-binding; (2) mutual benefit and respect; (3) respect for bilateral and regional cooperation; and (4) step-by-step approach with a long-term perspective (ACE 2009). This project falls under the ASEAN Plus Three Cooperation with ACE and Japan Oil, Gas and Metals National Cooperation as the secretariats. The aim here is to enhance energy security to sustain the economies in the region (ACE 2013c). However, as with other ASEAN documents and agreements, this project is equally open and non-binding to keep the rule of non-interference in internal matters and a ten-member rule in ASEAN policies.

ACE plays a key role in the regional integration of energy policies. Established in 1999, this intergovernmental organisation guided by the Governing Council is composed of senior officials on energy of member states as well as representatives from the ASEAN Secretariat. The organisation hopes to accelerate integration of energy strategies within ASEAN and to encourage economic growth and development in the region. Its task is to initiate, coordinate and facilitate regional, joint and collective activities. ACE coordinates different forums through the ASEAN Plan of Action for Energy Cooperation (1999–2004) with others, including:

- Heads of ASEAN Power Utilities/Authorities;
- ASEAN Council on Petroleum;
- ASEAN Forum on Coal;

- Energy Efficiency and Conservation Sub-Sector Network;
- New and Renewable Sources of Energy Subsector Network.

(ASEAN 2013)

Through energy cooperation plans, a new ASEAN Petroleum Security Agreement and Annex on Coordinated Emergency Response Measures have been drawn up. The two aim to help enhance the supply of petroleum to member states by raising the quality of energy supply through greater competition. In this, ASEAN Vision 2020 promises an establishment of an interconnection for electricity and gas through the APG and TAGP (ACE 2013c). From the current 11 bilateral power interconnection projects, the APG and TAGP hope to bring about cheaper electricity for all member countries and contribute not only to the sustainability of energy resources, but also energy efficiency (IEA 2007).

5 The Trans-ASEAN Gas Pipeline

Learning from various gas pipeline (network) projects in other regions of the world, namely Europe, Russia, North America (where gas is transmitted between Canada, Mexico and the US) and West Africa (gas pipelines connecting Benin, Ghana, Nigeria and Togo) – the TAGP is considered by many to be a leading project for ASEAN energy integration (see Figure 7.1). Estimated to be worth several billion dollars, this massive energy development project comprises several gas pipelines across ten countries in an area of around 4.5 million square kilometres connecting over 600 million people of ASEAN (ACE 2008). The advocates of TAGP suggest that the network could eventually connect to gas markets in the wider region, the likes of China, Japan or India, which would then become the largest pipeline system in the world, worth an estimated 93.6 billion dollars. This rosy and ambitious image aside, the project will prove to be difficult and tricky to accomplish given the financing issues and different energy interests within ASEAN (Sovacool 2009b).

According to Asia-Pacific Review 2003, there are a number of more specific key issues to be addressed in the development and management of the TAGP, namely:

- financing – the costs of construction and maintenance will be huge;
- technical specifications – the integrated network needs harmonised standards and protocols for construction, operation and maintenance;
- access and use – effective and stable contractual arrangements are needed for the supply;
- security of supply arrangements – measures to ensure uninterrupted flows of gas through the network;
- health, safety and environment – concerns for the livelihoods of people and environmental sustainability along the route of the TAGP;
- transit rights – acceptable measures facilitating the issue of permits, licenses, consents or other authorisations;
- taxation and tariff – harmonisation of taxation, tariffs, subsidies, controls on rate of return and other fiscal terms;

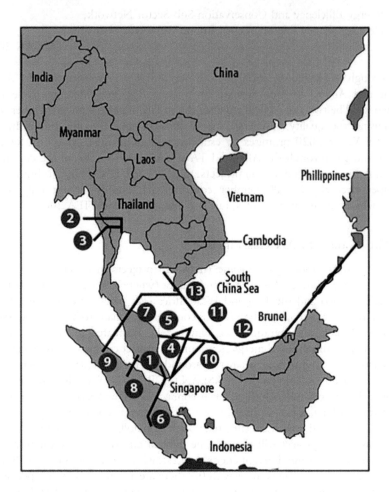

Figure 7.1 Map of the proposed Trans-ASEAN Gas Pipeline
Key: 1 Malaysia to Singapore (commissioned 1991); 2 Myanmar (Yadana) to Thailand
(Ratchaburi) (commissioned 1999); 3 Myanmar (Yetagun) to Thailand (Ratchaburi)
(commissioned 2000); 4 Indonesia (West Natuna) to Singapore (commissioned 2001);
5 Indonesia (West Natuna) to Malaysia (Duyong) (commissioned 2002); 6 Indonesia
(Grissik) to Singapore (commissioning scheduled 2003); 7 Thailand (joint development
area) to Malaysia (commissioning scheduled 2005); 8 Indonesia (South Sumatra) to
Malaysia (commissioning estimated 2005); 9 Indonesia (Arun) to Malaysia (commission-
ing estimated 2010); 10 Indonesia (East Natuna and West Natuna) to Malaysia (Kerteh)
and Singapore (commissioning estimated 2010); 11 Indonesia (East Natuna) to Thailand
(JDA-Erawan) (commissioning estimated 2012); 12 Indonesia (East Natuna) to Malaysia
(Sabah) and the Philippines (Palawan-Luzon) (commissioning estimated 2015); 13
Malaysia–Thailand (joint development area) to Vietnam (Block B) (commissioning estimated
2016).
Source: Redrawn from ACE map and information.

- abandonment – environmental obligations to ensure long-term commitments; and
- jurisdiction – maintenance of the principle of territorial integrity.

By connecting the gas markets in ASEAN together, ideally the TAGP should in turn integrate upstream components (drilling platforms and exploratory rigs) with downstream components (refineries and sweetening facilities) by directly linking gas fields with processing and enrichment centres, power plants and industrial users (Sovacool 2010). In effect, the project should mitigate monopoly control of gas reserves by any one company or country since gas would be flowing into the pipelines from a variety of suppliers and out of it to a variety of countries.

Despite talks and plans of the TAGP in the past two decades, much of the pipeline system proposed has not yet been put in place. There are some pipelines operating between Indonesia, Malaysia, Myanmar, Thailand and Singapore, but due to a lack of real interest and investment from banks/financiers, the project has failed to move as planned. Given that the TAGP is considered to be at the heart of regional energy cooperation of ASEAN, such a problem becomes collective. Thus, the TAGP might just turn out to be the test case of how far ASEAN's rhetoric of regionalism can be realised in practice (Sovacool 2009b).

5.1 Existing infrastructure

Prior to the finalisation of the TAGP Master Plan in 2001, the first cross-border gas pipeline in ASEAN was already in operation from 1991. This was a gas pipeline from Plentong, Johor, Malaysia to Senoko power plant in Singapore (see Figure 7.2). Five other cross-border gas pipelines in development/operation with a total pipeline length of 1,575 km followed (Wu et al. 2014). Today, there are 12 cross-border gas pipelines in operation with a total gas pipeline length of more than 3,000 km, including the latest one being a 150 km new pipeline connection from Myanmar to Thailand completed in 2013 (ACE 2013b).

Although only about 45 per cent or around 3,169 km of the total TAGP pipeline connections planned will be in operation by 2015, these initial achievements have shown great potential, making it possible to transmit gas from Myanmar to Vietnam or even to Indonesia (ACE 2013b).

5.2 Future development

The East Natuna gas resource in Indonesia remains the main source of energy in the ASEAN region for the future, containing about 46 trillion cubic feet in reserve – it is by far the largest in the region (Azwar 2013). As a result, it is not surprising to find that all proposed Trans-ASEAN pipelines require the development of the East Natuna gas field (IGU 2013). Assuming that the gas reserve can be exploited in the future, development of cross-border gas pipelines from East Natuna to various destinations in the ASEAN region would eventually provide a gas price that is affordable and competitive to alternative fuels, such as coal or oil. Requiring investment estimated to be around USD 30 billion, of which USD 24

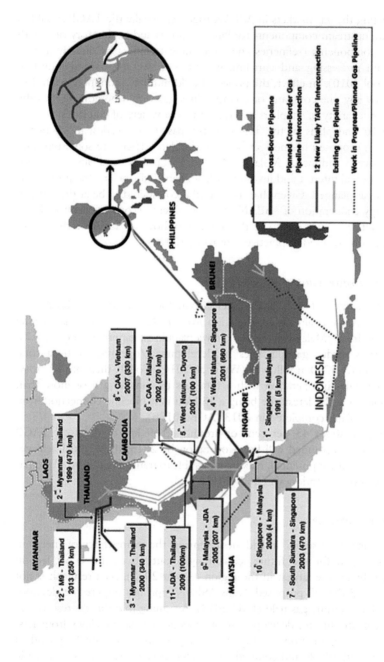

Figure 7.2 Map of the Trans-ASEAN Gas Pipeline in 2013
Source: Redrawn from ACE map and information.

billion is an investment credit, the East Natuna Block will be developed by a consortium of Pertamina, Exxon Mobil Corp and Total E&P Indonesie (ACE 2013b). Therefore, it can be argued that the success of the TAGP is heavily dependent on not only the cooperation of each member country of ASEAN but also those of the oil companies involved.

5.3 Stakeholders' analysis

Several scholars have reviewed the challenges and issues related to the development of the TAGP. One that stands out in terms of stakeholders' analysis of the TAGP project is by Benjamin K. Sovacool, who did extensive interviews with energy companies, oil and gas producers, trading firms, ASEAN with its institutes, government ministries and departments of member states, as well as the World Bank and Asian Development Bank (see Table 7.1). In this, the stakeholders of TAGP are divided into four categories – governments, corporations, banks and financiers and regional organisations.

From 121 semi-structured interviews with more than 40 representatives of institutions involved with the TAGP project during the period between September 2007 and December 2008, Sovacool managed to derive a set of eight interests. This set includes the major stakeholders but excludes elements of civil society, private-sector finance, university research institutes, consultants and interest groups that could also exert influence on the TAGP. Even without the latter group of even more diverse interests, the eight interests summarised in Table 7.2 clearly highlight the different interests that drive each stakeholder to be involved in the TAGP project.

5.4 Key issues to consider in taking the TAGP forward

Given that gas is the primary source in day-to-day power generation (especially electric) in all areas of life, it is clear that the TAGP would increase the level of economic activity which in turn would generate jobs and raise income for ASEAN's populations. The main concern is however in the fact that it is still difficult to estimate the exact amount of gas reserves in the region. Any assumption that the supply will always be there to meet the demand could fade quickly with rapid increases in consumption.

With climate change problems due to the usage of fossil fuels becoming more and more apparent, many researchers consider gas to be a much cleaner choice as gas creates less CO^2 and pollutants than other type of fuel – 25 to 30 per cent less than oil and 40 to 45 per cent less than coal (EIA 1998). Thus, this is one major environmental benefit for the development of the TAGP, although this benefit must be balanced against the potential danger and damage of natural gas projects to natural habitat and ecosystems by land degradation. Furthermore, gas projects also produce highly toxic chemicals which pose risks to human health (Waskow and Welch 2005).

Table 7.1 The Trans-ASEAN Gas Pipeline stakeholders (list)

Category	Description	Specific stakeholders	Number of stakeholders
Governments	Foreign affairs, economic, trade and energy ministries and departments	The governments of Brunei, Cambodia, Indonesia, Laos, Malaysia, Myanmar, the Philippines, Singapore, Thailand and Vietnam	10
Corporate	Energy companies and corporations needed to explore, extract, produce, refine and distribute natural gas and operate its associated infrastructure	British Petroleum (United Kingdom), ExxonMobil (United States), Chevron (United States), ConocoPhillips (United States), Gulf Indonesia (Indonesia), Keppel Corporation (Singapore), Myanmar Oil and Gas Enterprise (Myanmar), Nippon Oil (Japan), Pertamina (Indonesia), Petronas (Malaysia), PGN (Indonesia), Premier Oil (United Kingdom), PTT (Thailand), Repsol-YPF (Spain), Santos (Australia), SembGas (Singapore), Singapore Power (Singapore), Talisman (Canada), TotalFinalElf (France) and Triton Oil Company (Thailand)	20
Banks and financiers	Multilateral and regional development banks	Asian Development Bank, Japan International Cooperation Agency, Japanese Bank for International Cooperation, International Finance Corporation and World Bank	5
Regional institutions	Southeast Asian multilateral organisations and institutions	ASEAN and Asia-Pacific Economic Cooperation	2

Source: Sovacool 2009a.

Table 7.2 The Trans-ASEAN Gas Pipeline stakeholders (interests)

Stakeholders	Category	Interests
Thailand	Government	To maintain Thailand's commitment to the domestic use of natural gas and diversify domestic supply. To promote sustainable development and social responsibility. To attract foreign investment and continue the economic recovery from the Asian financial crisis.
Myanmar	Government	To solidify government authority and control through natural gas exports. To use remaining natural gas reserves as a geopolitical bargaining chip.
Petronas (Malaysia)	State-owned energy company	To assist in the strategic management of Malaysia's natural gas reserves and create possible gas export opportunities. To facilitate strong international engagement and technology transfer with other companies. To promote Malaysian-style economic growth and development.
PGN (Indonesia)	State-owned energy company	To accrue natural gas revenues to eventually move beyond pipelines. To expand natural gas supply to keep domestic prices low and extend the delivery of energy services.
ExxonMobil (United States)	Transnational energy corporation	To match global capital with local resources and integrate Southeast Asia with international energy markets.
Asian Development Bank	Multilateral development bank	To utilise natural gas investment to fight poverty and expand private sector development. To promote market liberalisation and restructuring. To increase environmental protection. To enhance regional and sub-regional cooperation.
Japan Bank for International Cooperation	Bilateral development bank	To secure natural gas imports for Japan. To create export opportunities for Japanese construction and consulting firms. To counterbalance Chinese influence in the region.
ASEAN	Regional institution	To create an interconnected network of regional natural gas (and eventually energy and electricity) supply. To facilitate economic growth and development. To enhance peace and stability through regional cooperation.

Source: Sovacool 2009a.

Vast differences in legal structures and frameworks of ASEAN members mean that investors are unsure whether their money will be protected once cross-border disputes arise from unforeseen situations. This could have major effects on the progress of the entire project or even worse stop it from moving ahead completely. The key here is that the individual countries involved need to get their domestic legal structures and frameworks fully in place.

Arguably, the most pressing political challenge to the success of the TAGP is the territorial disputes among ASEAN members. Since the late 1990s, Vietnam, the Philippines, Indonesia, Malaysia and Brunei together with China and Taiwan are involved in claims over natural gas reserves found in East Natuna and the Spratly Islands area (Cossa and Khanna 1997). Apart from this, many ASEAN projects in the past also highlight a lack of commitment and leadership among ASEAN members, often causing delays and postponements

The local development that comes with the TAGP could be significant for job creation and income generation. This can be achieved only if the management incorporates the needs and rights of the communities involved with their construction and operation effectively. Communities should have active participation in decision making concerning the project activities – this is, however, questionable in countries such as Myanmar, Laos and Cambodia.

5.5 Market impact

By filling the gaps between gas supply and demand, the project will undeniably have significant impacts on the region as a whole. According to the International Gas union, the project will enhance the overall integration of gas markets in Southeast Asia, bringing the following benefits:

- augmenting energy supply security and promoting energy diversification to reduce dependence on oil;
- monetising and maximising value of excess indigenous natural gas resources in the region (e.g. Myanmar and Indonesia);
- enhancing foreign income earnings for gas-exporting countries (e.g. for Myanmar and Indonesia);
- creating local gas infrastructure/market and other spin-offs to industrialise the economies in the region;
- promoting the use of natural gas, a more environmentally friendly fuel; and
- promoting regional cooperation to enhance energy security and reduce reliance on energy/gas imports from outside ASEAN, dampening the external effect relating to energy/gas supply uncertainties and gas price volatilities.

(IGU 2013)

Due to differences in the economic structure of each ASEAN nation, the extent to which the TAGP will bring these anticipated benefits to each country will depend mainly on the state of their economy. Other specific factors include energy mix, diversity, domestic gas production and contribution of gas revenue to GDP (ACE 2013b).

6 Energy security in ASEAN

As discussed earlier in the chapter, the meaning of energy security according to ASEAN member states is varied, due to differences in the economic structure of each nation and the development process tied to it. This said, the overriding concern for ASEAN as a region and individual member countries is to ensure energy security in the sense of stability of supply (both quantity and quality) without disruption or resorting to acquire resources through conflicts with other countries. Basic observations of the current economic system with its interdependence on sustainable access to energy allow us to argue that the energy market and stakeholders involved are key to the economic development of the region. To put it simply, these can be divided into public and private identities that include: (1) producing countries, (2) consuming countries and (3) energy companies.

ASEAN countries are increasingly dependent on industrial development. With this form of economic development being energy-driven, mostly oil for electricity, competition for a steady and stable supply of fuel has been fierce in recent years. The rising energy competition among members of ASEAN, mainly Indonesia, Thailand, Malaysia, Singapore, the Philippines and Brunei therefore posts serious challenges to regional energy cooperation, especially in the case of interrelated issues such as inflation, economic slowdown and fiscal constraints.

The scale of differences in terms of energy resources, demands and interests among the ASEAN members as highlighted in the earlier sections is rather diverse. This means that a consensus on an integrated ASEAN energy market will certainly not come easily. For instance, in terms of demands, Indonesia as the region's largest energy user (36 per cent) consumes 66 per cent more energy than Thailand as the second-largest user in ASEAN, and over 50 times more than Brunei Darussalam which has the lowest consumption among members (IEA 2013). In terms of resources, on the other hand, despite the fact that Indonesia and Thailand possess rich natural resources, their actual consumption needs are significantly higher and in contrast with Brunei who is self-sustainable through its oil export. Similar to Indonesia and Thailand but virtually without natural resources to rely upon, Singapore has been struggling to meet its domestic energy demands. It is not surprising therefore to find that these three ASEAN tigers are working toward finding new ways of cooperation within the region. In this, while Thailand and Indonesia are planning to diversify their electricity sectors, Singapore is aiming to become the "oil and gas refining hub" of ASEAN (Institute of Southeast Asian Studies 2009).

Recent economic expansions in ASEAN have not only highlighted the movements of energy sectors in those richer member countries (ASEAN Six – Brunei, Indonesia, Malaysia, the Philippines, Thailand and Singapore), but also those of poorer member countries (ASEAN Four – Cambodia, Laos, Myanmar, Vietnam). For instance, Myanmar, the poorest and least developed member with a controversial government in terms of transparency, has been in intensive energy cooperation with China and its neighbour Thailand for a few years. This has resulted from the country being more open to the rest of the world with ambition for reform. As a result, Myanmar's massive hydropower and natural gas capacities are currently one of the most lucrative on the world energy market. Similarly, great potentials are being seen in other less-developed ASEAN members, Cambodia and Laos. Although not as rich in terms of natural resources when compared to Myanmar, both have much to offer. While Laos is bound to 11 lower Mekong dam projects to generate hydropower (so far mainly for Thailand and China), Cambodia's mineral resources have remained largely unexplored with the possibility of oil and gas reserves (ACE 2009).

The stakes in ASEAN regional energy cooperation are high also for Malaysia as the country finds itself "somewhere in the middle" with its energy consumption, being the 3rd largest in ASEAN. Despite rich oil and gas reserves allowing them to export, growing domestic demands mean that the Malaysian government also aims to become a major energy hub of the region (through exploration of its own capacities, or cooperation with other regional partners, particularly for energy transport, to ease costs) (IEA 2013). Such energy cooperation would also be beneficial to member countries such as Vietnam and the Philippines. This is due to the fact that both countries, like Indonesia and Thailand, are heavily dependent on energy imports with rapid rises in domestic energy demands.

An important indicator when looking at stakes of ASEAN members is not only the resources-exports realm, but also overall access to electricity. This varies so widely that large-scale energy integration through energy projects on a regional level that accounts for all members' interests would greatly help move the region forward. Of course, this is much easier said than done.

Looking beyond the region, the energy security approach may include countries from the "Plus Three" countries as well (under the cooperation framework of ASEAN Plus Three). This includes China, as the second biggest economy in the world, which accounts for 12.1 per cent of the world's energy consumption (the US is at 24 per cent), Japan and South Korea as the second- and sixth-largest energy importers in the world, respectively. China's ambition of pushing their development through trade liberalisations has meant that its demand of oil has increased by 4.9 percent annually (compared to the world average of 1.9 percent) (CIA 2013). Japan and South Korea both import almost all of their energy to cope with surging consumption within the countries. This has meant that for the last few decades, securing energy has been one of the top priorities of these "Plus Three" countries (Park 2013).

7 The role of ASEAN Plus Three

Following the 1997 Asian financial crisis, the process of ASEAN Plus Three (APT) cooperation began with the ten ASEAN members and the Plus Three countries (China, Japan and Korea) agreeing to work together to make the region stronger economically, politically and socially. Since then, APT cooperation has broadened and deepened with cooperation in the areas of politics and security; transnational crime; trade and investment; finance; tourism; food, agriculture, fishery and forestry; minerals; small and medium enterprises; information and communication technology; energy; environment and sustainable development; poverty alleviation, promotion and development of vulnerable groups; culture and people-to-people contact; education; science and technology; public health; and disaster management (ASEAN Secretariat 2014).

Today, it is clear that despite the differences in their own economies, the power and influence of the Plus Three (China, Japan and Korea) in the ASEAN network is clear. This is highlighted in activities through both bilateral cooperation with individual members and regional cooperation in the ASEAN Plus Three networks. The thirst for new energy sources to fuel economic growth and/or rising consumption in the Plus Three countries has also resulted in efforts to reach new energy cooperation, again both bilaterally and regionally. The greater energy integration of ASEAN therefore offers new opportunities for these East Asia countries to secure energy sources from their Southeast Asian neighbours and have extensive ties to a potential new player on the world's energy market. Such new opportunities, however, create difficult situations due to competitive relationships between China, Japan and Korea, with their race for influence in the region. Thus, the question of whether APT cooperation will thrive in the energy sector will therefore depend very much on how beneficial it will be to the national energy interests of China, Japan and Korea.

The first consultations between ASEAN and the Plus Three countries took place in 2002 resulting in the APT energy ties of today through a summarised five-point programme with various components (USAID 2005):

- the creation of an emergency network;
- the development of oil stockpiling;
- joint studies on the ASEAN oil market;
- the improvement of natural gas development;
- the improvement of energy efficiency and renewable energy.

Building on APT energy ties, the ASEAN Ministers on Energy Meeting was held in Langkawi in July 2003. The meeting called for intensified cooperation in the development and exploitation of the energy resource potentials in the ASEAN region, as well as in attracting private-sector participation and investment in the ASEAN energy sector. In this, the ministers agreed to work collectively in moving forward the TAGP and the ASEAN Power Grid projects to provide greater stability and security of energy supply in the ASEAN region (ASEAN Secretariat 2013). More recently, at the 8th AMEM Plus Three (September 2013) in Phnom Penh, ASEAN ministers have pointed towards balancing energy security with economic competitiveness along environmental sustainability promising to strengthen commitment to the APT energy cooperation towards a sustainable energy future (ACE 2013a).

As the process of APT integration moves forward, the picture is becoming clearer in terms of the Plus Three's influences within the region. China already actively participates in numerous bilateral agreements with several ASEAN member countries and is playing a central role in terms of investments in the less-developed ASEAN members. Some of these agreements include exploration projects of energy resources in Myanmar, dam-building projects on Mekong connected to Cambodia and Laos (Wu et al. 2014). Japan has also been extremely active mainly through the Ministry of Economy, Trade and Industry, where consultations were established in the year 2000. Their activities have been mainly through the Regional Energy Policy and Planning Sub-Sector Network (ASEAN Sustainable Energy 2014) with country assistance in developing the ASEAN Energy Database on the website of ACE and in numerous other projects focused on energy analysis and regional approaches to the energy sector (USAID 2005). Korea, on the other hand, has been trying to secure energy resources by helping various ASEAN member countries with technical expertise through infrastructure development and encouraging dialogue on sustainable energy (Koyama 2013).

The overall discussion of cooperation through the APT network in terms of energy clearly highlights the importance of the Plus Three. For instance, the ambitious TAGP is such a huge project that it does not only depend on much needed investment but also improvement on both the management and technology infrastructure which will benefit from expertise provided by the Plus Three countries. The involvement of the East Asia trio in the ASEAN TAGP project will involve elements of cooperation and competition. Japan may have a key advantage in being part of the main stakeholders with several banking institutions taking part, China and Korea will want to get involved as they are already holding some of the bilateral agreements. These will be testing times not only for ASEAN Plus Three integration but also for the development of the ASEAN network as a whole, as competitive tension will rise among the Plus Three economic giants.

8 Thinking ahead and beyond

Once completed, the TAGP has great potential of expansion outside the borders of ASEAN. To many analysts, the idea of extending the gas pipelines from Myanmar, Laos or Vietnam to the southern Chinese provinces is not at all unrealistic. In fact, the Asian Development Bank has already had this in mind with Yunnan province being part of its Greater Mekong Sub Region Program focusing on economic cooperation, including the energy sector (ACE 2013b, 2013a). Furthermore, Thailand has already signed an agreement to import power from China's Yunnan, thus, the pipeline could lead from Yunnan through south China and then up north to near Shanghai. This could potentially develop into another cooperation project connecting East Asia to West Asia. Although these are hypothetical scenarios, the TAGP once/if fully completed and operational will be a strong foundation for ASEAN and its partners from the wider region to work towards extending this network for mutual benefits.

Rapid economic development within the ASEAN region during the past few decades has resulted in huge increases in energy demands across all member countries of the region. Although the energy mix in terms of resources and consumption is varied from country to country, it is clear that all are increasingly concerned about their energy needs. In this, while the more developed ASEAN Six (Brunei, Indonesia, Malaysia, the Philippines, Singapore and Thailand) view energy security to be a key factor to fuel their economic ambitions, the less-developed ASEAN Four (Cambodia, Laos, Myanmar and Vietnam) see it to be an important aspect of their daily lives. Therefore, the increasing demands for energy in ASEAN overall come from both economic and social drivers – with high economic growth and fast urbanisation as consequences of the region taking the road of capitalist industrialisation.

In an effort to overcome their heavy reliance on Middle East oil, the ASEAN members have turned to their neighbours for energy cooperation. This has led to an ambitious project, the Trans-ASEAN Gas Pipeline Master Plan, which is considered to be the backbone in the process of the region's energy integration. To outsiders, the project is seen to be the toughest test case of how ASEAN's rhetoric of regional cooperation and integration would fare in practice. Its extensive pipeline networks covering several countries are not only cost-intensive but also labour-intensive in term of construction and operation, involving many stakeholders. The success of the project therefore is up to the actors involved to compromise, invest, construct, operate and manage – to integrate Southeast Asia into one energy region. The initial phase in the building of what would eventually become one of the largest integrated natural gas pipeline networks in the world has already been achieved with a number of stakeholders including governments, corporations, banks and multilateral institutions both in ASEAN and ASEAN Plus Three, who have invested substantial financial, human and natural resources.

Whether the TAGP will be a success as envisioned only time will tell as there are several hurdles yet to be cleared. As Tables 7.1 and 7.2 show, there are complex interests among the powerful stakeholders; the project will remain to be an arena full of conflict and compromise as it develops. The mutual benefits, however, are too high for anyone to want to be left behind as the TAGP continues to present great opportunities politically, economically and socially for the actors involved – whether it will be to promote economic growth and development, attract foreign investment, secure a scarce resource or enhance political control. And if the TAGP becomes a reality, cooperative relations plus a secure energy situation may well lead to a more stable ASEAN Plus Three region.

References

ACE. 2008. *ASEAN Plan of Action for Energy Cooperation 2010–2015.* Jakarta: ACE.
ACE. 2009. *ASEAN's Perspectives on Energy Security and Expectations towards an Enhanced Regional Cooperation Mechanism.* Jakarta: ACE.
ACE. 2011. *The 3rd ASEAN Energy Outlook: The Energy Data and Modelling Center.* Jakarta: ACE.
ACE. 2013a. *ASEAN Energy Outlook.* Jakarta: ACE.
ACE. 2013b. *Development of ASEAN Energy Sector.* Jakarta: ACE.
ACE. 2013c. *Ensuring Energy Security in ASEAN.* Jakarta: ACE.

ASEAN. 2013. *ASEAN Statistical Cooperation.* Available at: www.asean.org/resources/ca tegory/asean-statistics-2.

ASEAN Secretariat. 2013. *ASEAN Ministers on Energy Meeting (AMEM).* ASEAN Secretariat. Available at: www.asean.org/communities/asean-economic-community/ca tegory/asean-ministers-on-energy-meeting-amem.

ASEAN Secretariat. 2014. *ASEAN Plus Three Cooperation.* ASEAN Secretariat, http:// www.asean.org/news/item/asean-plus-three-cooperation.

ASEAN Sustainable Energy. 2014. *Regional Energy Policy and Planning in ASEAN for Sustainable Development.* Available at: www.asean-sustainable-energy.net/dsp_page.cfm? view=page&select=7.

Asia Pacific Review. 2013. "Building the Trans-ASEAN Gas Pipeline". *Asia Pacific Review,* July: 15–20.

Azwar, Amahl S. 2013. "Govt Looks to Approve East Natuna Bid". *Jakarta Post.* Available at: www.thejakartapost.com/news/2013/08/14/govt-looks-approve-east-natuna-bid. html.

Chang, Youngho and Yanfei Li. 2012. "Power Generation and Cross-Border Grid Planning for the Integrated ASEAN Electricity Market: A Dynamic Linear Programming Model". *Energy Strategy Reviews.* 1–8.

CIA. 2013. *The World Fact Book,* Vol. 2013–2014, Langley, VA: Central Intelligence Agency.

Cossa, Ralph A. and Jane Khanna. 1997. "East Asia: Economic Interdependence and Regional Security". *International Affairs,* 73(2): 219–234.

EIA. 1998. *Natural Gas: ssues and Trends.* Washington, DC: US Department of Energy.

EIA. 2013. *International Energy Outlook 2013.* Washington, DC: US Department of Energy.

IEA. 2007. "Contribution of Renewables to Energy Security". In *IEA Information Paper.* Paris: IEA.

IEA. 2013. "Southeast Asia Energy Outlook". In *World Energy Outlook Special Report.* Paris: IEA.

IGU. 2013. "World LNG Report". In *2013 Edition.* Vevey: International Gas Union.

Institute of Southeast Asian Studies. 2009. *Energy and Geopolitics in the South China Sea: Implications for ASEAN and Its Dialogue Partners.* Singapore: Institute of Southeast Asian Studies.

Karki, Shankar K., Michael D.Mann and Salehfar Hossein. 2005. "Energy and Environment in the ASEAN: Challenges and Opportunities". *Energy Policy,* 33: 499–509.

Koyama, Ken. 2013. "Growing Importance of ASEAN+3 Energy Cooperation". *A Japanese Perspective on the International Energy Landscape,* March (special bulletin).

KPMG Global Energy Institute. 2013. *The Energy Report: Philippines: Growth and Opportunities in the Philippine Electric Power Sector.* Tokyo: KPMG Global Energy Institute.

Park, Sungwoo. 2013. *South Korea Seeks Broad Fuel Base for Energy Security.* Available at: www. bloomberg.com/news/2013-10-16/south-korea-seeks-broad-fuel-base-for-energy-securit y-yoon-says.html.

SEE. 2013. *Innovations for Sustainable and Secure Energy.* Available at: www.seeforum. net/countryreport/index.html.

Sovacool, Benjamin K. 2009a. "A Critical Stakeholder Analysis of the Trans-ASEAN Gas Pipeline (TAGP) Network". *Land Use Policy,* 27: 788–797.

Sovacool, Benjamin K. 2009b. "Energy Policy and Cooperation in Southeast Asia: The History, Challenges, and Implications of the Trans-ASEAN Gas Pipeline (TAGP) Network". *Energy Policy,* 37: 2356–2367.

Sovacool, Benjamin K. 2010. *The Routledge Handbook of Energy Security*. Hoboken, NJ: Taylor and Francis.

UN. 2013. *Cambodia Energy Sector Strategy*. Available at: www.un.org/esa/agenda21/na tlinfo/countr/cambodia/energy.pdf.

UNDP. 2013. *Accelerating Energy Access for all in Myanmar*. New York: United Nations Development Programme.

USAID. 2005. "Case Studies of Regional Energy Cooperation Programs: APEC and ASEAN". *Energy for South Asia*, January.

Vongchanh, Kinnaleth. 2013. *The Need for Sustainable Renewable Energy in Lao PDR*. Available at: www.seeforum.net/countryreport/laopdr.html.

Waskow, D. and C. Welch. 2005. "The Environment, Social, Human Rights Impacts of Oil Development". In S. Tsalik and A. Schriffrin (eds), *Covering Oil: A Reporter's Guide to Energy and Development*. New York: Open Society Institute, 101–23.

WEF, Asian Development Bank and Accenture. 2013. *New Energy Architecture: Myanmar*. Tokyo: WEF, Asian Development Bank and Accenture.

Wu, Yanrui, Fukunari Kimura and Xunpeng Shi. 2014. *Energy Market Integration in East Asia: Deepening Understanding and Moving Forward*. Abingdon: Routledge.

8 ASEAN cooperation on marine environment

Soparatana Jarusombat

1 Introduction

Southeast Asia is a region endowed with abundant natural resources; however, the situation of many environmental sources is currently in a stage of deterioration. According to the ASEAN 4th State of the Environment Report (2009), Southeast Asia has one of the fastest rates of deforestation in the world (around 1.11 per cent from the global average of 0.16 per cent annually); the mangrove areas were reduced by 18 per cent between 1980 and 2005. The same report highlighted that an estimated 88 per cent of coral reefs are threatened by human activities; the high volume of illegal wildlife trade could wipe out between 13 and 42 per cent of the region's plant and animal species in this century; most of the region's main rivers are reported to be polluted; the marine fish stock had fallen by 50 per cent; air pollution levels in Southeast Asian cities were amongst the highest in the world; and the burning of vegetation related to agriculture often spreads and creates serious trans-boundary haze pollution affecting people in vast areas. The region is also threatened by climate-change consequences like the rise of sea levels, downward trend of rainfall and the emergence of various natural disasters.

Since most Southeast Asian countries (except Singapore) are developing countries and there is still a high percentage of the population living in poverty and depending on agriculture and fishing, the resulting tension between economic development, sustaining basic livelihoods of the rural poor and environmental protection is a serious problem for ASEAN countries. In particular, how to promote the sustainable development of natural resources, prevent or alleviate trans-boundary pollution harmful effects and resolve environmental disputes are major challenges faced by ASEAN. In order to tackle these problems more effectively, the ASEAN environmental cooperative mechanism needs to be further enhanced.

This chapter aims to explore possible approaches to promote sustainability and ocean governance in this region. Based on the concept of sustainable development and the strengths and deficiencies of the current cooperation, a procedural perspective is taken to discuss the future development of the ASEAN cooperation mechanism on marine environment. The procedural approach is useful in highlighting the concerns at any given point in time, allowing the reader to understand how effectiveness is built gradually and highlighting what else needs to be done.

1.1 The need for regional cooperation to address environmental problems

Environmental problems are a type of non-traditional security threat to human-kind that creates worldwide effects. People in different parts of the world will be suffering from the impact of environmental problems as their impacts are not restricted to a specific territory. Since environmental problems have severe world-wide impacts, international organisations such as the United Nations remain very active in issuing environmental policies and agendas related to the environment. However, collaboration on environmental issues should also exist at the regional level. As ASEAN country members realise that Southeast Asia is among the regions that are highly vulnerable to environmental impacts, they have become more active in responding to the issue. Solving the problem of the environment in specific countries may not be the only effective solution as there are trans-boundary environment issues to manage. In addition, it would be considerably difficult for ASEAN to achieve the goal of creating prosperity if environmental problems remain unsolved. If societal well-being remains a basic goal of nations, then the rising standards of living which comes from development must also be assessed alongside public health issues which are tied to environmental problems. It can be said that environmental concerns impact many dimensions of human well-being. Without the well-being of the people in ASEAN, it may be impossible that ASEAN will grow strong and that will definitely become a barrier for the unity of ASEAN country members in the present and future. The central feature of environmental management is that it depends on people's habits and activities, both economic and non-economic. Besides promoting the concept of ASEAN unity in diversity, it is time to create ASEAN people's awareness toward the problem of environment. Creating awareness is a crucial step that will lead to the success of regional environmental policy implementation. When citizens of ASEAN countries are educated about the impacts and become aware that there is an urgent need to respond to the problem, people will be more eager to participate in activities that help to reduce greenhouse gas emission, which is one of the most significant causes of environmental degradation.

At the country level, if ASEAN country members established a strong colla-borative network for tackling environmental problems, it would be of benefit for the region and the world as a whole. On the other hand, if the problem of the environment is overlooked, it would lead to the suffering of the ASEAN and global population in the near future. A firm collaborative partnership of ASEAN country members will lead to an effective solution for the environmental issue. The important question is whether ASEAN country members promptly and effectively combat environmental problems.

Several studies have recognised the significance of regional organisations in effectively addressing the issue and it is fitting to examine how ASEAN, as an organisation that is often highlighted as a model region of cooperation among developing countries, is combating this security issue.

Elliott (2003) stressed the need for environmental cooperation in Southeast Asia for two reasons: first, she noted that the ASEAN Secretariat observed in its review of functional cooperation in 1994, any drastic irreversible reduction in the region's resources will have far-reaching implications to the region's quality of life; second, environmental cooperation somehow leads to a constructing (imagining) of a regional identity and therefore confirms the relevance of ASEAN's normative attachment to the principle of the *ASEAN way.*

1.2 Overview of environmental cooperation in ASEAN

"When ASEAN was established in 1967, environmental management was not expressly recognized as a concern" (Koh and Robinson 2011: 4). However, an increased population and rapid economic growth, combined with the existing and region-wide social inequities among the ASEAN countries, have essentially exerted increasing pressures on the natural resources of the region and brought along various common or trans-boundary environmental issues. Under such circumstances, ASEAN has since 1977 cooperated closely in promoting environmental cooperation among its member states and this process has been integrated into ASEAN's complex system of regional consultations on economic, social, technical and scientific development.

ASEAN cooperation on the environment is related to various issues, such as animals, health, energy, natural resources and climate change. ASEAN also focuses on harmonising environmental policies and databases and prioritises the development of environmental education, public participation and environmentally sound technology.

The increasing environmental awareness and ongoing environmental cooperation within ASEAN and the member's states certainly provide a foundation for further extending environmental cooperation to ASEAN's dialogue partners: ASEAN Plus Three (China, Japan and South Korea) and two ASEAN dialogue partners (Australia and New Zealand). Considering the environmental threats faced by ASEAN, the necessity of taking cooperative measures has been recognised by ASEAN countries. Meanwhile, attention should also be paid to the approach that ASEAN uses to promote regional cooperation, namely the *ASEAN way.*

The *ASEAN way,* as a collaborative approach, is derived from global principles and the local, social-cultural and political milieu in Southeast Asia (Nguitragool 2011: 28). Guided by the principle of non-interference in the internal affairs of member states, it relies on consensus building and cooperative programmes rather than legally building treaties and shows a preference to the national implementation of programmes rather than a reliance on a strong region-wide bureaucracy (Koh and Robinson 2011).

Its influence on ASEAN's success and failure is a highly controversial issue. In reality, it seems that the environmental objectives of ASEAN are often surpassed by various narrow self-interests represented by its member states. Within ASEAN, conflicts are dealt with by postponing and evading difficult issues, compartmentalising an issue so that it does not interface with other areas of cooperation, and with quiet diplomacy (Narine 2002: 31). This position suggests that ASEAN is better equipped to deal with issues where members' interests converge than where members have opposing interests. In addition, it is also argued that ASEAN's emphasis on consensus and capacity building is ill-equipped to deal with urgent events. Moreover, even if member states could reach consensus on a specific issue, ASEAN seem to lack measures (punitive or otherwise) to secure an effective compliance, since the consensus reached by member states is not in the form of legally binding agreements. This said, there are merits in continuing to work towards this approach.

This chapter will focus on ASEAN's approach to, and record of managing the common marine environment. The importance of ASEAN's marine environment can be underscored by the fact that ASEAN has a coastline of 173,000 km with a total area of 4.5 million km. This region has 35 per cent of the world's mangrove forests and about 30 per cent of the coral reefs.[1] According to Global Security, "more than half of the world's annual merchant fleet tonnage passes through the Straits of Malacca, Sunda, and Lombok, with the majority continuing on to the South China Sea".[2] And in terms of fishing as an industry and livelihood, the ASEAN Ten countries accounted for a quarter of global fish production. Fish and seafood is a main source of food and livelihood in ASEAN, and in terms of export trade, fishing accounts for a sizeable portion in ASEAN's agricultural product trade with the rest of the world.[3]

1.3 International legal approaches for marine environment protection

To date, many treaties regulating marine pollution have been conducted. Concerning treaty practice, three basic approaches can be identified (Tanaka 2015). The first approach is the source-specific approach. This approach seeks to regulate and control a specified source or substance of marine pollution, such as vessel-source pollution. On a specific substance, such as oil spill, state regulatory practice has shown that from the 1960s to 1970s the majority of global conventions adopted a source-or-substance-specific approach. A typical example may be provided by the International Convention for the Prevention of Pollution from Ships. This instrument seeks to achieve the complete elimination of international pollution from the marine environment from a specific source, that is to say, a vessel. Another important example in this category is the 1972 London Dumping Convention. This Convention, as amended in 1978, 1980, 1989, 1993 and 1996, seeks to prevent marine pollution caused by a specific source, that is to say, dumping at the global level.

With respect to the pollution of the marine environment, the United Nations Convention on the Law of the Sea creates an overarching and general obligation on coastal states to protect and preserve the marine environment. More specifically in the context of pollution from seabed activities, coastal states have an obligation to adopt national laws and take measures to prevent, reduce and control pollution of the marine environment arising from or in connection with seabed activities subject to their jurisdiction and dumping within their jurisdiction.

The second approach is the regional approach which aims to regulate marine pollution within a certain region. The regional treaties adopting this approach cover: the Baltic Sea, the northeast Atlantic, the Mediterranean Sea, the southeast Pacific, the south Pacific, the Caribbean Sea, the West and Central African region, the Red Sea and Gulf of Aden, the Indian Ocean and the Arabian/Persian Gulf. These treaties seek to regulate various sources of marine pollution in a (quasi-)comprehensive manner.

The third approach is the regional source-specific approach, which combines the source-specific approach with the regional approach. A case in point is the 1974 Convention for the Prevention of Marine Pollution from Land-Based Source. This Convention sought to prevent marine pollution from a specific, land-based source, in the northeast Atlantic area. In addition to this, there are several protocols for the regulation of land-based marine pollution in certain regions.

2 Marine environment in Southeast Asia

2.1 Natural resources: fact and figures

Coastal and marine resources provide essential ecological, economic and social services in the ASEAN region. Coastal and marine water serve as sinks for waste from land-based sources, provide livelihood directly and indirectly to millions of people in ASEAN, provide food, maintain water cycles, regulate climate conditions and maintain the complex balance of coastal and marine ecosystems. The marine resources of the region are economically important to most countries. However, the fast-growing economies and populations of Southeast Asia are putting the region's marine ecosystem under increasing stress. A major cause of concern throughout the region is over-fishing and the use of destructive fishing techniques, particularly in the highly diverse coral reef systems. Most fish stocks throughout the region are currently being fully harvested, while some are being exploited at unsustainable levels.

There is a substantial loss of coastal habitats in Southeast Asia as mangroves are used for the construction of shrimp ponds and for paddy rice cultivation. These activities affect, indirectly, commercial demersal fisheries that rely on mangroves as nursery areas. Thailand and the Philippines are typical examples, where some 208,218 hectares and 200,000 hectares (during 1961–93), respectively, were cleared. Coastal construction, particularly for tourist facilities and inland mining, and poor land-use practices have resulted in increased sediment loads in coastal waters in countries such as Malaysia, Indonesia and Thailand. The increased sediment has adverse impacts on sensitive coral reef systems, but in Thailand there has been a significant improvement in the condition of the reefs as a result of the efforts of non-governmental organisations (NGOs) and local people (OEPP 1996).

2.2 Marine pollution

Coastal and marine water pollution in this region is mainly due to direct discharges from rivers, surface run-off and drainage from port areas, domestic and industrial effluent discharges through outfalls and various contaminants from ships. Marine pollution also arises from sea-based activities, including marine transportation and offshore mineral exploration and production activities. Accidental oil spills are frequently reported in this region, e.g., there were 25,000 tons of oil spilled in Singapore on 15 October 1997. Then, on 1 April 2000 about 160,000 kilolitres of oil spill occurred on the southern coast of Central Java, Indonesia and on 22 January 2002, 100,000 litres of oil spilled into Rayong Bay in Thailand. In the Straits of Malacca alone, 490 shipping accidents were reported between 1988 and 1992, resulting in a considerable amount of oil spillage at sea.[4]

2013 has been a bad year for oil spills affecting ASEAN countries, with three separate petro-chemical spills polluting the waters, endangering biodiversity and livelihoods. In Thailand on 27 July 2013, there was an oil spill in which 50,000 litres of oil drenched the beaches of the tourist island Koh Samet. Soon after this came news of a massive spill in Indonesia. On 31 July 2013, an oil tanker carrying a reported 7 million litres of diesel and gasoline ran aground at the Indonesian island of Ternate in the Coral Triangle, an area that covers six Asia Pacific nations and is a top priority for marine conservation. On 9 August 2013, the Philippines awoke to the news of another disaster, with reports of up to half a million litres of diesel spilling into Manila Bay, affecting several coastal towns in Cavite province. A state of emergency has been declared in one town after officials reported the spill has damaged coral reefs and has driven local fishing boats out of the water amid serious contamination of fish catches (Soriano 2013).

The frequency and density of international and regional marine traffic passing through the sea lanes of ASEAN along with numerous development projects which have marine environmental implications require a comprehensive plan of deployment to quickly and effectively contain the inevitable oil spills that threaten its marine environment.

3 Regional initiatives to respond to problems of the marine environment

3.1 Development of ASEAN strategies and programmes

In recent decades, the economic potentiality of Southeast Asia attracts many investors from both inside and outside the region and it has experienced fast-paced economic growth. Natural resources are utilised for accelerating the growth and the polluting rate continues to rise. The lack of an appropriate environmental management system has led to environmental deterioration, which urgently needs to be tackled. Marine pollution is an issue related to environmental deterioration that requires close cooperation among countries in Southeast Asia as it is a threat at regional level. Therefore, ASEAN member countries have developed schemes and frameworks for collaborating on marine pollution.

ASEAN has been working on environmental cooperation, especially on marine pollution, for a few decades. At the first stage, ASEAN country members prioritised cooperation on the security issue. Cooperation on environment did not gain much attention until 1977. The first ASEAN Environmental Program (ASEP) was the starting point of cooperation (Elliott 2003). Cooperation on the area related to marine pollution is also listed in ASEP I. After ASEP I was created, many projects and plans have been implemented.

3.1.1 ASEAN Environmental Program I (1978–82)

In 1977, the Regional Advisory of the United Nations Environment Program (UNEP) met with governments from five ASEAN member countries, including Indonesia, Malaysia, the Philippines, Singapore and Thailand. The information gained from the discussion was beneficial and a drafted programme (ASEP I) was initiated. It mentioned issues that needed firm cooperation. In order to strengthen cooperation among countries, the list of projects and activities were included in the draft. ASEP I emphasised "marine environment; environmental management, including environmental impact assessment; nature conservation and terrestrial ecosystems; industry and the environment; environmental education and training; and environmental information" (Koh 2009). At this stage, marine environment was included in the area of environmental cooperation.

3.1.2 ASEAN Environmental Program II (1983–7)

In 1984 ASEP II was launched. The five existing countries who cooperated in ASEP I continued to collaborate in ASEP II and Brunei expressed its intention about taking part in ASEP II projects and activities, which covered various activities concerning environmental education, e.g., "Development of Prototype Curriculum Materials for Environmental Education (in-school), Development of Curriculum Materials for Non-Formal Education, and Training and Development of Institutional Materials for Environmental Education (in-school)" (ASEAN 2012).

3.1.3 ASEAN Environmental Program III (1988–92)

In 1988–92, UNEP supported the implementation of ASEP III. ASEP III was known as the continual phase of ASEP I and II and its implementation remained a significant step for latter project implementation. It is noticeable that after this period the issue related to environmental concerns and pollution has gained more attention. It could be supported by the time when pollution issues were emphasised in the discussion between the ASEAN Ministerial Meeting on Environment and ASEAN Senior Officials on Environment (ASOEN) as the following indicates: "ASEAN environment ministers agreed to develop minimum regional standards for ambient air and river water quality; they established an ASEAN Urban Air Pollution Monitoring and Control Program and a contingency plan for the control and mitigation of marine pollution" (ASEAN Secretariat 2012).

3.1.4 *Plans and strategies related to marine pollution management*

After the ASEAN Environmental Programs (ASEP I, II and III) were implemented, the ASEAN Strategic Plan of Action was initiated. By providing a forum
for discussion, a platform for developing consensus and a set of education and
training activities, ASEP I, II and III provided the basis for further action.
ASEAN's Hanoi 1998 Plan of Action listing activities to protect the environment
and promote sustainable development has, in particular, actions which were related to the marine environment. Frameworks and regional action plans were also
created as tools to support the cooperation.

3.2 *The evolution of a cooperative and monitoring system*

Cooperation among the ASEAN countries in the field of marine science and
marine environments has been carried out through three distinct regional bodies,
namely, the Coordinating Body on the Seas of East Asia (COBSEA), the ASOEN
Working Group on ASEAN Seas and Marine Environment (WGASME) and the
COST Sub-Committee on Marine Science (SCMS). While WGASME and SCMS
are official ASEAN bodies, the latter being under the purview of the ASEAN
Committee on Science and Technology, COBSEA comes under the purview of
UNEP.

The environmental cooperation in ASEAN is supported by an organisational
structure. To understand environmental cooperation in ASEAN, one needs to
consider the background and function of ASOEN. The establishment of the
agency ASOEN and its operation plan made the environmental programmes
become more systematically organised. ASOEN was formerly called the ASEAN
Expert Group on the Environment, which was created under the ASEAN Committee on Science and Technology in 1978. The creation of the Group marked a
good start to environmental cooperation and in 1989 it changed to be ASOEN.
With functional planning for environmental cooperation, ASOEN members
worked closely and initiated environmental programmes: "The cooperative programs and projects of ASOEN are carried out with the assistance of currently three
working groups and these are the working groups on Nature Conservation and
Biodiversity chaired by the Philippines, Coastal and Marine Environment chaired
by Thailand and Multilateral Environmental Agreements chaired by Malaysia"
(ASEAN 1999). That Thailand has assumed the chair of Coastal and Marine
Environment reflects the country's commitment and key role it will play in this
aspect of the environment.

In addition to the functional planning for environmental cooperation, ten strategic thrusts under the ASEAN Strategic Action Plan on the Environment 1994–8
were developed in 1994, a product from the ASOEN meeting in 1993 in Bangkok. In this case, cooperation on marine pollution was included in "Strategy 6:
promote the protection and management of coastal zones and marine resources"
(ASEAN Strategic Plan of Action 1994). The two sub-issues under this strategy
are "to improve regional marine and coastal environmental coordination and

develop a framework for the integrated management of regional coastal zones"
(ASEAN Strategic Plan of Action 1994).

3.2.1 ASEAN cooperation on marine pollution 2009–15

The balance in ecosystems in the ocean and sea has much impact on coastal and
marine resources. Without appropriate rules and regulations, coastal and marine
resources might be overused. The governments of ASEAN country members were
aware of this issue. They therefore engaged in the plans and programmes for
protecting the coastal and marine environment in the region. Their engagement
was also mentioned in the ASEAN Socio-Cultural Community Blueprint 2009–2015,
which demonstrates that ASEAN has developed a systematic approach for
cooperating on marine pollution.

In 2002 the ASEAN Marine Water Quality Criteria was approved, the purpose
of which was to protect marine waters. The collaboration on marine water is not
limited to ASEAN leaders only; the Australian government also plays a crucial role,
especially in financial and technical terms. With collaboration and assistance from
the Australian government, the ASEAN Marine Water Quality Criteria: Management Guidelines and Monitoring Manual 2008 was distributed (ASEAN Cooperation on Environment 2013). It was considered a mechanism at the regional
level that contained guidelines, monitoring and analytical functions for creating
the sustainability of marine waters. The guidelines reflect objectives that ASEAN
member states share in common. It contained information related to other
approaches that may be applicable to the marine water issues in ASEAN. Also, the
guidelines are created on the basis that they are applicable to all ASEAN member
states as they have some differences in terms of financial status, institution and
human resources. On top of that, monitoring processes, such as data analysis and
reporting, are chosen in accordance with the principle of sustainability. The
guidelines are thus a tool that helps to protect the marine water in the ASEAN
region.

It is essential to note that cooperation on marine pollution needs an integrated
knowledge for tackling the problem. Since marine pollution is trans-boundary, it
requires close collaboration among countries. Therefore, activities have to be
operated by different working groups, such as from the agricultural sector and
marine technology and from different countries in the region.

3.3 Regional mechanisms to protect the marine environment

3.3.1 Marine protected areas in the ASEAN region

Southeast Asia is endowed with rich natural resources that provide food, shelter,
clothing and other biological goods and ecosystems services to over 500 million
people. These vast resources, comprising a regional commons for ASEAN, however, are facing serious threats due to human activities and natural calamities. In
Southeast Asia, the establishment of a marine protected area had long been used

as a means to safeguard the region's natural wealth, as well as regulate their uses. Over the years, the number of marine protected areas has increased both in the terrestrial and marine realms. Based on aggregate current information sources from the World Database on Protected Areas and marine protected area gap analysis reports of ASEAN member states, Thailand registered the highest percentage of marine areas protected at 4.4 per cent, followed by the Philippines (2.5 per cent), Malaysia (2 per cent), Vietnam (1.7 per cent), Brunei Darussalam (1.4 per cent) and Singapore (1.4 per cent), while Myanmar has the smallest marine protected area coverage with only 0.31 per cent (ASEAN Centre for Biodiversity 2010: 1).

The establishment of marine protected areas was officially adopted by the Convention on Biological Diversity (CBD) through its Program of Work on Protected Areas during the Seventh Meeting of the Conference of the Parties in 2004, as a means to reduce biodiversity loss worldwide by at least 10 per cent. The programme's overall objective is for CBD parties to establish and maintain a comprehensive, effectively managed and ecologically representative system of protected areas by 2010 for terrestrial areas and by 2012 for marine areas. This goal is carried over through CBD's Strategic Goal 2020 with a new target of conserving at least 17 per cent of terrestrial and inland waters, and 10 per cent of coastal and marine areas, especially areas of particular importance for biodiversity and ecosystem services. It envisioned that these areas will be conserved through effectively and equitability managed, ecologically representative and well-connected systems of protected areas and other effective area-based conservation measures. Special focus is given to integrating them into the wider landscape and seascapes. The marine protected areas in ASEAN that meet narrowly defined biological goals are generally presented as "successes". However, these same areas may, in fact, be failures when social evaluation criteria are applied (Christie 2004). Moreover, results of various assessments conducted by ASEAN member states also revealed that in spite of increased areas of protection, the loss of biodiversity has not been effectively addressed.

3.3.2 Trans-boundary pollution from offshore oil and gas activities

Exploratory drilling and offshore oil production taking place in the vicinity of maritime boundaries between contiguous states are an obvious source of potential trans-boundary pollution which may be resolved through bilateral measures. In Southeast Asia, however, this concerns a substantial yet minor part of offshore development along the maritime border between Malaysia and Brunei, Malaysia and Indonesia and Vietnam and Malaysia south of the Gulf of Thailand. Pollution from many of the hydrocarbon fields currently in production close to maritime boundaries is likely to involve more than two states. Pollution from production sites in the Gulf of Thailand could for instance involve more than two coastal states due to the geographical characteristics of the respective borders. The same is true of pollution from hydrocarbon sites located in northeast Sabah, where the Philippines coast can be affected as well as Indonesia and Malaysia (Lyons 2012: 5).

Given the number of countries potentially involved, regional cooperation is necessary to establish a transnational regime aimed at preventing pollution from offshore oil and gas activities, and if pollution does occur, to mitigate the impact on the marine environment and ensure compensation for the victims of the ensuing pollution and remediate the environment. The 2004 ASEAN Vietnam Action Program, the 2007 ASEAN Singapore Declaration on Environmental Sustainability and the Roadmap for an ASEAN Community 2009–2015 emphasised the need for coordination in the management and protection of the marine environment.

3.3.3 Oil spill response and preparedness

Southeast Asia has played an important role as a transit route between the Pacific and Indian Oceans, between Japan and other countries of northeast Asia and the Indian Ocean, and between northeast Asia and Australia/New Zealand. Any large spill that occurs in the region can potentially lead to a trans-boundary spill affecting the coasts of neighbouring countries and can therefore require a substantial amount of international cooperation among countries in the region. Governments are aware of this problem and there have been various measures taken to deal with this concern, including the establishment of regional agreements and arrangements. These basically provide a framework that promotes cooperation and facilitates mutual assistance from other countries in the region in the event of an oil spill that exceeds the national response capacity, such as:

- ASEAN Oil Spill Response Plan: in 1993, six ASEAN countries (Brunei, Indonesia, Malaysia, Singapore, the Philippines and Thailand) established the Plan which is aimed at improving the marine oil spill combating capacity of each ASEAN country by providing mutual assistance from member states in the event of an oil spill that exceeds the national response capacity (ASEAN 1993).
- Tripartite Oil Spill Contingency Plan: known as the Standard Operating Procedure for Joint Oil Spill Combat in the Straits of Malacca and drawn up following the establishment of the Revolving Fund and forged in April 1984 among Indonesia, Malaysia and Singapore. The Procedure covers topics such as the response areas and division of responsibility among the littoral states, contact points, communication, information-sharing procedures, inter-state assistance and reimbursement procedures. The objectives are to facilitate early information sharing and prompt a coordinated response to any oil spill incident.

Other regional agreements also exist, including:

- Sulawesi Sea Oil Spill Network Response Plan: in 1980, Indonesia, Malaysia and the Philippines developed the Plan, which aimed to establish a coordinated response system to deal with oil spills in the Straits of Lombok, Makassar and the Sulawesi Sea.

- The Brunei Bay Oil Spill Contingency Plan: in 1994, Brunei and Malaysia developed this Plan to complement Sulawesi Sea Plan and address oil spills in both Brunei and Malaysian waters. The objective was to establish a coordinated oil spill response system to deal with oil spills in the terrestrial waters and exclusion economic zones of the states of Sabah and Sarawak for Brunei and Malaysia. The Brunei Bay Plan covers topics similar to those in the Standard Operating Procedure for Joint Oil Spill Combat in the Straits of Malacca, including the response and communication protocols to facilitate effective inter-state assistance and movement of personnel, craft and equipment across states.
- The Strait of Malacca and Singapore Revolving Fund: in 1981, a memorandum of understanding was signed between the governments of Indonesia, Malaysia, Singapore and the Malacca Strait Council (Japanese NGOs) to establish a resolving fund of 400 million yen. The fund enables the three littoral states to draw cash in advance from the Revolving Fund for use in combating oil pollution caused by ships. The amount drawn will be repaid to the Fund when the state recovers the clean-up costs from the parties responsible.

4 Strengths and weaknesses of the cooperation

Regional cooperation in marine environment is a challenging task, with numerous difficulties even among developed countries. As a region mainly comprised of developing countries and facing fierce competition over natural resources, any progress achieved under ASEAN is not easy and the evolution of ASEAN environmental cooperation is a long process.

From the developments highlighted in the previous sections of this chapter, ASEAN is most effective in developing dialogues and highlighting points of action. Controversial issues remain in environmental management (especially in the area of trans-boundary marine pollution and even the more basic issue of marine territorial disputes), but at this stage, postponing controversial issues requires a realistic and constructive approach. Although dialogue does not result in any direct solution to these complicated problems, it could contribute to trust building among member states, and to promoting inter-state and regional stability, which are crucial in cultivating good will. Moreover, the overall development of marine environmental cooperation could further raise member state and public awareness on marine environmental issues and help ASEAN and its member states gain more experience. Therefore, over the long term, the flexibility of the *ASEAN way* may, in fact, help ASEAN to build a stronger basis for regional action and effective policy making regarding marine environment.

ASEAN seemed to be a model of regionalism with a very well-designed central environmental management structure (ASOEN) and many good strategic plans serving its strong commitment towards sustainable development. However, its past actions appeared not to be that effective for the following reasons.

First, since the ASEAN governing body relies more on national institutions than the central bureaucracy (Elliott 2003), its environmental policies are also dependent on each member state's environmental practices. This situation means that any action from ASEAN is constrained by the state capacity of individual member countries and national environmental values which tend to have a "low-future value" and are reflected in a very weak sense of common ecological identity. These reasons, as well as the poor implementation records for implementing the programmes under the environmental strategic plans, are a result of ASOEN's limited budget allocated to environmental activities and some other institutional failures like poor planning coordination, overlapping and conflicting jurisdictions, understaffing of relevant agencies and a lack of technical and legal expertise. These cause inefficiency in actions regardless of how perfect the plans are.

Second; due to the ASEAN diplomatic norms of "consensus decision-making", "non-interference in a member country's internal affairs" and "the rule of compromise with no-fault-finding", ASEAN failed to produce efficient and strategically meaningful decisions in many policy issues including managing the environment (Mushkat 2003). One good example was the case of an ineffective regional response to the 1997–8 haze caused by forest fires in Indonesia that eventually spread across Southeast Asia. Despite the cooperation plan on transboundary pollution launched to cope with the crisis, the plan was found to be based on volunteerism without any legal instrument to impose any action on the polluters. Following the *ASEAN way* principle, the other victim countries avoided blaming Indonesia and claiming that the haze was Indonesia's legitimate responsibility, but instead provided technical assistance. Other regional strategies or declarations regarding environments were mostly stated as "soft-law" and "non-binding plans" rather than in a form of "treaties". This ASEAN decision-making approach had distinct strengths in flexibility and conflict avoidance but weakness in low efficiency and ineffectiveness.

5 The role and involvement of the Plus Three countries

As East Asia's largest industrial economies, China, Japan and South Korea contribute disproportionately to the marine shipping traffic passing through the Straits of Malacca, Lomba and Sunda. And as wealthy developed countries, these Plus Three countries can contribute financial support, country technical expertise and best practices to marine environmental management in ASEAN.

There are existing collaborative platforms in East and Southeast Asia. Partnerships in Environmental Management for the Seas of East Asia, or PEMSEA, is initiated by UNDP and includes several key ASEAN countries and China, Japan and both North and South Korea.[5] The PEMSEA vision shares many of the same objectives as ASEAN in the protection of the marine environment of the East Asian (broadly defined to include northeast and southeast Asia) seas, including sustainable development and the protection of livelihoods, marine habitat protection and controlling marine pollution. The East Asian Seas Congress, which includes a ministerial forum, is hosted by PEMSEA and can be viewed as a regular forum to highlight and discuss issues related to marine management.

The conflict in the South China Sea claims among the disputed parties are unlikely to be solved in the near future. The issue is not just with territorial claims but the areas of conflict are also rich with oil and fishing resources. In addition, the ten member ASEAN countries have different outlooks with regard to these conflicts. However, as with many of the difficult issues which ASEAN has dealt with in the past, the road ahead has to be dealt with through soft diplomacy channels and viewed from a procedural viewpoint, where small steps are added onto existing platforms.

At present, there are few cooperation mechanisms to protect marine environment and prevent marine pollution in ASEAN. Whether ASEAN+3 can be a driving force for ASEAN to be concerned about this issue or whether the inclusion of three economic giants with their own national interests will complicate the issue remains to be seen.

6 Conclusion and recommendations for future cooperation

The marine environment is truly an ASEAN regional heritage and an important regional commons, a fact that has been recognised from the very beginning of ASEAN cooperation. Among the first actions by the ASEAN countries, with catalytic support from UNEP, was the adoption of an Action Plan for the Protection and Development of the Marine Environment and Coastal Areas of the East Asia Region. The Southeast Asian seas are the natural habitat for 2,500 species of fish and invertebrates. They provide 11 per cent of the world's supply of marine products and are a source of livelihood for many of the region's fishermen. All ASEAN countries have extensive fishing industries. However, many of the major near-shore fishing areas in the region are overfished and polluted from land-based sources and oil spills. The Straits of Malacca, for example, is one of the world's major shipping lanes for crude oil transport and is vulnerable to oil spills. There has been a notable increase in the occurrence of red tides which is attributed to domestic sources of pollution. This incidence poses not only a health hazard but also affects export earnings. Similarly, many mangroves are disappearing to make room for brackish water prawn farming, housing and industrial development. Coral reefs are also being degraded and require rehabilitation. Accordingly, there is an urgent need for a more coordinated, proactive and collective action to protect ASEAN's marine resources.

Based on the above analysis, it can be concluded that ASEAN has the political willingness to promote ASEAN cooperation on marine environment. The deepening of cooperation inside ASEAN and the improvement of relevant countries' domestic environmental protection could contribute to this process as well. Moreover, the *ASEAN way* is estimated to have a profound impact on this process, especially regarding the choice of priority areas, preference for cooperative programmes and national implementation. Some possible recommendations for ASEAN cooperation on marine environment could be as follows.

First, the region's feasibility in adopting the legal or economic instruments in the intra-region's marine environmental management should be carefully studied in the specific environmental issues, for example, oil spill control, illegal fishing or species trading, or greenhouse gas emission mitigation.

Second, to learn and position ASEAN actively in external environmental relations or global environmental negotiations, since nowadays most financial sources for the region's marine environmental activities are from external supports through many cooperation channels with UNEP, China, Japan, South Korea, Australia, USAID, etc. Also many marine environmental initiatives are triggered by international environmental pressures like the United Nations Convention on the Law of the Sea, International Convention for the Prevention of Pollution from Ships, Kyoto Protocol or other multilateral environmental agreements, World Summit on Sustainable Development, UNEP, etc., rather than the internal inspiration. This could indirectly but effectively improve the performance of environmental governance and mainstream the environmental value of the region.

Third, ASEAN should allow opportunities for non-state actors like local environmental groups, civilians or NGOs to play more proactive roles in the region's policy setting and planning networks, e.g. in the ASOEN sub-committee meeting. This actor could have more socio-ecological information than the member state's representatives in local environmental situations with less national or private conflicts and could also be advantageously connecting with the marine environmental networks at a global level.

Fourth, ASEAN should integrate marine environmental issues into other development strategies, e.g. trade negotiation. Free trade agreements within or between ASEAN and external trade partners should consider the issue of the growth–environment balance in the form of an assessment of environmental impacts from trade-specific investment or from gross economic growth.

Finally, they would need to expand marine environmental cooperation to new, emerging issues like climate change and disaster management which are nowadays becoming more frequent and devastating in the region, in aspects of common policy, technical and financial support and preparation networking.

Notes

1 See http://environment.asean.org, retrieved 27 June 2012.
2 See www.globalsecurity.org/military/world/war/spratly-ship.htm, retrieved 13 September 2014.
3 See http://investasean.asean.org/index.php/page/view/fisheries, retrieved 13 September 2014.
4 See www.rrcap.ait.asia/apeo/Chp1g-marine.html, retrieved on 10 April 2013.
5 See www.pemsea.org/, accessed 14 September 2014.

References

ASEAN. 2009. *Fourth ASEAN State of the Environment Report.* Jakarta: ASEAN Secretariat.
ASEAN Centre for Biodiversity. 2010. *Protected Areas Gap Analysis in the ASEAN Region.* Laguna: ASEAN Centre for Biodiversity.

ASEAN Cooperation on Environment, Association of Southeast Asian Nations. Available at: http://environment.asean.org/46-2/ (accessed 7 March 2014).

Australian Marine Science and Technology. 2008. *ASEAN Marine Water Quality Management Guidelines and Monitoring Manual.* Jakarta: ASEAN Secretariat.

Elliott, Lorraine. 2003. "ASEAN and Environmental Cooperation: Norms, Interests and Identity". *Pacific Review,* 16(1): 29–52.

Koh, Kheng-Lian, ed. 2009. *ASEAN Environmental Law, Policy and Governance: Selected Documents, Volume 1.* Singapore: World Scientific.

Koh, Kheng-Lian and Nicholas A. Robinson. 2011. *Regional Environmental Governance: Examining the Association of Southeast Asian Nations (ASEAN) Model,* 9 February, Available at: http://environment.research.yale.edu/documents/downloads/h-n/koh.pdf.

Lyons, Youna. 2012. "Trans-Boundary Pollution from Offshore Oil and Gas Activities in the Seas of Southeast Asia". Available at: http://cil.nus.edu.sg/wp/wp-content/uploads/2010/08/YounaLyons-Transboundary-Pollution-From-Offshore-Platforms.pdf.

Mushkat, Roda. 2003. "Globalization and the International Environmental Legal Response: The Asia Context". *Asian-Pacific Law and Policy Journal:* 49–81.

Patrick, Christie. 2004. "Marine Protected Areas as Biological Successes and Social Failures in Southeast Asia". *American Fisheries Society Symposium,* 42: 155–165.

Soriano, Zelda. 2013. "Asia Needs to Act to Prevent Pollution". *Nation,* 15 August. Available at: www.nationmulti-media.com/opion/.

Tanaka, Yoshifumi. 2015. *The International Law of the Sea.* Cambridge: Cambridge University Press.

Appendix 1
Regional map

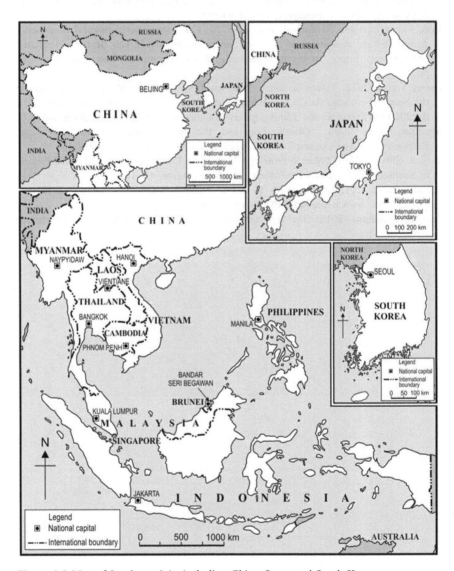

Figure A.1 Map of Southeast Asia, including China, Japan and South Korea

Appendix 2
Country surveys

BRUNEI DARUSSALAM

CAPITAL	**BANDAR SERI BEGAWAN**	
CURRENCY	**BRUNEI DOLLAR (BDN)**	

SURFACE AREA [1] **5,770 SQ KM**

OFFICIAL LANGUAGE **MALAY**

LIFE EXPECTANCY AT BIRTH [2] (YEARS)

	1990	2000	2011
BOTH SEXES	73.7	76.2	78.1
FEMALE	75.8	78.6	80.5
MALE	71.6	74.0	75.8

POPULATION

TOTAL IN 2012 (millions) [3] **0.4**

ANNUAL GROWTH RATE 2012 [4] **1.6%**

ETHNIC GROUPS [5] (2011) — PERCENTAGE

MALAY 65.7% CHINESE 10.3% OTHER 20.6% OTHER (indigenous) 3.4%

RELIGIOUS AFFILIATIONS [6] (2011) — PERCENTAGE

MUSLIM (official) 78.8% CHRISTIAN 8.7% BUDDHIST 7.8% OTHER (incl. indigenous beliefs) 4.7%

NET INTERNATIONAL MIGRATION RATE [7] — PER 1,000 POPULATION

1990 to 1995	2000 to 2005	2010 to 2015
2.2	3.1	3.5	2.0	1.8

AGE STRUCTURE [8] (2012) — PER AGE GROUP

0 — 14	15 — 64	65+
25.7%	70.3%	4.0%

LABOUR FORCE [9] (1995) — BY OCCUPATION

AGRICULTURE 2.5% INDUSTRY 8.9% SERVICES 88.6%

GROSS DOMESTIC PRODUCT (GDP) AT PURCHASING POWER PARITY (PPP) — CURRENT US$

MILLIONS [10]

1980	1985	1990	1995	2000	2005	2010	2012
7,367	7,888	9,232	12,164	14,113	17,567	19,973	21,635

PER CAPITA [11]

| 38,163 | 35,366 | 35,934 | 41,235 | 42,536 | 47,760 | 49,861 | 52,482 |

KEY IMPORTS [12] iron & steel, motor vehicles, machinery & transport equipment, manufactured goods, food, chemicals

KEY EXPORTS [13] crude oil, natural gas, garments

FOOTNOTES
1. *World Bank Open Data*, s.v "Surface area," accessed March 1, 2014, http://data.worldbank.org .
2. Asian Development Bank, *Key Indicators for Asia and the Pacific 2013*, accessed March 1, 2014, http://www.adb.org/ .
3&4. Ibid.
5. *The World Factbook*, s.v. "Brunei," accessed March 1, 2014, https://www.cia.gov/library/publications/the-world-factboo
6. *The World Factbook*, s.v. "Brunei," accessed March 1, 2014, https://www.cia.gov/library/publications/the-world-factbook
7. Asian Development Bank, *Key Indicators for Asia and the Pacific 2013*, accessed March 1, 2014, http://www.adb.org/ .
8&9. Ibid.
10. *World Bank Open Data*, s.v "GDP, PPP," accessed March 1, 2014, http://data.worldbank.org .
11. *World Bank Open Data*, s.v "GDP per capita, PPP," accessed March 1, 2014, http://data.worldbank.org .
12. *The World Factbook*, s.v. "Brunei," accessed March 1, 2014, https://www.cia.gov/library/publications/the-world-factbo
13. Ibid.

CAMBODIA

CAPITAL	**PHNOM PENH**	SURFACE AREA [1]	**181,040 SQ KM**
CURRENCY	**CAMBODIAN RIEL (KHR)**	OFFICIAL LANGUAGE	**KHMER**

LIFE EXPECTANCY AT BIRTH [2]
(YEARS)

	1990	2000	2011
BOTH SEXES	**55.4**	**57.5**	**63.0**
FEMALE	**57.1**	**58.4**	**64.4**
MALE	**53.8**	**56.5**	**61.6**

POPULATION

TOTAL IN 2012 (millions) [3]	**14.8**
ANNUAL GROWTH RATE 2012 [4]	**1.7%**

ETHNIC GROUPS [5]

KHMER — VIETNAMESE — CHINESE — OTHER

90% 5% 1% 4%

PERCENTAGE

RELIGIOUS AFFILIATIONS [6]
(2008 est.)

BUDDHIST (official) — MUSLIM — CHRISTIAN — OTHER

96.9% 1.9% 0.4% 0.8%

PERCENTAGE

NET INTERNATIONAL MIGRATION RATE [7]

1990 to	1995 to	2000 to	2005 to	2010 to	2015
3.4	3.0	1.6	-1.8	-3.7	

PER 1,000 POPULATION

AGE STRUCTURE [8]
(2012)

| 0 | 14 | 15 | 64 | 65+ |

31.0% 64.0% 5.0%

PER AGE GROUP

LABOUR FORCE [9]
(2012)

AGRICULTURE — INDUSTRY — SERVICES

71% 10% 19%

BY OCCUPATION

GROSS DOMESTIC PRODUCT AT PURCHASING POWER PARITY (PPP)

MILLIONS [10]

1980	1985	1990	1995	2000	2005	2010	2012
			7,424	11,474	20,143	30,615	36,477

PER CAPITA [11]

1995	2000	2005	2010	2012
689	939	1,508	2,131	2,454

CURRENT US$

KEY IMPORTS [12]
petroleum products, cigarettes, gold, construction materials, machinery, motor vehicles, pharmaceutical products

KEY EXPORTS [13]
clothing, timber, rubber, rice, fish, tobacco, footwear

FOOTNOTES
1. World Bank Open Data, s.v "Surface area," accessed March 1, 2014, http://data.worldbank.org .
2. Asian Development Bank, Key Indicators for Asia and the Pacific 2013, accessed March 1, 2014, http://www.adb.org/ .
3&4. Ibid.
5. The World Factbook, s.v. "Cambodia," accessed March 1, 2014, https://www.cia.gov/library/publications/the-world-factbook/
6. Ibid.
7. Asian Development Bank, Key Indicators for Asia and the Pacific 2013, accessed March 1, 2014, http://www.adb.org/ .
8. Ibid. Age structure of Cambodia is adapted from raw data (2012) which is not equal to 100%: 1) Population aged 0-14 years (%): 31.1%; 2) Population aged 15-65 years (%): 63.6%; 3) Population aged 65 years (%): 5.2%
9. Asian Development Bank, Key Indicators for Asia and the Pacific 2013, accessed March 1, 2014, http://www.adb.org/ . Labor force by occupation of Cambodia is adapted from raw data (2012) which is not equal to 100%: 1. Agriculture: 71.1%; 2. Industry: 9.7%; 3. Services: 19.3%
10. World Bank Open Data, s.v "GDP, PPP," accessed March 1, 2014, http://data.worldbank.org .
11. World Bank Open Data, s.v "GDP per capita, PPP," accessed March 1, 2014, http://data.worldbank.org .
12. The World Factbook, s.v. "Cambodia," accessed March 1, 2014, https://www.cia.gov/library/publications/the-world-factbook/ .
13. Ibid.

INDONESIA

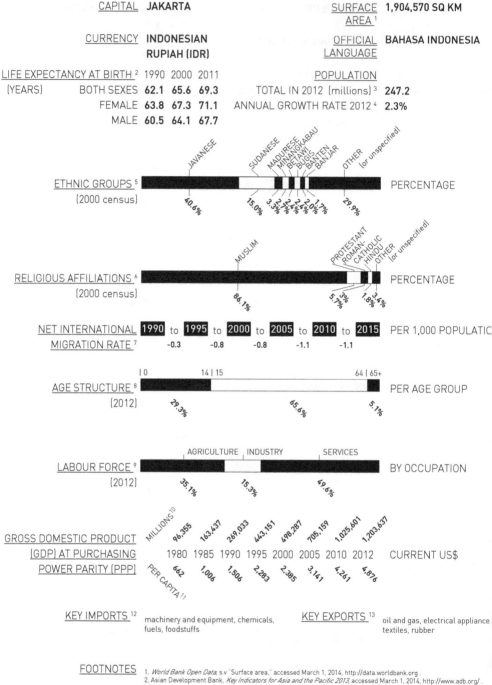

CAPITAL **JAKARTA**

SURFACE AREA [1] **1,904,570 SQ KM**

CURRENCY **INDONESIAN RUPIAH (IDR)**

OFFICIAL LANGUAGE **BAHASA INDONESIA**

LIFE EXPECTANCY AT BIRTH [2] (YEARS)

	1990	2000	2011
BOTH SEXES	**62.1**	**65.6**	**69.3**
FEMALE	**63.8**	**67.3**	**71.1**
MALE	**60.5**	**64.1**	**67.7**

POPULATION

TOTAL IN 2012 (millions) [3] **247.2**

ANNUAL GROWTH RATE 2012 [4] **2.3%**

ETHNIC GROUPS [5] (2000 census) — PERCENTAGE

JAVANESE 40.6% / SUDANESE 15.0% / MADURESE 3.3% / MINANGKABAU 2.7% / BETAWI 2.4% / BUGIS 2.4% / BANTEN 2.0% / BANJAR 1.7% / OTHER (or unspecified) 29.9%

RELIGIOUS AFFILIATIONS [6] (2000 census) — PERCENTAGE

MUSLIM 86.1% / PROTESTANT 5.7% / ROMAN-CATHOLIC 3% / HINDU 1.8% / OTHER (or unspecified) 3.4%

NET INTERNATIONAL MIGRATION RATE [7] — PER 1,000 POPULATION

1990 to **1995**	to **2000**	to **2005**	to **2010**	to **2015**
-0.3	-0.8	-0.8	-1.1	-1.1

AGE STRUCTURE [8] (2012) — PER AGE GROUP

| 0 | 14 | 15 | 64 | 65+ |

29.3% / 65.6% / 5.1%

LABOUR FORCE [9] (2012) — BY OCCUPATION

AGRICULTURE 35.1% / INDUSTRY 15.3% / SERVICES 49.6%

GROSS DOMESTIC PRODUCT (GDP) AT PURCHASING POWER PARITY (PPP) — CURRENT US$

MILLIONS [10]

1980	1985	1990	1995	2000	2005	2010	2012
96,355	163,437	269,033	443,151	498,287	705,159	1,025,601	1,203,637

PER CAPITA [11]

| 662 | 1,006 | 1,506 | 2,283 | 2,385 | 3,141 | 4,261 | 4,876 |

KEY IMPORTS [12] machinery and equipment, chemicals, fuels, foodstuffs

KEY EXPORTS [13] oil and gas, electrical appliance, textiles, rubber

FOOTNOTES

1. *World Bank Open Data*, s.v "Surface area," accessed March 1, 2014, http://data.worldbank.org .
2. Asian Development Bank, *Key Indicators for Asia and the Pacific 2013*, accessed March 1, 2014, http://www.adb.org/ .
3&4. Ibid.
5. *The World Factbook*, s.v. "Indonesia," accessed March 1, 2014, https://www.cia.gov/library/publications/the-world-factbo
6. Ibid.
7. Asian Development Bank, *Key Indicators for Asia and the Pacific 2013*, accessed March 1, 2014, http://www.adb.org/ .
8&9. Ibid.
10. *World Bank Open Data*, s.v "GDP, PPP," accessed March 1, 2014, http://data.worldbank.org .
11. *World Bank Open Data*, s.v "GDP per capita, PPP," accessed March 1, 2014, http://data.worldbank.org .
12. *The World Factbook*, s.v. "Indonesia," accessed March 1, 2014, https://www.cia.gov/library/publications/the-world-factb
13. Ibid.

LAO PDR

CAPITAL **VIENTIANE**	SURFACE AREA [1] **236,800 SQ KM**
CURRENCY **LAO KIP (LAK)**	OFFICIAL LANGUAGE **LAO**

EXPECTANCY AT BIRTH [2]
(RS)

	1990	2000	2011
BOTH SEXES	**54.3**	**61.4**	**67.4**
FEMALE	**55.6**	**62.7**	**68.9**
MALE	**53.1**	**60.2**	**66.0**

POPULATION

TOTAL IN 2012 (millions) [3]	**6.5**
ANNUAL GROWTH RATE 2012 [4]	**2.0%**

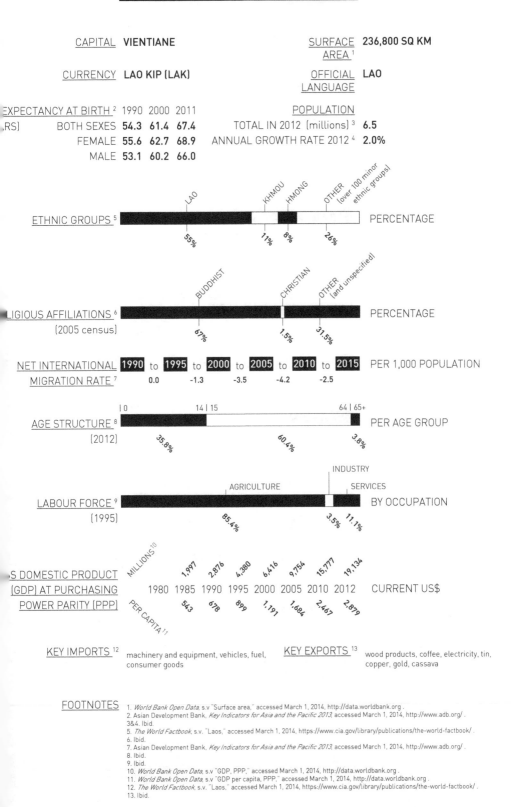

ETHNIC GROUPS [5] — PERCENTAGE

LAO 55% | KHMOU 11% | HMONG 8% | OTHER (over 100 minor ethnic groups) 26%

RELIGIOUS AFFILIATIONS [6] (2005 census) — PERCENTAGE

BUDDHIST 67% | CHRISTIAN 1.5% | OTHER (and unspecified) 31.5%

NET INTERNATIONAL MIGRATION RATE [7] — PER 1,000 POPULATION

1990 to 1995	to 2000	to 2005	to 2010	to 2015
0.0	-1.3	-3.5	-4.2	-2.5

AGE STRUCTURE [8] (2012) — PER AGE GROUP

| 0 | 14 | 15 | 64 | 65+ |
| 35.8% | | 60.4% | | 3.8% |

LABOUR FORCE [9] (1995) — BY OCCUPATION

AGRICULTURE 85.4% | INDUSTRY 3.5% | SERVICES 11.1%

GROSS DOMESTIC PRODUCT (GDP) AT PURCHASING POWER PARITY (PPP) — CURRENT US$

MILLIONS [10]

1980	1985	1990	1995	2000	2005	2010	2012
		1,997	2,876	4,380	6,416	9,754	15,777	19,134

PER CAPITA [11]

| | | 543 | 678 | 899 | 1,191 | 1,684 | 2,467 | 2,879 |

KEY IMPORTS [12]
machinery and equipment, vehicles, fuel, consumer goods

KEY EXPORTS [13]
wood products, coffee, electricity, tin, copper, gold, cassava

FOOTNOTES
1. *World Bank Open Data*, s.v "Surface area," accessed March 1, 2014, http://data.worldbank.org .
2. Asian Development Bank, *Key Indicators for Asia and the Pacific 2013*, accessed March 1, 2014, http://www.adb.org/ .
3&4. Ibid.
5. *The World Factbook*, s.v. "Laos," accessed March 1, 2014, https://www.cia.gov/library/publications/the-world-factbook/ .
6. Ibid.
7. Asian Development Bank, *Key Indicators for Asia and the Pacific 2013*, accessed March 1, 2014, http://www.adb.org/ .
8. Ibid.
9. Ibid.
10. *World Bank Open Data*, s.v "GDP, PPP," accessed March 1, 2014, http://data.worldbank.org .
11. *World Bank Open Data*, s.v "GDP per capita, PPP," accessed March 1, 2014, http://data.worldbank.org .
12. *The World Factbook*, s.v. "Laos," accessed March 1, 2014, https://www.cia.gov/library/publications/the-world-factbook/ .
13. Ibid.

MALAYSIA

CAPITAL	**KUALA LUMPUR**	**SURFACE AREA** [1] **330,800 SQ KM**
CURRENCY	**MALAYSIAN RINGGIT (MYR)**	**OFFICIAL LANGUAGE** **BAHASA MALAYSIA**

LIFE EXPECTANCY AT BIRTH [2] (YEARS)	1990	2000	2011
BOTH SEXES	70.1	72.1	74.3
FEMALE	72.1	74.3	76.5
MALE	68.1	70.0	72.1

POPULATION
TOTAL IN 2012 (millions) [3] **29.3**
ANNUAL GROWTH RATE 2012 [4] **1.3%**

ETHNIC GROUPS [5] (2004 est.) — PERCENTAGE

MALAY 50.4% CHINESE 23.7% INDIGENOUS 11% INDIAN 7.1% OTHERS 7.8%

RELIGIOUS AFFILIATIONS [6] — PERCENTAGE

MUSLIM 60.4% BUDDHIST 19.2% CHRISTIAN 9.1% HINDU 6.3% CONFUCIANISM, TAOISM & OTHER (traditional chinese) 2.6% OTHER (or unknown) 1.5% NONE 0.8%

NET INTERNATIONAL MIGRATION RATE [7] — PER 1,000 POPULATI[ON]

1990 to 1995	2000 to 2005	2010 to 2015		
5.4	3.3	3.8	3.2	0.6

AGE STRUCTURE [8] (2012) — PER AGE GROUP

| 0 | 14 | 15 | 64 | 65+ |

26.5% 68.3% 5.2%

LABOUR FORCE [9] (2012) — BY OCCUPATION

AGRICULTURE 12.6% INDUSTRY 18.1% SERVICES 69.3%

GROSS DOMESTIC PRODUCT (GDP) AT PURCHASING POWER PARITY (PPP) — CURRENT US$

	1980	1985	1990	1995	2000	2005	2010	2012
MILLIONS [10]	33,827	55,963	90,961	161,330	221,398	313,496	429,358	494,696
PER CAPITA [11]	2,445	3,550	4,995	7,784	9,453	12,131	15,185	16,919

KEY IMPORTS [12]
electronics, machinery, petroleum products, plastics, vehicles, iron and steel products, chemicals

KEY EXPORTS [13]
semiconductors and electroni[cs], palm oil, petroleum and liquef[ied] gas, wood and wood products, rubber, textiles, chemicals, so[...]

FOOTNOTES
1. *World Bank Open Data*, s.v "Surface area," accessed March 1, 2014, http://data.worldbank.org .
2. Asian Development Bank, *Key Indicators for Asia and the Pacific 2013*, accessed March 1, 2014, http://www.adb.org/ .
3&4. Ibid.
5. *The World Factbook*, s.v. "Malaysia," accessed March 1, 2014, https://www.cia.gov/library/publications/the-world-factb[ook].
6. Ibid.
7. Asian Development Bank, *Key Indicators for Asia and the Pacific 2013*, accessed March 1, 2014, http://www.adb.org/ .
8. Ibid.
9. Ibid.
10. *World Bank Open Data*, s.v "GDP, PPP," accessed March 1, 2014, http://data.worldbank.org .
11. *World Bank Open Data*, s.v. "GDP per capita, PPP," accessed March 1, 2014, http://data.worldbank.org .
12. *The World Factbook*, s.v. "Malaysia," accessed March 1, 2014, https://www.cia.gov/library/publications/the-world-fac[tbook].
13. Ibid.

MYANMAR

CAPITAL	**NAYPYIDAW**		SURFACE AREA [1]	**676,590 SQ KM**
CURRENCY	**MYANMAR KYAT (MMK)**		OFFICIAL LANGUAGE	**BURMESE**

LIFE EXPECTANCY AT BIRTH [2] (YEARS)

	1990	2000	2011
BOTH SEXES	**57.3**	**61.9**	**65.2**
FEMALE	**58.7**	**63.3**	**66.9**
MALE	**55.9**	**60.5**	**63.5**

POPULATION

TOTAL IN 2012 (millions) [3]	**61.0**
ANNUAL GROWTH RATE 2012 [4]	**1.0%**

ETHNIC GROUPS [5] — PERCENTAGE

BURMAN 68%, SHAN 9%, KAREN 7%, RAKHINE 4%, CHINESE 3%, INDIAN 2%, MON 2%, OTHER 5%

RELIGIOUS AFFILIATIONS [6] — PERCENTAGE

BUDDHIST 89%, CHRISTIAN (Baptist) 3%, CHRISTIAN (Roman Catholic) 1%, MUSLIM 4%, OTHER 2%, ANIMIST 1%

NET INTERNATIONAL MIGRATION RATE [7] — PER 1,000 POPULATION

1990 to 1995	1995 to 2000	2000 to 2005	2005 to 2010	2010 to 2015
-0.7	-0.6	0.0	-4.4	-2.1

AGE STRUCTURE [8] (2012) — PER AGE GROUP

0	14	15	64	65+
25.3%		69.5%		5.2%

LABOUR FORCE [9] (1995) — BY OCCUPATION

AGRICULTURE 64.1%, INDUSTRY 9.1%, SERVICES 26.8%

GROSS DOMESTIC PRODUCT (GDP) AT PURCHASING POWER PARITY (PPP) [10] — CURRENT US$

MILLIONS

1980	1985	1990	1995	2000	2005	2010	2012
					49,207	92,419	109,813

PER CAPITA

2005	2010	2012
888	1,546	1,801

KEY IMPORTS [11]

fabric, petroleum products, fertilizer, plastics, machinery, transport equipment, cement, construction materials, crude oil, food products, edible oil

KEY EXPORTS [12]

natural gas, wood products, pulses, beans, fish, rice, clothing, jade and gems

FOOTNOTES

1. *World Bank Open Data*, s.v "Surface area," accessed March 1, 2014, http://data.worldbank.org .
2. Asian Development Bank, *Key Indicators for Asia and the Pacific 2013*, accessed March 1, 2014, http://www.adb.org/ .
3&4. Ibid.
5. *The World Factbook*, s.v. "Burma," accessed March 1, 2014, https://www.cia.gov/library/publications/the-world-factbook/ .
6. Ibid.
7. Asian Development Bank, *Key Indicators for Asia and the Pacific 2013*, accessed March 1, 2014, http://www.adb.org/ .
8&9. Ibid.
10. Ibid
11. *The World Factbook*, s.v. "Burma," accessed March 1, 2014, https://www.cia.gov/library/publications/the-world-factbook/ .
12. Ibid.

PHILIPPINES

CAPITAL	**MANILA**
CURRENCY	**PHILIPPINE PESO (PHP)**

SURFACE AREA [1]	**300,000 SQ KM**
OFFICIAL LANGUAGE	**FILIPINO, ENGLISH**

LIFE EXPECTANCY AT BIRTH [2] (YEARS)

	1990	2000	2011
BOTH SEXES	**65.2**	**66.8**	**68.8**
FEMALE	**68.0**	**70.0**	**72.2**
MALE	**62.5**	**63.7**	**65.5**

POPULATION

TOTAL IN 2012 (millions) [3] **95.8**

ANNUAL GROWTH RATE 2012 [4] **1.7%**

ETHNIC GROUPS [5] (2000 census) — PERCENTAGE

TAGALOG	CEBUANO	ILOCANO	BISAYA/BINISAYA	HILIGAYNON-ILONGGO	BIKOL	WARAY	OTHER
28.1%	13.1%	9%	7.6%	7.5%	6%	3.4%	25.3%

RELIGIOUS AFFILIATIONS [6] (2000 census) — PERCENTAGE

CATHOLIC (Roman Catholic)	CATHOLIC (Aglipayan)	MUSLIM	EVANGELICAL	IGLESIA NI KRISTO	OTHER (Christian)	OTHER	UNSPECIFIED	NONE
80.9%	2%	5%	2.8%	2.3%	4.5%	1.8%	0.6%	0.1%

NET INTERNATIONAL MIGRATION RATE [7] — PER 1,000 POPULATION

1990 to 1995	1995 to 2000	2000 to 2005	2005 to 2010	2010 to 2015
-1.0	-2.1	-2.1	-2.8	-2.8

AGE STRUCTURE [8] (2012) — PER AGE GROUP

0 – 14	15 – 64	65+
34.5%	61.7%	3.8%

LABOUR FORCE [9] (2012) — BY OCCUPATION

AGRICULTURE	INDUSTRY	SERVICES
32.1%	9%	58.9%

GROSS DOMESTIC PRODUCT (GDP) AT PURCHASING POWER PARITY (PPP) — CURRENT US$

	1980	1985	1990	1995	2000	2005	2010	2012
MILLIONS [10]	64,253	77,727	114,267	143,483	185,642	260,987	365,336	419,583
PER CAPITA [11]	1,356	1,431	1,845	2,061	2,391	3,041	3,910	4,339

KEY IMPORTS [12]
electronic products, mineral fuels, machinery and transport equipment, iron and steel, textile fabrics, grains, chemicals, plastic

KEY EXPORTS [13]
semiconductors and electronic transport equipment, garments products, petroleum products, oil, fruits

FOOTNOTES

1. *World Bank Open Data*, s.v. "Surface area," accessed March 1, 2014, http://data.worldbank.org .
2. Asian Development Bank, *Key Indicators for Asia and the Pacific 2013*, accessed March 1, 2014, http://www.adb.org/ .
3 & 4. Ibid.
5. *The World Factbook*, s.v. "Philippines," accessed March 1, 2014, https://www.cia.gov/library/publications/the-world-fac
6. Ibid.
7. Asian Development Bank, *Key Indicators for Asia and the Pacific 2013*, accessed March 1, 2014, http://www.adb.org/ .
8. Ibid.
9. Ibid.
10. *World Bank Open Data*, s.v "GDP, PPP," accessed March 1, 2014, http://data.worldbank.org .
11. *World Bank Open Data*, s.v "GDP per capita, PPP," accessed March 1, 2014, http://data.worldbank.org .
12. *The World Factbook*, s.v. "Philippines," accessed March 1, 2014, https://www.cia.gov/library/publications/the-world-fa
13. Ibid.

SINGAPORE

CAPITAL	**SINGAPORE**		SURFACE AREA [1]	**710 SQ KM**
CURRENCY	**SINGAPORE DOLLAR (SGD)**		OFFICIAL LANGUAGE	**MANDARIN, ENGLISH, TAMIL, MALAY**

LIFE EXPECTANCY AT BIRTH [2] (YEARS)

	1990	2000	2011
BOTH SEXES	**75.6**	**78.1**	**81.9**
FEMALE	**78.0**	**80.1**	**84.3**
MALE	**73.3**	**76.1**	**79.6**

POPULATION

TOTAL IN 2012 (millions) [3]	**5.3**
ANNUAL GROWTH RATE 2012 [4]	**2.5%**

ETHNIC GROUPS [5] (2012 est.) — PERCENTAGE

CHINESE 74.2% | MALAY 13.3% | INDIAN 9.2% | OTHER 3.3%

RELIGIOUS AFFILIATIONS [6] (2010 est.) — PERCENTAGE

BUDDHIST 33.9% | MUSLIM 14.3% | TAOIST 11.3% | CATHOLIC 7.1% | HINDU 5.2% | OTHER (Christian) 1.1% | OTHER 0.7% | NONE 16.4%

NET INTERNATIONAL MIGRATION RATE [7] — PER 1,000 POPULATION

1990 to 1995	1995 to 2000	2000 to 2005	2005 to 2010	2010 to 2015
8.5	14.3	13.7	11.4	30.9

AGE STRUCTURE [8] (2012) — PER AGE GROUP

0 — 14	15 — 64	65+
16.5%	73.8%	9.7%

LABOUR FORCE [9] (2012) — BY OCCUPATION

AGRICULTURE 0.1% | INDUSTRY 14.3% | SERVICES 85.5%

GROSS DOMESTIC PRODUCT (GDP) AT PURCHASING POWER PARITY (PPP) — CURRENT US$

	1980	1985	1990	1995	2000	2005	2010	2012
MILLIONS [10]		17,622	31,665	55,871	94,991	136,481	193,557	292,201	322,996
PER CAPITA [11]	7,300	11,573	18,336	26,952	33,884	45,374	57,557	60,800

KEY IMPORTS [12] — machinery and equipment, mineral fuels, chemicals, foodstuffs, consumer goods

KEY EXPORTS [13] — machinery and equipment (including electronics and telecommunications), pharmaceuticals and other chemicals, refined petroleum products

FOOTNOTES
1. *World Bank Open Data*, s.v "Surface area," accessed March 1, 2014, http://data.worldbank.org .
2. Asian Development Bank, *Key Indicators for Asia and the Pacific 2013*, accessed March 1, 2014, http://www.adb.org/ .
3&4. Ibid.
5. *The World Factbook*, s.v. "Singapore," accessed March 1, 2014, https://www.cia.gov/library/publications/the-world-factbook/ .
6. Ibid.
7. Asian Development Bank, *Key Indicators for Asia and the Pacific 2013*, accessed March 1, 2014, http://www.adb.org/ .
8. Ibid.
9. Ibid.
10. *World Bank Open Data*, s.v "GDP, PPP," accessed March 1, 2014, http://data.worldbank.org .
11. *World Bank Open Data*, s.v "GDP per capita, PPP," accessed March 1, 2014, http://data.worldbank.org .
12. *The World Factbook*, s.v. "Singapore," accessed March 1, 2014, https://www.cia.gov/library/publications/the-world-factbook/ .
13. Ibid.

THAILAND

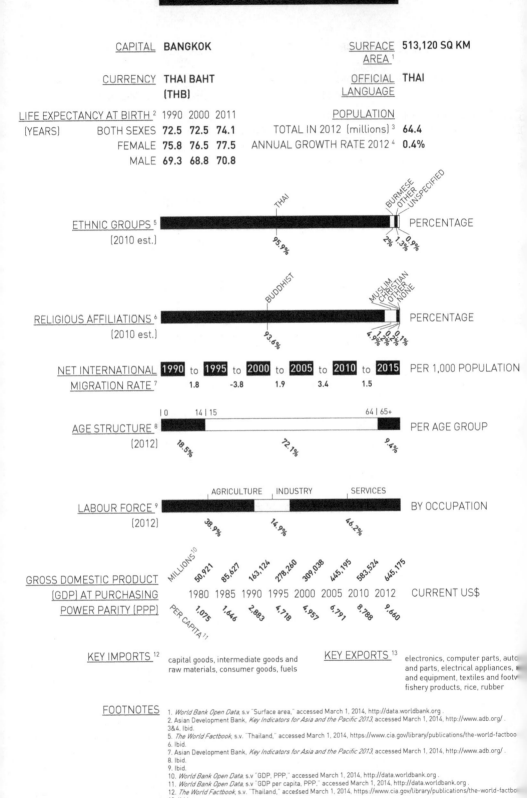

CAPITAL **BANGKOK**

SURFACE AREA [1] **513,120 SQ KM**

CURRENCY **THAI BAHT (THB)**

OFFICIAL LANGUAGE **THAI**

LIFE EXPECTANCY AT BIRTH [2]
(YEARS)

	1990	2000	2011
BOTH SEXES	72.5	72.5	74.1
FEMALE	75.8	76.5	77.5
MALE	69.3	68.8	70.8

POPULATION
TOTAL IN 2012 (millions) [3] **64.4**
ANNUAL GROWTH RATE 2012 [4] **0.4%**

ETHNIC GROUPS [5]
(2010 est.)

THAI 95.9%
BURMESE 2%
OTHER 1.3%
UNSPECIFIED 0.9%
PERCENTAGE

RELIGIOUS AFFILIATIONS [6]
(2010 est.)

BUDDHIST 93.6%
MUSLIM 4.9%
CHRISTIAN 1.2%
OTHER 0.2%
NONE 0.1%
PERCENTAGE

NET INTERNATIONAL MIGRATION RATE [7]

1990 to	1995 to	2000 to	2005 to	2010 to	2015	PER 1,000 POPULATION
1.8	-3.8	1.9	3.4	1.5		

AGE STRUCTURE [8]
(2012)

| 0 | 14 | 15 | | 64 | 65+ | PER AGE GROUP |
18.5% — 72.1% — 9.4%

LABOUR FORCE [9]
(2012)

AGRICULTURE 38.9% | INDUSTRY 14.9% | SERVICES 46.2%
BY OCCUPATION

GROSS DOMESTIC PRODUCT (GDP) AT PURCHASING POWER PARITY (PPP)

MILLIONS [10]	50,921	85,627	163,124	278,260	309,038	445,195	583,524	645,175
	1980	1985	1990	1995	2000	2005	2010	2012
PER CAPITA [11]	1,075	1,646	2,883	4,718	4,957	6,791	8,788	9,660

CURRENT US$

KEY IMPORTS [12]
capital goods, intermediate goods and raw materials, consumer goods, fuels

KEY EXPORTS [13]
electronics, computer parts, auto and parts, electrical appliances, and equipment, textiles and footw fishery products, rice, rubber

FOOTNOTES
1. *World Bank Open Data*, s.v "Surface area," accessed March 1, 2014, http://data.worldbank.org .
2. Asian Development Bank, *Key Indicators for Asia and the Pacific 2013*, accessed March 1, 2014, http://www.adb.org/ .
3&4. Ibid.
5. *The World Factbook*, s.v. "Thailand," accessed March 1, 2014, https://www.cia.gov/library/publications/the-world-factboo
6. Ibid.
7. Asian Development Bank, *Key Indicators for Asia and the Pacific 2013*, accessed March 1, 2014, http://www.adb.org/ .
8. Ibid.
9. Ibid.
10. *World Bank Open Data*, s.v "GDP, PPP," accessed March 1, 2014, http://data.worldbank.org .
11. *World Bank Open Data*, s.v "GDP per capita, PPP," accessed March 1, 2014, http://data.worldbank.org .
12. *The World Factbook*, s.v. "Thailand," accessed March 1, 2014, https://www.cia.gov/library/publications/the-world-factbo
13. Ibid.

VIET NAM

CAPITAL **HANOI**

SURFACE AREA [1] **330,957 SQ KM**

CURRENCY **VIETNAMESE DONG (VND)**

OFFICIAL LANGUAGE **VIETNAMESE**

LIFE EXPECTANCY AT BIRTH [2] (YEARS)

	1990	2000	2011
BOTH SEXES	65.5	71.9	75.1
FEMALE	67.4	73.8	77.1
MALE	63.7	70.2	73.1

POPULATION

TOTAL IN 2012 (millions) [3] **88.8**

ANNUAL GROWTH RATE 2012 [4] **1.1%**

ETHNIC GROUPS [5] (1999 census) — PERCENTAGE

KINH (VIET) 85.7%
TAY 1.9%
THAI 1.8%
MUONG 1.5%
KHMER 1.5%
HMONG 1.2%
NUNG 1.1%
OTHERS 5.3%

RELIGIOUS AFFILIATIONS [6] (1999 census) — PERCENTAGE

BUDDHIST 9.3%
CATHOLIC 6.7%
HOA HAO 1.5%
CAO DAI 1.1%
PROTESTANT 0.5%
MUSLIM 0.1%
NONE 80.8%

NET INTERNATIONAL MIGRATION RATE [7] — PER 1,000 POPULATION

1990 to 1995	1995 to 2000	2000 to 2005	2005 to 2010	2010 to 2015
-1.0	-0.9	-0.8	-1.1	-1.0

AGE STRUCTURE [8] (2012) — PER AGE GROUP

| 0 | 14 | 15 | 64 | 65+ |

22.9% / 70.6% / 6.5%

LABOUR FORCE [9] (2012) — BY OCCUPATION

AGRICULTURE 47%
INDUSTRY 15%
SERVICES 38%

GROSS DOMESTIC PRODUCT (GDP) AT PURCHASING POWER PARITY (PPP) — CURRENT US$

MILLIONS [10]							
		33,010	48,641	81,390	123,687	193,945	289,835	336,221
1980	1985	1990	1995	2000	2005	2010	2012
PER CAPITA [11]		561	737	1,130	1,593	2,354	3,334	3,787

KEY IMPORTS [12] machinery and equipment, petroleum products, steel products, raw materials for the clothing and shoe industries, electronics, plastics, automobiles

KEY EXPORTS [13] clothes, shoes, electronics, seafood, crude oil, rice, coffee, wooden products, machinery

FOOTNOTES

1. *World Bank Open Data*, s.v "Surface area," accessed March 1, 2014, http://data.worldbank.org .
2. Asian Development Bank, *Key Indicators for Asia and the Pacific 2013*, accessed March 1, 2014, http://www.adb.org/ .
3&4. Ibid.
5. *The World Factbook*, s.v. "Vietnam," accessed March 1, 2014, https://www.cia.gov/library/publications/the-world-factbook/ .
6. Ibid.
7. Asian Development Bank, *Key Indicators for Asia and the Pacific 2013*, accessed March 1, 2014, http://www.adb.org/ .
8. Ibid.
9. Ibid. Labor force by occupation is aggregated from raw data which is not equal to 100%:1) Agriculture: 47.4%; 2) Industry: 14.4%; 3) Services: 38.3%
10. *World Bank Open Data*, s.v "GDP, PPP," accessed March 1, 2014, http://data.worldbank.org .
11. *World Bank Open Data*, s.v "GDP per capita, PPP," accessed March 1, 2014, http://data.worldbank.org .
12. *The World Factbook*, s.v. "Vietnam," accessed March 1, 2014, https://www.cia.gov/library/publications/the-world-factbook/ .
13. Ibid.

CHINA

CAPITAL	**BEIJING**	SURFACE AREA [1]	**9,600,001 SQ KM**
CURRENCY	**CHINESE YUAN RENMINBI (CNY)**	OFFICIAL LANGUAGE [2]	**STANDARD CHINESE OR MANDARIN**

LIFE EXPECTANCY AT BIRTH [3] (YEARS)

	1990	2000	2011
BOTH SEXES	69.5	71.2	73.5
FEMALE	71.1	72.9	75.3
MALE	67.9	69.6	71.8

POPULATION

TOTAL IN 2012 (millions) [4]	**1,354**
ANNUAL GROWTH RATE 2012 [5]	**0.5%**

ETHNIC GROUPS [6&7] — PERCENTAGE

HAN CHINESE 91.6% · ZHUANG 1.3% · OTHER 7.1% (includes: Hui, Manchu, Uyghur, Miao, Yi, Tujia, Tibetan, Mongol, Dong, Buyi, Yao, Bai, Korean, Hani, Li, Kazakh, Dai and other nationalities)

RELIGIOUS AFFILIATIONS [8] — PERCENTAGE

UNAFFILIATED 52.2% · FOLK RELIGION 21.9% · BUDDHIST 18.2% · CHRISTIAN 5.1% · MUSLIM 1.8% · HINDU <0.1% · JEWISH <0.1% · OTHER 0.7% (includes, Daoist/Taoist)

NET INTERNATIONAL MIGRATION RATE [9] — PER 1,000 POPULATION

1990 to	1995 to	2000 to	2005 to	2010 to	2015
0.0	-0.1	-0.1	-0.4	-0.3	

AGE STRUCTURE [10] (2012) — PER AGE GROUP

0 – 14	15 – 64	65+
18.0%	73.3%	8.7%

LABOUR FORCE [11] (2012) — BY OCCUPATION

AGRICULTURE	INDUSTRY	SERVICES
33.6%	30.3%	36.1%

GROSS DOMESTIC PRODUCT (GDP) AT PURCHASING POWER PARITY (PPP) — CURRENT US$

	1980	1985	1990	1995	2000	2005	2010	2012
MILLIONS [12]	248,285	532,972	907,923	1,826,284	2,998,272	5,364,251	10,036,535	12,268,638
PER CAPITA [13]	253	507	800	1,516	2,375	4,115	7,503	9,083

KEY IMPORTS [14] electrical and other machinery, oil and mineral fuels; nuclear reactor, boiler, and machinery components; optical and medical equipment, metal ores, motor vehicles; soybeans

KEY EXPORTS [15] Electrical and other machinery, data processing equipment, and telephone handsets, textiles, in circuits

FOOTNOTES

1. *World Bank Open Data*, s.v "Surface area," accessed March 1, 2014, http://data.worldbank.org .
2. In addition to the official national language, many provinces have their own official language.
3. Asian Development Bank, *Key Indicators for Asia and the Pacific 2013*, accessed March 1, 2014, http://www.adb.org/ .
4&5. Ibid.
6. *The World Factbook*, s.v. "China," accessed March 1, 2014, https://www.cia.gov/library/publications/the-world-factbook
7. As of 2010, the Chinese government officially recognizes 56 ethnic groups.
8. *The World Factbook*, s.v. "China," accessed March 1, 2014, https://www.cia.gov/library/publications/the-world-factbook
9. Asian Development Bank, *Key Indicators for Asia and the Pacific 2013*, accessed March 1, 2014, http://www.adb.org/ .
10&11. Ibid.
12. *World Bank Open Data*, s.v "GDP, PPP," accessed March 1, 2014, http://data.worldbank.org .
13. *World Bank Open Data*, s.v "GDP per capita, PPP," accessed March 1, 2014, http://data.worldbank.org .
14. *The World Factbook*, s.v. "China," accessed March 1, 2014, https://www.cia.gov/library/publications/the-world-factbook
15. Ibid.

JAPAN

CAPITAL	**TOKYO**	SURFACE AREA [1]	**377,955 SQ KM**
CURRENCY	**JAPANESE YEN (JPY)**	OFFICIAL LANGUAGE	**JAPANESE**

LIFE EXPECTANCY AT BIRTH [2] (YEARS)

	1990	2000	2011
BOTH SEXES	**78.8**	**81.1**	**82.6**
FEMALE	**81.9**	**84.6**	**85.9**
MALE	**75.9**	**77.7**	**79.4**

POPULATION

TOTAL IN 2012 (millions) [3] **127.6**

ANNUAL GROWTH RATE 2012 [4] **-0.2%**

ETHNIC GROUPS [5] — PERCENTAGE

JAPANESE 98.5%
KOREANS 0.5%
CHINESE 0.4%
OTHER 0.6%

RELIGIOUS AFFILIATIONS [6&7] — PERCENTAGE

SHINTOISM 83.9%
BUDDHISM 71.4%
CHRISTIANITY 2%
OTHER 7.8%

NET INTERNATIONAL MIGRATION RATE [8] — PER 1,000 POPULATION

1990 to	1995 to	2000 to	2005 to	2010 to	2015
-1.0	0.7	0.0	0.1	0.4	

AGE STRUCTURE [9] (2012) — PER AGE GROUP

0 14	15 64	65+
13%	63%	24%

LABOUR FORCE [10] (2012) — BY OCCUPATION

AGRICULTURE 3.8%
INDUSTRY 16.5%
SERVICES 79.7%

GROSS DOMESTIC PRODUCT (GDP) AT PURCHASING POWER PARITY (PPP) — CURRENT US$

	1980	1985	1990	1995	2000	2005	2010	2012
MILLIONS [11]		995,563	1,583,102	2,370,774	2,871,614	3,287,034	3,889,582	4,290,995	4,487,301
PER CAPITA [12]	8,525	13,110	19,191	22,893	25,909	30,441	33,668	35,178

KEY IMPORTS [13]

petroleum 15.5%; liquid natural gas 5.7%; clothing 3.9%; semiconductors 3.5%; coal 3.5%; audio and visual apparatus 2.7% (2011 est.)

KEY EXPORTS [14]

motor vehicles 13.6%; semiconductors 6.2%; iron and steel products 5.5%; auto parts 4.6%; plastic materials 3.5%; power generating machinery 3.5%

FOOTNOTES

1. *World Bank Open Data*, s.v "Surface area," accessed March 1, 2014, http://data.worldbank.org .
2. Asian Development Bank, *Key Indicators for Asia and the Pacific 2013*, accessed March 1, 2014, http://www.adb.org/ .
3&4. Ibid.
5. *The World Factbook*, s.v. "Japan," accessed March 1, 2014, https://www.cia.gov/library/publications/the-world-factbook/ .
6. Ibid.
7. Total adherents exceeds 100% because many Japanese identify themselves as both Shintoist and Buddhist. No census taken.
8. Asian Development Bank, *Key Indicators for Asia and the Pacific 2013*, accessed March 1, 2014, http://www.adb.org/ .
9. Age structure of Japan is adapted from raw data (2012) which is not equal to 100%:1) Population Aged 0–14 Years (%): 13.1%; 2) Population Aged 15–64 Years (%): 62.5%; 3) Population Aged 65 Years and Over (%): 24.3%.
10. Asian Development Bank, *Key Indicators for Asia and the Pacific 2013*, accessed March 1, 2014, http://www.adb.org/ .
11. *World Bank Open Data*, s.v. "GDP, PPP," accessed March 1, 2014, http://data.worldbank.org .
12. *World Bank Open Data*, s.v "GDP per capita, PPP," accessed March 1, 2014, http://data.worldbank.org .
13. *The World Factbook*, s.v. "Japan," accessed March 1, 2014, https://www.cia.gov/library/publications/the-world-factbook/ .
14 Ibid.

SOUTH KOREA

CAPITAL	**SEOUL**		SURFACE AREA [1]	**99,900 SQ KM**
CURRENCY	**SOUTH KOREAN WON (KRW)**		OFFICIAL LANGUAGE	**KOREAN**

LIFE EXPECTANCY AT BIRTH [2] (YEARS)

	1990	2000	2011
BOTH SEXES	**71.3**	**75.9**	**80.9**
FEMALE	**75.5**	**79.6**	**84.4**
MALE	**67.3**	**72.3**	**77.5**

POPULATION

TOTAL IN 2012 (millions) [3]	**50.0**
ANNUAL GROWTH RATE 2012 [4]	**0.5%**

ETHNIC GROUPS [5]

HOMOGENEOUS (Korean) (except for about 20,000 Chinese)

<100%

PERCENTAGE

RELIGIOUS AFFILIATIONS [6]
(2010 survey)

PERCENTAGE

CHRISTIAN (protestant) 24%
CHRISTIAN (roman catholic) 7.6%
BUDDHIST 24.2%
OTHER (or unknown) 0.9%
NONE 43.3%

NET INTERNATIONAL MIGRATION RATE [7]

1990 to	1995 to	2000 to	2005 to	2010 to	2015
	2.1	-2.9	-2.3	-0.4	-0.1

PER 1,000 POPULATIO

AGE STRUCTURE [8]
(2012)

| 0 | 14 | 15 | 64 | 65+ |

15.3% 72.9% 11.8%

PER AGE GROUP

LABOUR FORCE [9]
(2012)

AGRICULTURE 6.2%
INDUSTRY 16.7%
SERVICES 77.1%

BY OCCUPATION

GROSS DOMESTIC PRODUCT (GDP) AT PURCHASING POWER PARITY (PPP)

MILLIONS [10]

	1980	1985	1990	1995	2000	2005	2010	2012
	90,599	178,098	341,246	562,092	808,404	1,096,741	1,413,760	1,540,151
PER CAPITA [11]	2,376	4,364	7,960	12,465	17,197	22,783	28,613	30,801

CURRENT US$

KEY IMPORTS [12]

machinery, electronics and electronic equipment, oil, steel, transport equipment, organic chemicals, plastics

KEY EXPORTS [13]

semiconductors, wireless telecommunications equipment, vehicles, computers, steel, ships petrochemicals

FOOTNOTES

1. *World Bank Open Data*, s.v "Surface area," accessed March 1, 2014, http://data.worldbank.org .
2. Asian Development Bank, *Key Indicators for Asia and the Pacific 2013*, accessed March 1, 2014, http://www.adb.org/ .
3&4. Ibid.
5. *The World Factbook*, s.v. "Korea, South," accessed March 1, 2014 ttps://www.cia.gov/library/publications/the-world-fact
6. Ibid.
7. Asian Development Bank, *Key Indicators for Asia and the Pacific 2013*, accessed March 1, 2014, http://www.adb.org/ .
8&9. Ibid.
10. *World Bank Open Data*, s.v "GDP, PPP," accessed March 1, 2014, http://data.worldbank.org .
11. *World Bank Open Data*, s.v "GDP per capita, PPP," accessed March 1, 2014, http://data.worldbank.org .
12. *The World Factbook*, s.v. "Korea, South," accessed March 1, 2014, https://www.cia.gov/library/publications/the-world-f
13. Ibid.

Appendix 3

Timeline of key ASEAN milestones
Azmi Mat Akhir and Alice D. Ba

1967	Birth of ASEAN
1969	Establishment of a Fund for ASEAN
1971	Declaration on Zone of Peace, Freedom and Neutrality (ZOPEAN)
1975	First ASEAN Labour Ministers Meeting
	First ASEAN Economic Ministers Meeting
1976	Treaty of Amity and Cooperation in Southeast Asia (TAC)
	First Leaders ASEAN summit
	ASEAN/Bali Concord 1
	Agreement on the Establishment of the ASEAN Secretariat
1977	ASEAN Preferential Trading Arrangements
	ASEAN Sswap Arrangements
	First Meeting of the ASEAN Education Ministers
1978	First Meeting of ASEAN Inter-Parliamentary Organization (became ASEAN Inter-Parliamentary Assembly (AIPA) in 2007)
	Establishment of the ASEAN Cultural Fund
1979	Agreement on ASEAN Food Security Reserve (AFSR)
	First Meeting of the ASEAN Agriculture and Forestry Ministers
1980	First ASEAN Energy Ministers Meeting
	First ASEAN Health Ministers Meeting
1981	First ASEAN Environment Ministers Meeting
	Basic Agreement on ASEAN Industrial Complementation (AIC)
1983	Basic Agreement on ASEAN Industrial Joint Ventures (AIJV)
1984	Brunei Darussalam joined ASEAN
1986	First ASEAN Law Ministers Meeting (regularized in 1993)
	Agreement on ASEAN Energy Cooperation
	ASEAN Petroleum Security Agreement
1987	Declaration on Political, Economic and Functional Cooperation
	Protocol on Amending Treaty of Amity and Cooperation
1989	Basic Agreement on ASEAN Industrial Projects (AIP)
1992	Agreement on the Common Effective Preferential Tariff (CEPT) Scheme for ASEAN Free Trade Area (AFTA)

	Framework Agreement on Enhancing ASEAN Economic Cooperation
1994	Establishment of Fund for ASEAN
	First ASEAN Regional Forum (ARF)
1995	Treaty on the Southeast Asia Nuclear Weapons-Free Zone (SEANWFZ)
	ASEAN Framework Agreement on Services (AFAS)
	Socialist Republic of Vietnam joined ASEAN
	First ASEAN Ministerial Meeting on Youth
1996	First ASEAN Transport Ministers Meeting
	Basic Agreement on ASEAN Industrial Cooperation (AICO)
1997	Laos and Myanmar joined ASEAN
	Memorandum of Understanding on the Establishment of the ASEAN Foundation
	First ASEAN Fnance Ministers Meeting
	Declaration on Transnational Crime
	First ASEAN Ministerial Meeting on Transnational Crime
	ASEAN Vision 2020
1998	Second Protocol on Amending Treaty of Amity and Cooperation
	First Meeting of ASEAN Tourism Ministers
	First Informal Meeting of ASEAN Ministers on Rural Development and poverty eradication
	Agreement on ASEAN Investment Area (AIA)
	Hanoi Plan of Action (HPA)
1999	Cambodia joined ASEAN
	ASEAN Surveillance Process
2000	First meeting of High Level Task Force on the AFTA-CER Free Trade Area (AFTA-CER-FTA)
	ASEAN Troika
	Declaration on Cultural Heritage
	Political Declaration in Pursuit of a Drug Free ASEAN 2015
	e-ASEAN Framework Agreement
2001	First ASEAN meeting of Telecommunications and IT Ministers
	Rules of Procedure of the High Council of TAC
2002	ASEAN Agreement on Transboundary Haze Pollution
2003	Conference of the Parties to the ASEAN Agreement on Transboundary Haze Pollution
	Declaration on Strengthening Participation in Sustainable Youth Employment
	Bali Concord II
	First ASEAN Ministerial Meeting on Disaster Management
2004	Declaration on the Elimination of Violence Against Women in the ASEAN Region
	Vientiane Action Programme (VAP) 2004–2010
	ASEAN Security Community (ASC) Plan of Action

	ASEAN Economic Community (AEC) Plan of Action
	ASEAN Socio-Cultural Community (ASCC) Plan of Action
	ASEAN Plan of Action on Narrowing the Development Gap (NDG)
	ASEAN Framework Agreement for the Integration of Priority Sectors
	ASEAN Declaration against Trafficking in Persons Particularly Women and Children
2005	Statement on "One Vision, One Identity, One Community"
	Kuala Lumpur Declaration on Establishment of ASEAN Charter
	Agreement to Establish and Implement the ASEAN Single Window
	Establishment of the ASEAN Development Fund
	Coordination Agreement on Technical Assistance and Training to Combat Money Laundering and Terrorist Financing
	Memorandum of Understanding on the ASEAN SWAP arrangement (by all 10 central banks)
	ASEAN Agreement on Disaster Management and Emergency Response
2006	Inaugural ASEAN Defence Ministers Meeting (ADMM)
	Framework Agreement on Visa Exemption
2007	Singapore Declaration on Climate Change, Energy and the Environment
	Declaration towards One Caring and Sharing Community
	ASEAN Committee of Permanent Representatives created
	AEC Blueprint
	Declaration on Protection and Promotion of Rights of Migrant Workers
	Declaration on Acceleration of the Establishment of the ASEAN Community by 2015
	ASEAN Charter
2008	Statement on the ASEAN Charter
2009	Declaration on [ASEAN] Intergovernmental Commission on Human Rights (AICHR)
	APSC Blueprint
	ASCC Blueprint
	Roadmap for an ASEAN Community (2009–2015)
2010	Third Protocol on Amending Treaty of Amity and Cooperation
	ASEAN Commission on the Promotion and Protection of the Rights of Women and Children created
2011	Bali Concord III (RCEP/AFEED)
	Agreement on the Establishment of the ASEAN Coordinating Centre for Humanitarian Assistance on Disaster Management
	Ha Noi Declaration on the Adoption of the Master Plan on ASEAN Connectivity

2012	ASEAN Comprehensive Investment Agreement enacted
	Joint Declaration of the ASEAN Defense Ministers on Enhancing ASEAN Unity for a Harmonized and Secure Community
	First ASEAN Ministerial Meeting on Women
	ASEAN Human Rights Declaration
2015	First Dateline for Achieving the ASEAN Community

Appendix 4

Timeline of key ASEAN+3 milestones
Azmi Mat Akhir and Alice D. Ba

1997	First ASEAN-Japan Summit
	First ASEAN–Republic of Korea Summit
	First ASEAN–China Summit
	First (Informal) Meeting of ASEAN+3
1999	First East Asia Cooperation/ASEAN+3 Summit (Joint Statement on East Asia Cooperation)
	First APT Finance Ministers and Central Bank Governors Meeting
2000	First Meeting of ASEAN Economic Ministers+3
	First ASEAN+3 Foreign Ministers Meeting
	Chiang Mai Initiative
2001	First ASEAN Agriculture and Forestry Ministers+3 Meeting
	First ASEAN+3 Labour Ministers Meeting
	East Asian Vision Group (EAVG) Report: "Towards an East Asian Community: Region of Peace, Prosperity and Progress"
2002	First ASEAN+3 Tourism Ministers Meeting
	First ASEAN+3 Environment Ministers Meeting
	Final report of East Asian Study Group (EASG)
	Asian Bond Market Initiative (ABMI)
2003	Establishment of ASEAN+3 Finance Cooperation
	Declaration on Revitalising Tourism for ASEAN+3
	APT meeting of Ministers of Cultures and Arts
	APT meeting of Ministers of Social Welfare and Development
	Track 1.5 East Asia Forum (EAF)
	Track 2 Network of East Asian Think Tanks (NEAT)
2004	First ASEAN+3 Ministerial Meeting on Transnational Crime (AMMTC+3)
	First ASEAN+3 Health Ministers Meeting
	First ASEAN+3 Ministerial Meeting for Social Welfare and Development
	First ASEAN+3 Telecommunications and IT Ministers Meeting (TELMIN)
	APT Ministerial Meeting on Transnational Crime
	APT Energy Ministers Meeting

2005	First East Asia summit
2007	Declaration on East Asian Energy Community
	East Asia Cooperation and the APT Cooperation Work Plan (2007–2017)
	APT Ministers Meeting on Youth
2008	Economic Research Institute for ASEAN and East Asia
	Asian Bond Market Initiative (ABMI) Roadmap
2009	Guidelines to implement the Second Joint Statement on East Asia Cooperation and the APT Cooperation Work Plan (2007–2017)
2010	Joint Declaration on APT Civil Service Cooperation
	ASEAN+3 Comprehensive Strategy on Food Security and Bioenergy Development (APTCS-FSBD) Framework and Strategic Plan of Action on Food and Energy Security (SAP-FES) 2010–2013
	Chiang Mai Initiative on Multilateralization (CMIM)
	Inclusion of United States and Russia into EAS
2011	Agreement on the ASEAN+3 Emergency Rice Reserve (APTERR)
	ASEAN+3 Macroeconomic Research Office (AMRO)
2012	Chiang Mai Initiative Multilateralisation (CMIM) Fund increased from US$120 billion to US$240 billion
	APT Plan of Action on Education: 2010–2017
	ASEAN+3 Conference on Civil Service Matters Work Plan (2012–2015)
	Work Plan on Enhancing APT Cooperation in Culture
	Work Plan on Enhancing APT Cooperation through Information and Media 2012–2017
	Work Plan to Implement the Asian Bond Market Initiative (ABMI) New Roadmap
	APT Emergency Rice Reserve Agreement
	Report of East Asia Vision Group
2013	Strengthening efforts to prevent and combat transnational crimes
	Revised East Asia Cooperation and the APT Cooperation Work Plan 2013–2017
	Asian Bond Market Initiative New Roadmap

Index

Entries in **bold** denote tables; entries in *italics* denote figures.

education migration; female migrants; retirement migration
money laundering 31
money transfers 133
morphine 33, 35, **38**, 42
multiculturalism: in advanced countries 78, 84; in South Korea 81–3, 85–6, 88, **91**, 92–3, 93n6
multinational corporations 130
Mutual Technical Cooperation 22
Myanmar: collaboration in drug control 47–50; drugs seized in **42**; economic growth in 135; and energy security 141, 145–6, 156–8, 160; financial sector in 133; food security in 12; gas pipelines 151; higher education in 104; illicit drug use in 32, 35–7, **38**, *39*; joining ASEAN 102; and marine environment 173; trade liberalisation 121

NAFTA 128
national interests: ASEAN prioritising 9; and food security 27; and regional commons 2
Natori, Miwa 65
natural disasters 3, 10, 12, 20, 164, 172; *see also* disaster management
natural gas: ASEAN country resources and use of 140, 142–7, 151, 158; disputes between ASEAN members over 156; environmental impacts of 153, 173–4; interconnection of ASEAN countries 149, 151 (*see also* TAGP)
natural resources: as commons 2; competition over 175; marine 168–9
needle and syringe exchange 35, 37, 40–1
new security issues 31, 49, 69, 165
New Zealand: in EAS 96; education migration to 55–6, 58; environmental cooperation with 166; FTA with ASEAN 119; retirement migration to 62
NGOs (non-governmental organisations): in ASEAN Rice Trade Forum 17; and drug trafficking 31, 48, 50; and marine environment 168, 175, 178; and migration flows 88, 92
NNCC (National Narcotics Control Commission, China) 41, 43
non-interference, in ASEAN 1, 9, 148, 166, 176
normative commons, regional 2
Northeast Asia 4, 29, 174
North Korea 86, 176
nursing homes 71

ocean governance 164
oil: and ASEAN pipeline 5; ASEAN resources of and demand for 126, 140, 142–7, 149; Chinese demand for 158; and electricity generation 157; exports of 121; pollution from 173–4 (*see also* oil spills)
oil production 5, 144, 146–7, 173
oil spills 167, 169, 174–5, 177–8
opium 32–7, 41, 50; poppy cultivation 35–7, 39, 41, 47, 50; seizures of **38**, **42**; trafficking 36–7

PEMSEA (Partnership in Environmental Management for the Seas of East Asia) 176
Penang Island 34
people-to-people relationships 6
personal security 34, 45
Pertamina 153–4
petro-chemical spills 169
PhD students 105, 108, 114
Philippines: drug manufacturing in 47; economic growth in 134–5; education migration to 56–7, 59; education spending in 137; and energy security 142, 146, 156–8; FDI in 131; food security in 10, 12; and food self-sufficiency 26; labour migration from 79; and marine environment 168–9, 173; retirement migration to 62–6, *67*, 69, 71, 73n16; trade liberalisation 121; typhoons in 8–9
Plan Metjack 63
Plus Three countries: economic growth in **136**; and education 105–6; and energy security 158–61; financial cooperation 132–3; and food security 9–10, 15–17, 22; and marine environment 176–7; and migration flows 92–3; trade among 122; and transnational crime 49
PMC (Post-Ministerial Conference) 30
policy dialogues 103, 109, 112
political security 3, 6n6, 45
pollution: air 176; from hydrocarbons 173–5; marine 167–72, 175–7; trans-boundary 164–6, 173, 175–6, 178
poverty headcount ratio **137**
poverty reduction: and economic growth 137; and economic integration 120; and food security 9, 13, 27; and rice reserves 20, 23

For Product Safety Concerns and Information please contact our
EU representative GPSR@taylorandfrancis.com Taylor & Francis
Verlag GmbH, Kaufingerstraße 24, 80331 München, Germany